Everyday Spelling

Authors

James Beers • Ronald L. Cramer • W. Dorsey Hammond

Scott Foresman
Addison Wesley

Editorial Offices: Glenview, Illinois • New York, New York
Sales Offices: Reading, Massachusetts • Duluth, Georgia • Glenview, Illinois
Carrollton, Texas • Menlo Park, California

1-800-552-2259
http://www.sf.aw.com

◾ ACKNOWLEDGMENTS

ILLUSTRATIONS

p. 10: Peter Pahl; **pp. 12-34:** Margaret Sanfilippo; **pp. 12, 38, 64, 90, 116, 142:** Tish Tenud; **pp. 40, 41, 44, 48, 52, 56, 60:** Vita Jay; **p. 58:** Christopher Byrne; **pp. 61, 176, 177, 213:** Brian Karas; **pp. 62, 63:** Larry Macintyre; **pp. 64-86:** Laura Cornell/Publishers Graphics; **pp. 81, 85:** Shelly Dietrichs; **pp. 86, 89, 112, 115, 139, 165, 175, 183, 188, 189, 214:** Mark Oldach Design; **p. 87:** Malcolm Farley; **pp. 88, 195:** Myron Grossman; **pp. 90-112:** Debbie Pinkney/Cliff Knecht; **pp. 113, 198, 199, 226, 227:** John Sanford; **p. 114:** Rob Porazinski; **p. 115:** Carolyn Croll; **pp. 116-138:** Michael McGurl; **pp. 121, 125, 133:** Patricia Barbee; **pp. 138, 140, 141, 214, 215:** Mary Lynn Blasuta; **pp. 139, 140, 304:** LeeLee Brazeal; **pp. 142-164:** Mary Thelen; **p. 164:** Michael Dinges; **pp. 165, 174, 175:** Patti Green; **pp. 166, 167:** Pauline Ellison; **pp. 170, 171:** Steve Mach; **pp. 172, 173:** Tim Jonke; **pp. 178, 179:** Adam Cohen; **pp. 180, 181:** Tom Bookwalter; **pp. 182, 183:** Lonnie Sue Johnson; **pp. 184, 185, 218, 219:** Jose Cruz; **pp. 190, 191:** Kirk Caldwell; **pp. 192, 193:** John Kane; **pp. 194, 195:** Kath Petrauskas; **pp. 196, 197:** Craig Smallish; **p. 197:** Mercury Engraving; **pp. 200, 201, 222, 223:** Phillippe Béha; **pp. 202, 203:** Kim Behm; **pp. 206, 207:** David Csicsko; **pp. 208, 209:** Normand Cousineau; **pp. 210, 211:** Rueben Ramos; **pp. 216, 217:** Sally Comport; **pp. 220, 221:** Precision Graphics; **p. 224:** Peter Hoey; **pp. 228, 229:** Gil Ashby; **p. 297:** Kathi Ember; **p. 299:** Don Wilson; **p. 306:** Rob Barber; **p. 310:** Ellen Joy Sasaki

PHOTOGRAPHS

pp. 28, 80, 110, 162: Marilyn Meyerhofer; **pp. 38, 39, 41, 43, 45-47, 53, 54, 57:** Christopher Rory Photography; **p. 185:** The Bettmann Archive; **pp. 186, 187, 250T, 250B, 260T, 272T, 272B, 276B, 280T, 290T:** Courtesy NASA; **p. 248B:** John Madeley/R.C. Photo Agency; **pp. 252B, 256T, 264T, 264B, 270B, 271, 287, 288T:** Cynthia Clampitt; **p. 254T:** © Crown; **p. 254B:** General Biological Supply House, Inc.; **p. 256B:** Courtesy Michelle E. Ryan; **p. 257:** By permission of the Controllers of Her Britannic Majesty's Stationery Office, British Crown copyright; **p. 258:** U.S. Department of Interior; **p. 259T:** The British Library, London; **p. 262T:** Joe F. Viesti; **p. 266T:** Robert Amft; **p. 267:** U.S. Department of the Interior, National Park Service, Edison National Historic Site; **p. 268T:** Courtesy Naval Photographic Center; **p. 268B:** Catherine Koehler; **p. 269:** National Park Service; **p. 274:** Robert B. Rolchin; **p. 277T:** Pottery by Byron Temple; **p. 278:** Bill Ivy; **p. 279:** United States Gypsum, a wholly-owned subsidiary of USG Corporation; **p. 290B:** Courtesy Center for Disease Control; **p. 301:** Comstock; **p. 308:** Craig Aurness/Westlight/Woodfin Camp and Associates

Unless otherwise acknowledged all photographs are the property of Addison-Wesley Educational Publishers Inc.

UNIT 1

■ CONTENTS

■ CONTENTS

UNIT 5

■ CONTENTS

Cross-Curricular Lessons

✻ FREQUENTLY MISSPELLED WORDS!

Lots of words on your spelling lists are marked with green asterisks ✻. These are the words that are misspelled the most by students your age.*

Pay special attention to these frequently misspelled words as you read, write, and practice your spelling words.

too	with	we're	house	almost
because	our	and	one	clothes
there	really	another	would	cousin
their	friends	sometimes	brother	everything
a lot	then	didn't	could	getting
Christmas	I	heard	pretty	I'm
were	always	little	caught	scared
said	finally	through	whole	was
went	again	off	morning	what
they	different	outside	took	everyone
favorite	they're	something	believe	found
when	once	thought	his	swimming
friend	until	Halloween	it's	very
know	where	people	started	who
that's	before	everybody	beautiful	
upon	presents	want	two	

* *Research in Action* is a research project conducted in 1990–1993. This list of frequently misspelled words is one result of an analysis of 18,599 unedited compositions. Words are listed in the order of their frequency of misspelling.

STRATEGY WORKSHOP

Steps for Spelling New Words

DISCOVER THE STRATEGY Here's a plan to use when you study your spelling words.

Step 1 Look at the word. **Say** it and listen to the sounds.

running

Step 2 Spell the word aloud.

r-u-n-n-i-n-g

Step 3 Think about its spelling. Is there anything special to remember?

There are three n's in running.

Step 4 Picture the word with your eyes shut.

running

Step 5 Look at the word and **write** it.

running
running

Step 6 Cover the word. Picture it and **write** it again. **Check** its spelling.

running

TRY IT OUT Now practice this step-by-step plan. Do the exercises on the next two pages.

Look at each word. **Say** it and listen to its sounds. Then **spell** the word aloud.

Words	Step 1 Look, Say	Step 2 Spell Aloud
away	▢	▢
little	▢	▢
airplane	▢	▢

Think about how each word is spelled. Why is it special? Write your idea. One is done for you.

Step 3

Word	Idea
away	It's a + way.
little	
airplane	

Share your ideas with a partner or group. You may have different ideas about the same word. That's fine, as long as what you say is true.

Next, close your eyes and **picture** the word. **Look** at the word and **write** it. **Cover** the word and **write** it again. **Check** its spelling.

Step 4 Picture	Step 5 Look, Write	Step 6 Cover, Write, Check
away	___	___
little	___	___
airplane	___	___

LOOK AHEAD   Look ahead at the next five lessons. Write down four list words that look hard to spell. Use the steps for spelling to study them.

Words with dr, sc, ft, nk

SPELLING FOCUS

The letters **dr** in **dry**, **sc** in **score**, **ft** in **soft**, and **nk** in **think** are blends.

■ **STUDY** Say each word. Read the sentence.

1.	dry	Warm, **dry** socks feel good.
2.	dream	I had a **dream** last night.
3.	drink	Give him water to **drink.**
4.	score	The **score** was tied, 7 to 7.
5.	soft	I sleep with a **soft** pillow.
6.	left	I write with my **left** hand.
7.	think	We **think** the answer is no.

8.	dragon	A knight fought a **dragon.**
9.	drum	Sam beat on the **drum.**
10.	scared ✳	The loud noise **scared** me.
11.	scarf	Wear a **scarf** in winter.
12.	gift	This necklace was a **gift.**
13.	thank	I said **thank** you for the gift.
14.	bank	She has a neat piggy **bank.**

WATCH OUT FOR FREQUENTLY MISSPELLED WORDS!

■ **PRACTICE** Write one word with both **dr** and **nk.** Then write
- four other words with **dr**
- three other words with **nk**
- six words with **sc** or **ft**

■ **WRITE** Choose six words. Write a sentence for each word.

CHALLENGE!

drawer
scanner
aircraft
prank

dry	dragon	score	gift	left
drink	thank	soft	scarf	bank
scared	dream	think	drum	

PATTERNS Match the letters on the left with the ones on the right to make list words. Write each list word once.

1. tha   arf

2. drag   ft

3. sc   on

4. so   nk

CLASSIFYING Write the list word that belongs in each group.

5. guess, study, ___
6. goal, point, ___
7. present, favor, ___
8. afraid, frightened, ___
9. bugle, flute, ___

10. nap, sleep,___
11. high, low; wet, ___
12. money, safe, ___
13. up, down; right, ___
14. sip, gulp, ___

STRATEGIC SPELLING

Using Steps for Spelling New Words

15–16. Think about words when you study them. Write two list words that are hard for you. Think about how each one is spelled. What makes it special? Write your idea next to the word.

☰	Make a capital.
/	Make a small letter.
∧	Add something.
ℓ	Take out something.
⊙	Add a period.
¶	New paragraph

PROOFREAD AN AD Find the four misspelled words and two punctuation errors Juan made in his advertisement. Correct them.

<u>Free Tickets</u>

Two tickets are lift Can you an a friend go to Funland Saturday? I cant! No need to think me Just call Juan at 555-1813.

PROOFREADING TIP
Can you tell where one sentence ends and another one begins? Each sentence should have punctuation at the end.

WRITE AN AD Write an advertisement for a neighborhood newspaper. Pretend you want to sell an old toy. Use some of your spelling words.

Word List

dry	dream	scarf
drink	score	drum
scared	soft	left
dragon	think	bank
thank	gift	

Personal Words 1.___ 2.___

Review

PUZZLE Fill in the puzzle to find a meaningful book.

1. a glass of water
2. all your points
3. not right
4. not hard
5. use your head
6. ideas while you sleep
7. not wet

dry		
dream		
drink		
score		
soft		
left		
think		

1. _ _ _ _ _ _
   i
2. _ _ _ _ _
3. _ _ _ _ _
   i
4. _ _ _ _
5. _ _ _ _ _
6. _ _ _ _
   r
7. _ _ _

Using a *Dictionary*

ALPHABETICAL ORDER

Q: Why is looking up a word in a dictionary as easy as *abc*?

A: The words are listed in **alphabetical order.**

Sometimes you need to look up words that start with the same letter. Then you must look at the second letter to find them in alphabetical order. If the words also have the same second letter, then look at the third letter.

Write the words below in alphabetical order.

scarf   soft   dream   score   drink   dragon

Words with ch, sh, th, ng

SPELLING FOCUS

Some words have two consonants together that are pronounced as one sound: **rich**, **finish**, **they**, **long**.

■ **STUDY** Say each word. Read the sentence.

WATCH OUT FOR FREQUENTLY MISSPELLED WORDS!

1. rich	The actor is **rich** and famous.
2. finish	The race had a close **finish**.
3. they ✳	I know **they** are my friends.
4. mother	The **mother** fed her baby.
5. something ✳	Explain **something** to me.
6. long	We take **long** walks at night.
7. morning ✳	She runs every **morning**.

8. chain	His bicycle **chain** slipped.
9. touch	We could **touch** the lambs.
10. shadow	At noon a **shadow** is small.
11. smash	You might **smash** the vase.
12. thick	The soup is **thick** and tasty.
13. tooth	She pulled a loose **tooth**.
14. ring	He wore a shiny gold **ring**.

CHALLENGE!

cheese
sandwich
dishwasher
belongings

■ **PRACTICE** Sort the words by writing
- one word with both **th** and **ng**
- seven other words with **th** or **ng**
- six words with **ch** or **sh**

■ **WRITE** Use two sentences in a paragraph.

shadow	chain	smash	something	touch
mother	ring	long	rich	finish
tooth	they	morning	thick	

OPPOSITES Complete each phrase with the list word that is the opposite of the underlined word.

1. not <u>sunlight</u>, but ___
2. not <u>father</u>, but ___
3. not <u>thin</u>, but ___
4. not <u>short</u>, but ___
5. not <u>start</u>, but ___
6. not <u>evening</u>, but ___

RHYME TIME Complete the silly sentences. Write a list word that rhymes with the underlined words.

7. The <u>king</u> will <u>bring</u> the queen a ___.
8. Can the <u>witch</u> <u>switch</u> to being ___?
9. She can make ___ out of <u>anything</u> or <u>nothing</u>.
10. I hope the <u>rain</u> won't <u>stain</u> the ___.
11. I won't ___ such a <u>crutch</u>.
12. There was a <u>crash</u> and a ___ as I made a <u>dash</u>.
13. Who's to <u>say</u> which <u>way</u> ___ <u>play</u>?

STRATEGIC SPELLING

Seeing Meaning Connections

| toothache |
| toothpaste |

14. Write the list word that is part of each word in the box.

Write the words from the box that match the clues.

15. Squeeze me and I'll fall all over you.
16. I'm a pain above the neck.

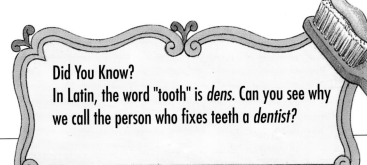

Did You Know?
In Latin, the word "tooth" is *dens*. Can you see why we call the person who fixes teeth a *dentist*?

19

≡	Make a capital.
/	Make a small letter.
∧	Add something.
ℓ	Take out something.
⊙	Add a period.
⊄	New paragraph

PROOFREAD A RECIPE Katy made pinwheels for her class. She also brought the recipe from home. Find two misspelled words and two handwriting mistakes and write them correctly.

Mexican Pinwheels

1. Spread a flour tortilla with soft cream cheese.
2. Put a little thik salsa on tup.
3. Roll up like a jellyroll and chill.
4. To finsh, cut into pinwheels.

PROOFREADING TIP
Did Katy write *tup* or *top*? If a letter is written too loosely, it may look like another letter.

WRITE A RECIPE Write a recipe for something you like to fix for yourself or for company at home. Use some of your spelling words if possible.

Word List

shadow	they	rich
mother	smash	thick
tooth	long	touch
chain	morning	finish
ring	something	

Personal Words 1.___ 2.___

Review

CROSSWORD PUZZLE Fill in the puzzle by writing the word from the box for each clue.

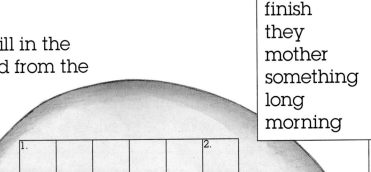

rich
finish
they
mother
something
long
morning

Across
1. father and ___
3. nothing and ___
6. start and ___
7. short and ___

Down
2. poor and ___
4. night and ___
5. we and ___

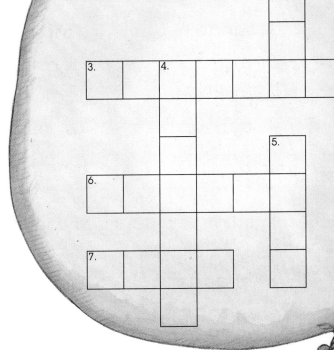

Multicultural *Connection*

LANGUAGES People of many cultures greet each other with "Good morning" or "Good day." Finish each sentence by writing the correct greeting.

Language	Greeting
Swahili	*Salam alekum*
Japanese	*Ohayō*
Spanish	*Buenos días*

1. In Spain, "Good day" is ___.
2. In Japan, they say ___.
3. In Zanzibar, Africa, you would hear ___.

21

Consonant Sounds /j/ and /s/

The consonant sound /j/ can be spelled **ge** and **j: large, jam.** The consonant sound /s/ can be spelled **c** and **s: center, silly.**

WATCH OUT FOR
FREQUENTLY
MISSPELLED
WORDS!

■ **STUDY** Say each word. Read the sentence.

1. large — We'll all fit in a **large** van.
2. page — My name is on the first **page.**
3. jam — He ate toast with **jam.**
4. center — Visit our tourist **center.**
5. pencil — You need **pencil** and paper.
6. sometimes ✳ — I daydream **sometimes.**
7. silly — My dad told a **silly** story.

8. orange — They drank **orange** juice.
9. jeans — She wore her new **jeans.**
10. joke — We laughed at the **joke.**
11. jelly — Grape **jelly** is purple.
12. circle — He drew a perfect **circle.**
13. cents — One nickel is five **cents.**
14. circus — A big top is a **circus** tent.

CHALLENGE!

bandage
journey
vegetables
concert

■ **PRACTICE** Sort the words by writing
- seven other words with /s/ spelled **c** or **s**
- three words with /j/ spelled **ge**
- four words with /j/ spelled **j**

■ **WRITE** Choose two sentences to write a slogan.

jeans   jelly   joke   pencil   circus
large   jam   silly   sometimes   circle
orange   page   cents   center

SYNONYMS Write a list word that means about the same as each word below.

1. middle
2. pants
3. pennies
4. riddle

5. funny
6. carnival
7. big
8. jelly

ALPHABETICAL ORDER Write the list word that fits alphabetically between each two-word set.

9. ozone/pain
10. peanut/people
11. open/otter

12. cinnamon/circus
13. somersault/sum

STRATEGIC SPELLING

Seeing Meaning Connections

14. Write the list word that is part of each word in the box.

Write a word from the box that fits each definition below.

jellyfish
jellybean

15. a small candy made of jellied sugar
16. a sea animal that looks like a lump of jelly

Did You Know?
Genoa, Italy, is famous for
Christopher Columbus and *jeans*.
The cloth we use for jeans was
first made there.

☰	Make a capital.
/	Make a small letter.
∧	Add something.
ℯ	Take out something.
⊙	Add a period.
℉	New paragraph

PROOFREAD A LIST Find three misspelled words in the list of supplies needed to make a class book of field trips. Write them correctly. Find one careless mistake and correct it.

1 sharp pensil

a paper punch

4 larg sheets of paper
   folded down the senter
   a label for the the cover

PROOFREADING TIP
If you proofread the list aloud, you'll find the repeated word.

CREATE A LIST Think of a project you may have to do at home or school. Make a list of what you need. Try to use some of your list words.

Word List

jeans	page	sometimes
large	joke	center
orange	silly	circus
jelly	cents	circle
jam	pencil	

Personal Words 1.___ 2.___

Review

CLASSIFYING Write the word from the box that finishes each set.

1. crayon, pen, ___
2. top, bottom, ___
3. always, never, ___
4. huge, big, ___
5. funny, stupid, ___
6. jelly, honey, ___
7. book, chapter, ___

large
page
jam
center
pencil
sometimes
silly

Word *Study*

ANTONYMS Words that have opposite meanings are called **antonyms.** There are different ways to write them.

Use a different word: large/small

Add **un-:** happy/unhappy

Below is a bad news note. Write an antonym for each word to change the bad-news note to a good-news note.

How (1) unlucky can you get! As the music (2) stopped and the lights went (3) off, everyone on the roller coaster began to (4) frown. It was (5) boring to be on the (6) slowest ride in the park.

Adding -s and -es

Add **-s** to most words, add **-es** to words that end in **ch, sh,** or **x,** and change **y** to **i** and add **-es** to words that end with a **consonant** and **y.**

WATCH OUT FOR FREQUENTLY MISSPELLED WORDS!

■ **STUDY** Notice how **-s** or **-es** is added.

friend	1. friends ✲
inch	2. inches
brush	3. brushes
fix	4. fixes
fly	5. flies
try	6. tries
penny	7. pennies

cracker	8. crackers
march	9. marches
stitch	10. stitches
rush	11. rushes
mix	12. mixes
lady	13. ladies
party	14. parties

CHALLENGE!

wasps
mailboxes
companies
batteries

■ **PRACTICE** Sort these words by writing
- five words with **y** changed to **i** before **-es** is added
- seven other words to which **-es** is added
- two words to which just **-s** is added

■ **WRITE** Write about a parade using three list words.

crackers	*marches*	*rushes*	*ladies*	*pennies*
friends	*stitches*	*fixes*	*parties*	*tries*
inches	*brushes*	*mixes*	*flies*	

MAKING CONNECTIONS Write the list word that matches each clue.

1. Thirty-six of these are in a yard.
2. Ten of these equal a dime.
3. Birthdays can be celebrated at these.
4. Hair, tooth, and paint are kinds of these.
5. You can sew using different kinds of these.
6. Graham, saltine, and animal are kinds of these.
7. Pals and buddies are these.
8. Too many of these pests ruin a picnic.

WORD MATH Do the word math and then write each list word.

9. lady **- y + i + es** =
10. rush **+ es** =
11. fix **+ es** =
12. march **+ es** =
13. try **- y + i + es** =
14. mix **+ es** =

STRATEGIC SPELLING

Building New Words

Add **-s** or **-es** to these words.
Remember what you learned.

15. touch
16. joke

FREQUENTLY MISSPELLED WORDS * FREQUENTLY MISSPELLED WORDS *

Friday ends your school week with your **friends.** Does this help you remember the spelling of *friends?*

PROOFREAD A SIGN Find the misspelled word in the photograph below. What rule did the sign maker forget? Write the word correctly.

NOW OPEN
3 PM
DAILY SPECIALS
HOT SANDWICHS
PIZZA

PROOFREADING TIP
Proofread your sign carefully before you display it. You want people to notice the sign, not a mistake.

CREATE A SIGN Make a sign advertising food. Choose words to make people hungry just reading it. Use some spelling words and a personal word.

Word List

crackers	brushes	parties
friends	rushes	flies
inches	fixes	pennies
marches	mixes	tries
stitches	ladies	

Personal Words 1.___ 2.___

Review

TONGUE TWISTERS A tongue twister is hard to say without making a mistake. What makes it so hard?

> If flies can flee, can fleas fly?

All or most of the words in a tongue twister begin with the same sound.

Write a word from the box to finish these tongue twisters.

1. Bruce's brown bike ___ bushes.
2. Terrific Tracy ___ terrible tricks twice.
3. Fernando ___ fancy phones for fun.
4. Francy and Fatima are fast ___ forever.
5. A feathered finch ___far fast.
6. Peggy put pretty ___ in piles.
7. Into the igloo the insect ___ .

| friends |
| inches |
| brushes |
| fixes |
| flies |
| tries |
| pennies |

Using a *Thesaurus*

ENTRY WORDS A **thesaurus** is a book of words with the same or nearly the same meaning. Writers use a thesaurus to help them find just the right word.

An **entry word** is a word in a thesaurus for which words of nearly the same meaning are given. Entry words in a thesaurus are usually base words. Write the entry word where you would find other words for these list words: **friends, flies, mixes.**

Look up those three entry words in your Writer's Thesaurus. Write a sentence using one synonym for each entry.

Adding -ed **and** -ing

When adding **-ed** and **-ing,** some base words do not change. Others do change.
- In words that end with **consonant-e,** the **e** is dropped.
- In words that end in **y,** the **y** is changed to **i** when adding **-ed** but kept when adding **-ing.**
- In one-syllable words that end with **consonant-vowel-consonant,** the final consonant is doubled.

■ **STUDY** Read the words in each row. Notice what happens when **-ed** and **-ing** are added.

❋
WATCH OUT FOR FREQUENTLY MISSPELLED WORDS!

start	1. started ❋	2. starting
smile	3. smiled	4. smiling
cry	5. cried	6. crying
plan	7. planned	8. planning

hope	9. hoped	10. hoping
fry	11. fried	12. frying
hop	13. hopped	14. hopping

■ **PRACTICE** Sort these words by writing
- four words in which final **e** is dropped
- four words with no spelling change
- two words in which **y** is changed to **i**
- four words in which the final consonant is doubled

■ **WRITE** Choose seven words to write in sentences.

CHALLENGE!

amazed
amazing
dragged
dragging

started   smiling   hopped   planning   cried
starting   hoped   hopping   fried   crying
smiled   hoping   planned   frying

WORD FORMS For each base word below, write the **-ed** and **-ing** forms.

start   hope   plan

1.___   3.___   5.___

2.___   4.___   6.___

WORDS IN CONTEXT Write the list word that is a form of the underlined word and fits the sentence.

7. Have you ever had a <u>fry</u> green tomato?
8. After school, Jody <u>hop</u> on her bike.
9. As the photographer said, "Cheese," Ken <u>smile</u>.
10. As the door opened, everyone <u>cry</u>, "Surprise!"
11. In this race, <u>hop</u> is allowed.
12. Is he <u>fry</u> eggs for breakfast?
13. The puppy was <u>cry</u> to go outside.
14. The actors were <u>smile</u> as they took their bows.

STRATEGIC SPELLING

Building New Words

Use the rules you learned as you add **-ed** and **-ing.**

15. circle

16. dry

≡	Make a capital.
/	Make a small letter.
∧	Add something.
ℓ	Take out something.
⊙	Add a period.
¶	New paragraph

PROOFREAD AN INVITATION Fix the two spelling errors and one capitalization error Kim made.

PROOFREADING TIP
Days of the week and months of the year should begin with a capital letter.

January 5, 20__

Dear Trish,

I planed a surprise party for Ed. Can you come to Funland on saturday at 2:00 P.M. ? Bring only a smileing face.

Kim

ANSWER AN INVITATION Answer Kim's invitation. Use some spelling words and a personal word.

Word List

started	fried	hopping
smiled	cried	planning
hoped	starting	frying
hopped	smiling	crying
planned	hoping	

Personal Words 1.___ 2.___

Review

CONTEXT CLUES Write the word from the box that best finishes each sentence.

started
starting
smiled
smiling
cried
crying
planned
planning

1. The Garcias are ___ a camping trip for next summer.
2. The baby ___ when his mother left the room.
3. "Keep ___!" Hoda said, as she snapped our picture.
4. The race ___ when the coach blew the whistle.
5. People watching the sad movie began ___.
6. He ___ when the teacher said, "Great work!"
7. Have you ___ what your costume will be?
8. We are ___ a new chapter in science today.

Word *Study*

SYNONYMS Words that have the same, or almost the same, meanings are called **synonyms.**

Write a list word that is a synonym for each underlined word. Does the story have the same meaning with the new words?

Bonzo, a sad-looking clown, (1) <u>wished</u> to change his image. He (2) <u>began</u> by changing his makeup. Then he stopped (3) <u>weeping</u> and began (4) <u>grinning</u>. In no time Bonzo was a new clown.

Review

Lesson 1: Words with dr, sc, ft, nk
Lesson 2: Words with ch, sh, th, ng
Lesson 3: Consonant Sounds /j/ and /s/

Lesson 4: Adding -s and -es
Lesson 5: Adding -ed and -ing

REVIEW WORD LIST

1. bank
2. dragon
3. dream
4. drink
5. gift
6. left
7. scared
8. scarf
9. thank

10. long
11. morning
12. mother
13. rich
14. ring
15. shadow
16. smash
17. something
18. tooth

19. center
20. cents
21. circus
22. jam
23. jelly
24. large
25. orange
26. silly
27. crackers

28. fixes
29. flies
30. friends
31. inches
32. ladies
33. pennies
34. crying
35. smiling

z a b = a b c

z = a   i = j   r = s
a = b   j = k   s = t
b = c   k = l   t = u
c = d   l = m   u = v
d = e   m = n   v = w
e = f   n = o   w = x
f = g   o = p   x = y
g = h   p = q   y = z
h = i   q = r   z = a

bank   cents   pennies
rich   thank

**Break the code and
write the list words.**

qhbg
bdmsr
odmmhdr
azmj
sgzmj

WHAT A NIGHTMARE

shadow
dream
scared
tooth
dragon

When Tony woke up in the morning, he wrote in his journal. Complete the sentences. Write each list word once.

I knew it was just a (1). I wanted to wake up, but I was too (2). A huge, purple (3) with an enormous, front (4) chased me the whole night. Suddenly its hulking body cast a giant (5) over me. Then Dad shook me to get up for school.

UNDER THE BIG TOP

Sue has begun writing a movie script. Use the list words to complete her ideas. Write each word once.

ladies   ring   circus   center   smiling   silly

Narrator: *(A long shot of the big (1) tent)* It's sundown as everyone enters the tent to witness the performances of the trained animals, the talented, but (2) clowns, and the daring trapeze artists.

Ringmaster: *(Inside the tent, the lights go down. A small, bright spotlight hits the ringmaster. He's (3) broadly.)* Welcome (4) and gentlemen. May I direct your attention to the (5) of the (6)?

BREAKFAST!

Who Needs It?

For her health project, Amy interviewed her grandmother. Use the list words to complete each question and answer. Write each word once.

jam
mother
morning
orange
drink

Q: Is it necessary to eat breakfast every (1)?

A: Yes, and it's also a good idea to (2) milk and (3) juice.

Q: Is toast with grape or strawberry (4) healthful?

A: I don't know, but I'll ask your (5) to get a jar so that I can read the label.

Annual Crafts Show Begins

In the Neighborhood section of the local newspaper, Pedro announced this upcoming event. Complete the announcement with list words. Write each word once.

crackers
scarf
jelly
friends
gift

Many holiday (1) ideas will come to mind if you visit the annual Crafts Fair at Prospect School. It will be held on Saturday, November 28, from 10:00 A.M. to 4:00 P.M. You will be able to buy a handmade (2) or a quilted pillow. Some of your (3) and neighbors will be selling homemade jam and (4) this year. Samples will be served on assorted (5).

What Fits?

Kimiko set up this puzzle for her classmates. Solve each puzzle. Write the list word that belongs in each group.

1. break, destroy,

2. walks, drives,

3. repairs, mends,

4. feet, yards,

5. small, medium,

fixes
inches
flies
smash
large

SIMON SAYS DO THE OPPOSITE

something
crying
left
long

Write the list word that is the opposite of each underlined word.

1. Simon says, "Turn <u>right</u>."
2. Simon says, "Everyone should be <u>laughing</u>."
3. Simon says, "Take a <u>short</u> step."
4. Simon says, "Everyone should say <u>nothing</u>."

Rhyming Helpers

DISCOVER THE STRATEGY   Jason uses rhymes to help him spell. Here's how he remembers that **clown** is spelled **c-l-o-w-n.**

Brown, town, and *down* help Jason because they rhyme with **clown** and they're spelled the same at the end. He calls this strategy rhyming helpers.

TRY IT OUT   Now you'll learn how to use rhyming helpers.

Write *thick* and *dream.* Then write a rhyming helper from the Word Bank. Underline the matching letters.

team	seem
ink	pick

Watch Out! Just because one word rhymes with another doesn't mean it's a good helper. Tell why *main* would be a good rhyming helper for *chain,* but *lane* would not.

Write *thank* and *clean.* Then think of and write a rhyming helper for each word. Underline the matching letters.

With a partner, check each other's work.

LOOK AHEAD   Look ahead at the next five lessons. Find two list words you could use this strategy with and write them.

Short e

SPELLING FOCUS

Short e is often spelled **e: sme<u>l</u>l**. It can also be spelled **ea: h<u>ea</u>d**.

■ **STUDY** Say each word. Read the sentence.

1.	smell	The cheese has a strong **smell.**
2.	then ✱	The sun rises, **then** sets.
3.	together	Everyone sat **together.**
4.	getting ✱	They are **getting** a new car.
5.	head	She put a hat on her **head.**
6.	ready	Class is **ready** to begin.
7.	instead	Say yes **instead** of maybe.

8.	fresh	The farmer sells **fresh** fruit.
9.	spelling	The **spelling** test is easy.
10.	else	Give someone **else** a turn.
11.	breakfast	I eat cereal for **breakfast.**
12.	dead	The toy has a **dead** battery.
13.	feather	A bird **feather** is soft.
14.	bread	Dad toasted our **bread.**

✱
WATCH OUT FOR FREQUENTLY MISSPELLED WORDS!

■ **PRACTICE** Sort the words by writing
▪ seven words with **short e** spelled **ea**
▪ seven words with **short e** spelled **e**

■ **WRITE** Choose two sentences to use in riddles or rhymes.

CHALLENGE!

arrest
pretend
heavier
jealous

getting   together   else   ready   smell
breakfast   dead   bread   then   instead
fresh   feather   spelling   head

LETTERS AND SOUNDS Change the underlined vowel in each word to make a list word with the **short e** sound.

1. sm<u>a</u>ll
2. f<u>a</u>ther
3. th<u>a</u>n
4. sp<u>i</u>lling
5. h<u>i</u>d

DEFINITIONS Write the list word that means the same as the underlined word or phrase. Use your Spelling Dictionary if necessary.

6. What time is <u>the first meal of the day</u>?
7. How about some <u>newly made</u> orange juice?
8. Do you want something <u>different</u> instead?
9. When can the pancakes be <u>prepared</u> to eat?
10. I'm <u>becoming</u> hungrier by the minute.
11. Can we work <u>in cooperation</u> to fix this meal?

STRATEGIC SPELLING

Using the Rhyming Helper Strategy

12–14. A rhyming helper rhymes with another word and is spelled the same at the end. The word *head* is a rhyming helper for three other list words. Write the other list words that go with *head*. Underline the matching letters.

Did You Know?
Breakfast means to "break a fast." To *fast* means to "go without food." In the morning we *break* the *fast* by eating *breakfast*.

41

═	Make a capital.
/	Make a small letter.
∧	Add something.
ℯ	Take out something.
⊙	Add a period.
¶	New paragraph

PROOFREAD A DESCRIPTION

Read Beth's description of her grandmother. Find three spelling errors and one incorrect verb. Correct them.

PROOFREADING TIP

Beth needs to watch the endings on her verbs. She should have written *grandma collects* instead of *grandma collect*. Proofread aloud to be sure everything sounds right.

My grandma collect old toys. When we're togather, she shows me her dolls, her games, and her marbles. Our family is almost redy for her birthday. But wat old toy can we get her?

WRITE A DESCRIPTION

Write a description of one of your friends or relatives. Use some of your spelling words and at least one personal word.

Word List

getting	feather	then
breakfast	else	head
fresh	bread	smell
together	spelling	instead
dead	ready	

Personal Words 1.___ 2.___

Review

PUZZLE Use words from the box to fill in the puzzle. The puzzle answers the riddle.

What day is everyone waiting for?

1. now and ___
2. apart or ___
3. you do it with your nose
4. giving and ___
5. highest part of your body
6. in another's place
7. ___, set, go

smell
then
together
getting
head
ready
instead

1. _ _ _ _ _
2. _ _ _ _ _ _ _
3. _ _ _ _ _
4. _ _ _ _ _ _
5. _ _ _ _
6. _ _ _ _ _ _ _
7. _ _ _ _ _

Multicultural Connection

FOODS People all over the world eat **breakfast.** In fact, many people in different countries enjoy foods that are alike but have different names. Use the information to answer the questions below.

The people of France often eat *les croissants* (crescent-shaped rolls) with *le beurre* (butter) and *café au lait* (coffee with milk).

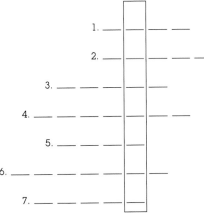

Italy
il pane (bread)
il burro (butter)
caffè latte (coffee with milk)

Russia
kasha (cooked cereal)

Japan
miso (a kind of soup)

Mexico
biscochos (sweet buns)
café con leche (coffee with hot milk)

1–2. In which countries do people eat a breakfast similar to the breakfast eaten in France?
3. In which country is cooked cereal often eaten?

Long e

SPELLING FOCUS

Long e can be spelled **y, ee,** and **e**: an**y**, w**ee**k, vid**e**o.

■ **STUDY** Say each word. Read the sentence.

1.	many	He has so **many** toys.
2.	any	You can pick **any** book.
3.	seem	They **seem** to be asleep.
4.	deep	Don't swim in **deep** water.
5.	week	A **week** is seven days.
6.	idea	Think of an **idea**.
7.	video	We will get to see a **video**.

8.	city	The **city** streets are crowded.
9.	lucky	My **lucky** number is seven.
10.	busy	The workers are **busy**.
11.	Halloween✳	I had a **Halloween** party.
12.	asleep	The baby fell **asleep** at last.
13.	secret	A friend will keep a **secret**.
14.	even	The ice was **even** and slick.

■ **PRACTICE** Sort the words by writing
- four words with **long e** spelled **e**
- five words with **long e** spelled **ee**
- five words with **long e** spelled **y**

■ **WRITE** Choose three sentences to rewrite as questions.

CHALLENGE!

trophy
activity
referee
torpedo

idea   city   secret   asleep   video
Halloween seem   deep   week   even
any   lucky   many   busy

LETTERS AND SOUNDS Change the underlined vowel in each word to make a list word with the **long e** sound.

1. ov<u>e</u>n   3. w<u>o</u>k
2. s<u>u</u>m   4. d<u>i</u>p

CLASSIFYING Write the list word that

  5. begins with a capital letter.
  6. begins with the letter *v*.
  7. has four letters and three are vowels.
  8. begins with *bus*.
  9. has the word *sleep* in it.
10. has *it* in the middle.
11. rhymes with *ducky*.
12. begins with an *s* and ends with a *t*.
13. rhymes with *many*.
14. has *man* in it.

Seeing Meaning Connections

Add *any* to each word to make a new word.

15. one

16. where

Take a Hint
The words *week* and *weak* sound alike. Remember a week has **seven** days.

≡	Make a capital.
/	Make a small letter.
∧	Add something.
ℯ	Take out something.
⊙	Add a period.
¶	New paragraph

PROOFREAD A STORY After a trip to the zoo, Jeff began to write a make-believe story. Find two misspelled words and one careless error. Correct them.

When I was a baby bear, I had a fuzzy, stuffed boy. I lived at the citie zoo with Mama and Papa. We very happy. I'd fall a sleep in our den with my cuddly boy right next to me.

PROOFREADING TIP
Jeff left a word out of his story. Read your work aloud to catch this kind of error.

WRITE A STORY Pretend you are an animal. Write a story about something in your life. Use some spelling words and one personal word.

Word List

idea	lucky	week
Halloween	secret	busy
any	deep	video
city	many	even
seem	asleep	

Personal Words 1.___ 2.___

Review

RHYMES Use a word from the box to finish each silly rhyme.

many
any
seem
deep
week
idea
video

1. Your bike wouldn't squeak,
   If you'd oiled it last ___.
2. She found a penny,
   But I didn't find ___.
3. Nightmare or dream—
   How very real they ___.
4. His ___ was great,
   But his homework was late!
5. Come on, let's go
   Rent a funny ___.
6. The ticket was cheap,
   But the cave was not ___.
7. "Just three cats," said Jenny,
   "You don't have ___."

Word *Study*

ACROSTICS An **acrostic** is a way of arranging words to tell what you know about something. To make an **acrostic,** write a noun from left to right. Then connect other words to it that describe the noun. Try it with *dinosaur.* Use the words in the word box or words of your own. One has been done for you.

many
huge
reptile
extinct

```
          a
d i n o s a u r
          l
          e
          e
          p
```

Short a and Long a

SPELLING FOCUS

Short a is often spelled **a**: <u>a</u>nd. **Long a** can be spelled **ai** and **ay**: t<u>ai</u>l, tod<u>ay</u>.

■ **STUDY** Say each word. Read the sentence.

1. last	He finished **last** in the race.
2. and ✳	You **and** I are best friends.
3. math	That **math** problem is easy.
4. began	The show **began** on time.
5. tail	The puppy wagged its **tail**.
6. afraid	He is **afraid** of the dark.
7. today	My birthday is **today**.

WATCH OUT FOR FREQUENTLY MISSPELLED WORDS!

8. camping	We use a tent for **camping**.
9. trail	They hiked along the **trail**.
10. aim	Take **aim** and throw the ball.
11. Maine	**Maine** is an eastern state.
12. holiday	Enjoy your **holiday** season.
13. crayon	She colors with a **crayon**.
14. spray	Red paint is in the **spray** can.

■ **PRACTICE** Sort the words by writing
- five words with **long a** spelled **ai**
- five words with **short a** spelled **a**
- four words with **long a** spelled **ay**

CHALLENGE!

fantastic
mechanic
complain
essay

■ **WRITE** Choose six words. Write a sentence for each word.

tail   camping last   math   holiday
crayon Maine   aim   began   spray
trail   and   today   afraid

TWO MEANINGS Write the list word that fits both phrases. Use your Spelling Dictionary.

1. a mountain ___
   ___ by three points

3. my ___ in life
   ___ at the target

2. a ___ of flowers
   a ___ from a hose

4. a dog's wagging ___
   ___ a suspect all day

MAKING CONNECTIONS Write a list word to complete each statement.

5. The one at the end of a line is ___.
6. A short word for *mathematics* is ___.
7. Another word for *also* is ___.
8. One state in the United States is ___.
9. A day off from school might be a ___.
10. The word *started* means the same as ___.
11. You can draw with a ___.
12. You might need a sleeping bag for a ___ trip.

STRATEGIC SPELLING

Using Steps for Spelling New Words

13–14. Write *today* and *afraid*. Think about how each one is spelled. What makes it special? Write your idea next to the word.

Word   **Idea**

___   ___

PROOFREAD A HOW-TO ARTICLE

Carla began to write some tips on packing for a trip. Correct her four spelling errors and two handwriting errors.

How to Pack for a Camping Trip

First, make a list of what you'll need on the tral. Next, sel out everything, an dont be a frad if it looks like too much. You'll pul most of it back anyway.

PROOFREADING TIP

Carla's handwriting is pretty good, but she didn't cross two letters. A **t** that is not crossed might look like an **l**.

WRITE A HOW-TO ARTICLE

Explain to someone how to load a camera with film or how to do something you're really good at. Try to use some spelling words and at least one personal word.

Word List

tail	and	began
crayon	last	afraid
trail	aim	holiday
camping	today	spray
Maine	math	

Personal Words 1.___ 2.___

Review

CROSSWORD PUZZLE Use the clues for words in the box that finish the puzzle.

last
and
math
began
tail
afraid
today

Across
1. started
3. school subject
4. this day
5. opposite of *first*

Down
2. scared
4. a dog wags it
6. red, white, ___ blue

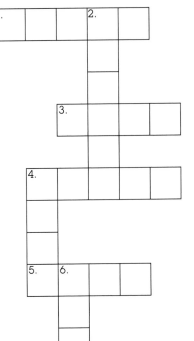

Using a *Dictionary*

GUIDE WORDS The two words at the top of a dictionary page are called **guide words.** They tell the first and last entry word on the page. You can find a word in a dictionary by using the guide words. Write the list word you would find on the page with each pair of guide words.

1. **tag/talk**   2. **match/matter**   3. **afford/again**

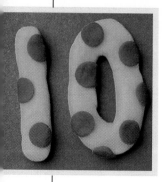

Short o and Long o

SPELLING FOCUS

Short o is often spelled **o: socks. Long o** can be spelled **o** and **oa: most, coat.**

■ **STUDY** Say each word. Read the sentence.

1.	body	The **body** needs sleep.
2.	socks	The team **socks** are blue.
3.	gold	The king has **gold** coins.
4.	most	He likes **most** of the people.
5.	ago	The tale happened long **ago.**
6.	coat	Button up your **coat.**
7.	toast	I eat **toast** for breakfast.

8.	monster	A **monster** movie is scary.
9.	collar	The dog lost its **collar.**
10.	Ohio	We live in Akron, **Ohio.**
11.	hello	Pa said **hello** cheerfully.
12.	road	The **road** has big potholes.
13.	coach	She likes her golf **coach.**
14.	load	Carry this **load** of laundry.

■ **PRACTICE** Sort the words by writing
- five words with **long o** spelled **o**
- four words with **short o** spelled **o**
- five words with **long o** spelled **oa**

■ **WRITE** Use two sentences in a paragraph.

CHALLENGE!

fossil
volleyball
potato
oatmeal

monster	ago	collar	socks	load
gold	coat	toast	body	most
road	Ohio	coach	hello	

PICTURE CLUES Write the list word that names each picture.

1.

2.

3.

RHYMES Write the list word that rhymes with each word below.

4. ghost

5. dollar

6. told

MEANING CONNECTIONS Write the list word that matches each clue.

7. Use this word to greet people.
8. This is a state in the Midwest.
9. You can walk or ride on this.
10. This can be heavy to carry.
11. This word describes an event that has happened in the past.

STRATEGIC SPELLING

Building New Words

12–14. Write *coach, body,* and *monster.* Add **-s** or **-es** to each. Remember what you learned about adding these endings.

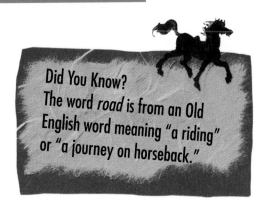

Did You Know?
The word *road* is from an Old English word meaning "a riding" or "a journey on horseback."

≡	Make a capital.
/	Make a small letter.
∧	Add something.
℮	Take out something.
⊙	Add a period.
¶	New paragraph

PROOFREAD AN INTERVIEW

Milo is getting ready to interview a new classmate for the school paper. He made three spelling errors and one capitalization error in his notes. Fix his mistakes.

1. Where were you born?

2. how long a go did you come to Ohio?

3. How do you say "hellow" in Greek?

4. What do you like moste about school?

PROOFREADING TIP
Milo didn't begin each sentence correctly. Proofread to make sure each sentence begins with a capital letter.

WRITE AN INTERVIEW Write some questions you would like to ask a person who has lived in or visited another country. Use some of your spelling words and one personal word if you can.

Word List

monster	Ohio	body
gold	collar	hello
road	toast	load
ago	coach	most
coat	socks	

Personal Words 1.___ 2.___

body
socks
gold
most
ago
coat
toast

Review

CONTEXT CLUES Read the story. Then write a word from the box to replace each underlined word or phrase.

A long time (1) <u>back</u>, people searched for (2) <u>a yellow metal</u> in Alaska. A miner needed many supplies, but some were more important than others. The (3) <u>very</u> important things for staying alive were food and clothing. Heavy (4) <u>stockings</u> and a heavy (5) <u>jacket</u> could keep a (6) <u>person</u> as warm as (7) <u>bread</u>.

Word *Study*

WORDS WITH MORE THAN ONE MEANING

Many words have more than one meaning. A **coat** of paint is not the same as a **coat** of arms or a warm **coat**. A football **coach** is not Cinderella's **coach.**

Read the sentences below. Write either *cake* or *bar* to complete each sentence. If you need to, use your Spelling Dictionary to help you with the different meanings.

1. We had milk and banana ___ for dessert.
2. She had a candy ___ in her pocket.
3. Mud will ___ as it dries.
4. There was a ___ across the barn door.

55

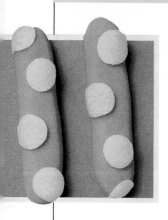

Short i and Long i

Short i is often spelled **i**: **his**. **Long i** can be spelled **igh** and **y**: **might**, **why**.

■ **STUDY** Say each word. Read the sentence.

1. still — It is hard to sit **still**.
2. with ✳ — I like cookies **with** milk.
3. his ✳ — That is **his** hat, not yours.
4. bright — The grass is **bright** green.
5. might — It **might** snow again.
6. my — These are **my** parents.
7. why — Ben always asks **why**.

8. visit — Jan will come for a **visit**.
9. picnic — We sat at a **picnic** table.
10. winter — He likes cold **winter** weather.
11. tight — My shoes are too **tight**.
12. sight — The river was a **sight** to see.
13. fly — We **fly** kites in March.
14. sky — The **sky** was clear blue.

✳
WATCH OUT FOR FREQUENTLY MISSPELLED WORDS!

■ **PRACTICE** Sort the words by writing
- four words with **long i** spelled **igh**
- four words with **long i** spelled **y**
- six words with **short i** spelled **i**

■ **WRITE** Use two sentences in a paragraph about summer.

CHALLENGE!

pumpkin
lightning
nightmare
recycle

with	*visit*	*sight*	*winter*	*might*
fly	*why*	*bright*	*sky*	*still*
tight	*picnic*	*my*	*his*	

BEFORE AND AFTER Write the list word that begins and ends like each word below.

1. stall
2. may
3. taught
4. slight
5. worth
6. fry

DEFINITIONS Write the list word that means the same as the phrase.

7. a party with a meal in the open air
8. giving much light
9. the coldest season of the year
10. for what reason
11. go to see
12. belonging to him

STRATEGIC SPELLING

Using the Rhyming Helper Strategy

13–14. A rhyming helper rhymes with another word and is spelled the same at the end. Write *might* and *sky*. Write a rhyming helper from the group below for each word. Underline the matching letters.

kite   try

eye   night

Take a Hint
Knock, knock.
Who's there?
Who **is it**
coming to
visit?

	Make a capital.
=	Make a capital.
/	Make a small letter.
∧	Add something.
ℓ	Take out something.
⊙	Add a period.
¶	New paragraph

PROOFREAD A CARTOON Julio showed his humor in a cartoon. But he made two spelling errors and one error in punctuation. Fix his errors.

PROOFREADING TIP
Punctuation errors aren't funny, even in a cartoon. Only **questions** are followed by **question marks.**

You must be the new kid.

I don't know whay you'd say that?

What was hs first clue?

MAKE A CARTOON Draw a cartoon of your own. What will your characters say? Use some spelling words and a personal word if you can.

Word List

with	picnic	sky
fly	sight	his
tight	bright	might
visit	my	still
why	winter	

Personal Words 1.___ 2.___

Review

CROSSWORD PUZZLE Fill in the crossword puzzle by writing a word from the box for each clue.

still
with
his
bright
might
my
why

Across

1. hot dog ___ everything
3. I, ___, mine
4. shiny
5. not moving

Down

1. where, when, ___
2. hers and ___
3. can, could; may, ___

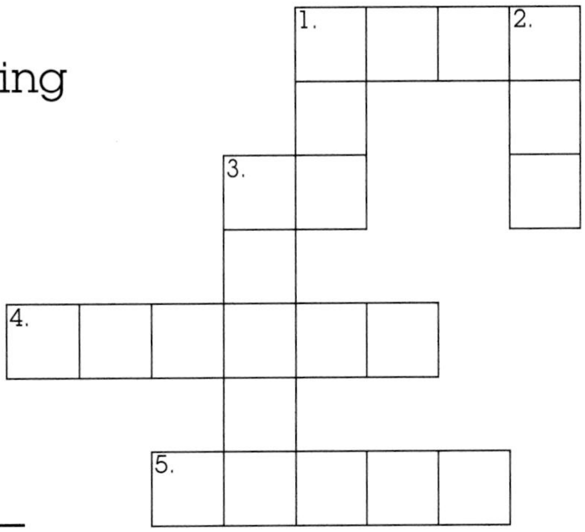

Word *Study*

WORD WEB To find out what you know about a subject, you can make a **word web.** Write words that tell about a picnic.

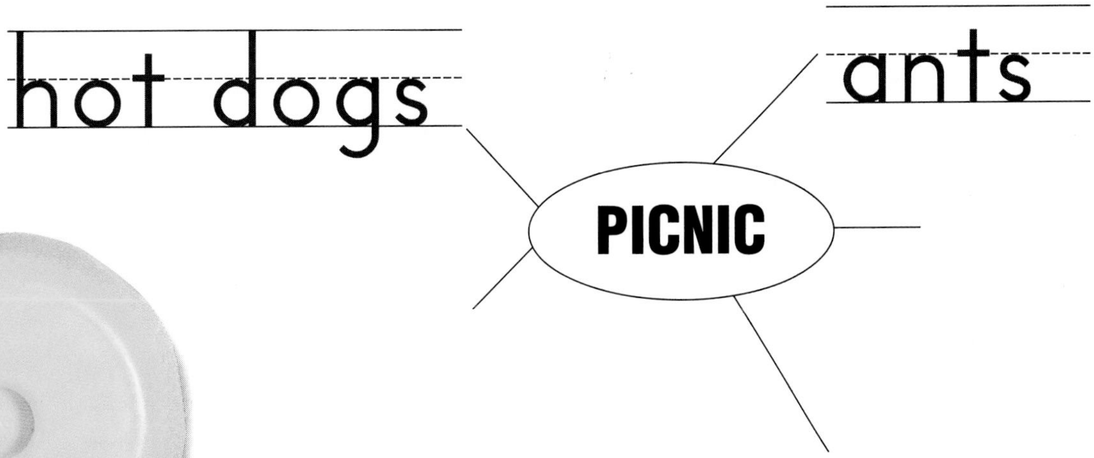

hot dogs

ants

PICNIC

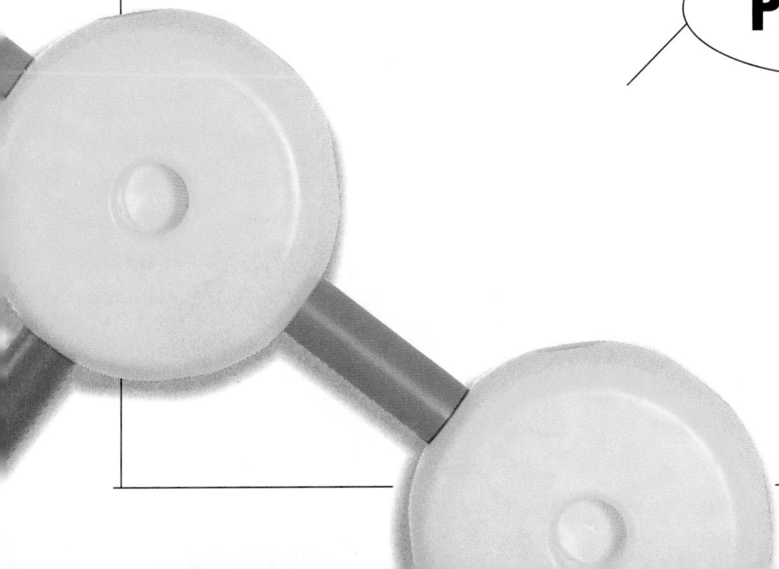

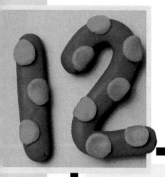

Review

Lesson 7: Short e
Lesson 8: Long e
Lesson 9: Short a and Long a

Lesson 10: Short o and Long o
Lesson 11: Short i and Long i

REVIEW WORD LIST

1. breakfast
2. fresh
3. getting
4. instead
5. ready
6. smell
7. spelling
8. together
9. asleep

10. city
11. even
12. lucky
13. many
14. secret
15. video
16. week
17. afraid
18. and

19. began
20. camping
21. math
22. today
23. ago
24. coat
25. load
26. road
27. fly

28. his
29. my
30. picnic
31. sky
32. visit
33. why
34. winter
35. with

opposites

asleep **ready** **today** **afraid**
fresh **began** **even**

Choose a list word that means the opposite
of each word at the right.

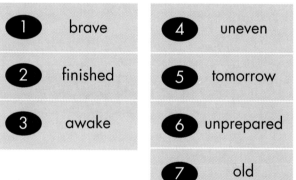

1 brave
2 finished
3 awake
4 uneven
5 tomorrow
6 unprepared
7 old

Duck and I

This poem rhymes. Write the list words once.

my   fly   why   sky

A duck can ___,

Up in the ___.

I don't know ___,

But I'd like to try; oh ___!

SUMMERTIME

Jace took a survey. Complete each answer with a list word.

Third-grade survey: I like summer vacation because…

**coat
smell
camping
city
spelling
together**

Theresa: I can lie in the grass and (1) the flowers in bloom.

Randy: I don't have to study (2), and I can read any book I choose.

Miguel: I never have to wear boots or a (3).

Seamus and Sean: We stay at our dad's house and go (4) and canoeing with our stepbrothers.

Becky: We get (5) with all our relatives for barbecues and picnics.

Khanh: I'm going to the (6) of Washington, D.C., to see the White House.

61

The Family Job Jar

lucky
winter
breakfast
getting
load
picnic

People in Tuan's house have chores. They pick cards from a jar to find out what job to do. Complete each card with a list word.

Go outside. Water the grass and wash off the (1) table and benches.

Put all the scarves, hats, and mittens away for next (3).

Your job is to fold a (2) of clothes.

Wash and dry the (4) dishes after we eat tomorrow morning.

The bookshelves are (5) dusty. Clean them today.

This is your (6) day! You do not have to do a job.

A Train Trip

Laura wrote some exciting news in her diary. Write each list word only once to complete her entry.

secret   with   visit   week   math

Dear Diary,

Today I sent Juanita a message in a (1) code. It looked like this:

9 1 13 7 15 9 14 7 15 14 1 20
18 9 16 14 5 24 20 23 5 5 11

I learned the code in (2) class. The message says:

I am going on a trip next (3).

I really am! Dad and I are taking a train to Austin! We'll (4) Grandma, and I'll play with all my cousins. Hey, Diary, I won't forget to take you (5) me!

STREET REPAIRS

Read this magazine story. Write the list words to complete the sentences. Use each word once.

his   many   road   video   and   ago   instead

Kids in Action

These third graders found (1) large holes in a main (2) near their school. They sent the mayor (3) the city council a (4) of the holes.

Each student had a chance to give (5) or her opinion to the council. The students asked why the city waited for the holes to get worse (6) of repairing the road long (7). The mayor told them that they would get an answer at the next council meeting.

Strategy Workshop

Problem Parts

DISCOVER THE STRATEGY We all have words that are hard for us to spell. Here's a strategy that will help.

Step 1 Ask yourself:

Which part of the word gives me problems?

Step 2 Underline your problem part.

wasn't which

Step 3 Picture the word. Focus on the problem part.

wasn't which

TRY IT OUT Now practice the problem-parts strategy below and on the next page.

Find four misspelled words and write them. Be sure to spell them right. Use a dictionary if you need help. Then underline the part of each word that gave the writer problems.

Almost every holaday we vizit our friends in Ohio. We go on a picknick in a big city park. We allways have a good time.

What are some words you've misspelled? List three of them. Be sure to spell them right. Use a dictionary if you need help.

Underline the part of each word that's a problem for you. Now study your list. Pay special attention to the underlined parts.

Have your partner or group quiz you on your words. Then check the results. How did you do?

LOOK AHEAD   Look ahead at the next five lessons. Find three list words you could use this strategy with and list them. Underline the part of each word that might cause you problems.

Using Just Enough Letters

SPELLING FOCUS

Pronouncing a word carefully and picturing how it looks helps you avoid writing too many letters.

■ **STUDY** Say each word. Read the sentence.

✻
WATCH OUT FOR FREQUENTLY MISSPELLED WORDS!

1.	found ✻	He **found** his lost glove.
2.	doing	She is **doing** homework.
3.	until ✻	We waited **until** five o'clock.
4.	one ✻	I ate **one** or two apples.
5.	sure	I'm **sure** I saw you.
6.	always ✻	The bus is **always** on time.
7.	almost ✻	She is **almost** ready to go.

8.	hasn't	The bell **hasn't** rung yet.
9.	couldn't	We **couldn't** forget you.
10.	alone	Don't leave the baby **alone.**
11.	a lot ✻	The comic laughs **a lot.**
12.	hadn't	We **hadn't** locked the door.
13.	angry	He spoke in an **angry** tone.
14.	hungry	I'm **hungry** for chili.

CHALLENGE**!**

chimney
computer
hundred
burglar

■ **PRACTICE** Sort the words by writing four or five words that are hardest for you to spell. Then write all the other words in any order you choose.

■ **WRITE** Use two sentences in a paragraph.

found	couldn't	alone	hadn't	always
hasn't	one	doing	almost	hungry
until	sure	a lot	angry	

CROSSWORD PUZZLE Use the clues to complete the crossword puzzle with list words.

DOWN
1. *had + not*
2. nearly all
4. upset; mad

ACROSS
3. *has + not*
5. working on

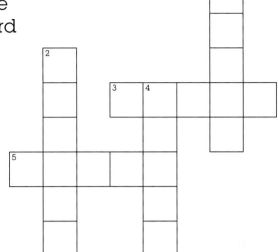

DEFINITIONS Write list words to complete the paragraph.

I like having the apartment to myself. Now I'm home (6) at last, even if it's only for (7) night. I'm (8) to have a good time. When I'm (9), I eat. When I'm tired, I sleep (10). I've (11) out that life (12) be finer for a cat like me.

Strategic Spelling

Using the Problem Parts Strategy

You might expect to see **ll** instead of **l** in *until* and *always*. Write the words and underline the single **l** in each to help you remember how to spell them.

FREQUENTLY MISSPELLED WORDS * FREQUENTLY MISSPELLED WORDS * FREQUENTLY

You won't find *a lot* under the **a**'s in the dictionary. You'll find it in the **l**'s under *lot*. Remember, it's two words, not one!

≡	Make a capital.
/	Make a small letter.
∧	Add something.
ℯ	Take out something.
⊙	Add a period.
¶	New paragraph

PROOFREAD A FORM Sally filled out a form to tell the owners what she thought about their restaurant. Correct three spelling errors and one handwriting error she made.

PROOFREADING TIP
Like most people, Sally sometimes rushes when she writes. Does her answer say *lung* or *long*?

How would you rate our service?

I was hungery, and it sure took a long time to get are food.

How would you rate our food?

The food was allways cold.

FILL OUT A FORM Fill out a form like the one above. Try to use one or two list words.

How would you rate our service?

How would you rate our food?

Word List

found	sure	almost
hasn't	alone	angry
until	doing	always
couldn't	a lot	hungry
one	hadn't	

Personal Words 1.___ 2.___

Review

CONTEXT CLUES Choose a word from the box that best completes each sentence.

found
doing
until
one
sure
always
almost

1. What were you ___ when the rain started?
2. I am ___ that I returned the library book.
3. Grandma ___ makes pancakes for Sunday breakfast.
4. We waited for you ___ noon.
5. I ___ my shoes under the bed.
6. Which ___ of you will go first?
7. Tyrell is ___ finished with his homework.

Word *Study*

HINK PINKS Play a rhyming game with a partner. Think of two short rhyming words that answer this question.

What do you call **an unhappy father?**

Your answer should be **a sad dad.**
Use the phrases in the box to answer the hink pinks.

a hot pot

a cook's books

a tall wall

a fat cat

a mad lad

a grape ape

1. What do you call **an angry boy?**
2. What do you call **a high fence?**
3. What do you call **a sizzling pan?**
4. What do you call **a chubby kitty?**
5. What do you call **a chef's novels?**
6. What do you call **a purple gorilla?**

Words with w and wh

■ **STUDY** Say each word. Read the sentence.

1. was ✻   He **was** here before me.
2. warm   We kept **warm** by the fire.
3. want ✻   I **want** you to learn this.
4. went ✻   Today we **went** to the park.
5. where ✻   Find out **where** he lives.
6. what ✻   They know **what** to do.
7. when ✻   It was late **when** she left.

✻
WATCH OUT FOR FREQUENTLY MISSPELLED WORDS!

8. watched   We **watched** TV after dinner.
9. wear   In winter you **wear** a coat.
10. would ✻   He said he **would** do it.
11. wheel   Turn the steering **wheel.**
12. whip   I will **whip** the cream.
13. whale   A killer **whale** surfaced.
14. while   Come sit with me for a **while.**

CHALLENGE!

warrior
weather
whether
whisper

■ **PRACTICE** Sort the words by writing
• seven words that begin with **wh**
• seven words that begin with **w**

■ **WRITE** Choose three sentences to write as questions.

was   wheel   would   when   went
watched   want   whip   whale   while
where   wear   what   warm

REBUSES Write the list word that matches each letter and picture clue below.

1. w +

2. w +

3. w+→

4. w +

5. w +

POEMS Write list words to complete the poems.

We watched a wh (6)__ while it was skimming
Across the sea to wh (7)__ more were swimming,
It we (8)__ where whales were ever brimming,
To where the whales were ever swimming.

We wa (9)__ a goose wh (10)__ it w (11)__ flying
Across the sky to where more were crying.
It wo(12)__ fly so high while it was trying,
To fly to where the geese were flying.

Strategic Spelling

Building New Words

13–14. Write *want* and *whip*. Write the forms of these words that complete the chart. Remember what you've learned.

Base Word	Add -ed	Add -ing
___	___	___
___	___	___

≡	Make a capital.
/	Make a small letter.
∧	Add something.
℮	Take out something.
⊙	Add a period.
⁋	New paragraph

PROOFREAD A WEATHER REPORT

Akemi broadcasts the school news every day. She wrote this weather report. Fix three spelling errors and two places where she used the wrong verb.

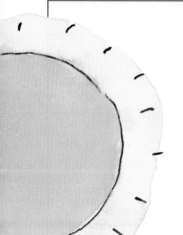

The rain along the coast wos cold. High winds brought worm air over the mountains. Then wen the warm air met the cold water, fog develop. The sun came out and make everything warm and sunny.

PROOFREADING TIP

Akemi used two incorrect verb forms. Which should it have been — *develop* or *developed*? Look at all the other verbs to be sure they are correct forms.

WRITE A WEATHER REPORT Write what the weather was like in your area today. Use some of your spelling words and one personal word.

Word List

was	wear	whale
watched	would	warm
where	whip	went
wheel	what	while
want	when	

Personal Words 1.___ 2.___

was	where
warm	what
want	when
went	

PUZZLE Write each letter of your answer on a separate line. Then use the numbered letters to solve the riddle.

1. I ___ happy to help you.

___ ___ ___ ___
$\quad\quad$ 9

2. Ruben ___ to the store with Dad.

___ ___ ___ ___
$\quad$ 3 $\quad$ 10

3. What do you ___ for your birthday?

___ ___ ___ ___
$\quad\quad\quad$ 4

4. I didn't hear ___ you said.

___ ___ ___ ___
$\quad\quad\quad$ 5

5. Practice was over ___ I got there.

___ ___ ___ ___
$\quad$ 6 $\quad$ 11

6. She asked, "___ did you find my book?"

___ ___ ___ ___ ___
$\quad$ 1 $\quad\quad\quad$ 7

7. The day was ___ and sunny.

___ ___ ___ ___
$\quad\quad$ 8 $\quad$ 2

Where do you find a cooking cowboy?

1	2	3		4		5	6	7		8	9	10	11
O				O								G	

Multicultural *Connection*

TRAVEL Gregorio lives in Puerto Rico. During the winter holiday he is going with his uncle to Fairbanks, Alaska. One of the things he knows will be different there is the weather. It is much colder. He wants to take the right kind of clothing with him.

Help Gregorio pack his suitcase. Write the items of clothing listed in the box that he should take.

down jacket	mittens	earmuffs
boots	wool scarf	sweatshirt
sandals	bathing suit	straw hat

Consonant Sounds /s/ and /k/

SPELLING FOCUS

The sound /s/ can be spelled **ce** and **se**: on**ce**, hou**se**. The sound /k/ is often spelled **ck**: tri**ck**.

■ **STUDY** Say each word. Read the sentence.

*
WATCH OUT FOR
FREQUENTLY
MISSPELLED
WORDS!

1.	once *	Ed called **once** or twice.
2.	chance	We have a **chance** to win.
3.	face	He made a funny **face**.
4.	house *	The **house** next door is tan.
5.	neck	Rub my stiff **neck**, please.
6.	trick	I taught the dog a **trick**.
7.	jacket	Wear a light **jacket** today.

8.	since	I'm lonely **since** you left.
9.	police	Ask that **police** officer.
10.	erase	Who will **erase** the board?
11.	chase	Hounds **chase** the fox.
12.	bucket	She put water in a **bucket**.
13.	ticket	Buy a **ticket** at the door.
14.	locker	My coat is in my **locker**.

■ **PRACTICE** Sort the words by writing
- six words with the sound /k/ spelled **ck**
- five words with the sound /s/ spelled **ce**
- three words with the sound /s/ spelled **se**

■ **WRITE** Use two sentences in a paragraph about school.

CHALLENGE!

furnace
violence
purpose
tackle

once	erase	house	face	locker
trick	chance	neck	chase	police
bucket	jacket	ticket	since	

MAKING CONNECTIONS Write the list word that will fit with each set of words or phrases below.

1. ___ officer, ___ man, ___woman
2. ___ or treat, card ___, magic ___
3. theater ___, parking ___, raffle ___
4. a smiling ___, a sad ___, a funny ___
5. a stiff ___, a pain in the ___, a ___ tie

DEFINITIONS Write the list word that means the same as each word or phrase. Use your Spelling Dictionary.

6. one time
7. run after to catch
8. small closet that can be locked
9. pail
10. short coat
11. from a past time till now
12. rub out
13. an opportunity

Strategic Spelling

Seeing Meaning Connections

greenhouse
doghouse
lighthouse

14. Write the list word that is related in spelling and meaning to the words in the box.

Complete the sentences with words from the box.

If a dog lives in a (15), does a light live in a (16)?
Does a houseplant live in a (17)?

Did You Know?
The word *erase* comes from a Latin word that means "scraped out."

☰	Make a capital.
/	Make a small letter.
∧	Add something.
℮	Take out something.
⊙	Add a period.
¶	New paragraph

PROOFREAD A WARNING LABEL

Tino rewrote the tiny warning label from a glass cleaner so that everyone would see it. Fix three spelling errors he made and two small letters that should be capitals.

PROOFREADING TIP
Be extra careful when you copy something. Titles and the first words of sentences should be capitalized.

<u>warning</u>

Keep in a safe place in the hous. Keep away from children ones the bottle is opened. hold by the neak of the bottle and spray away from yourself.

WRITE A WARNING LABEL Write a warning label for some classroom supply such as glue or rubber cement. Use some of your spelling words and at least one personal word.

Word List

once	jacket	chase
trick	house	since
bucket	neck	locker
erase	ticket	police
chance	face	

Personal Words 1.___ 2.___

once
chance
face
house
neck
trick
jacket

PUZZLE   Use words from the box to find the answer to the puzzle question: What is the most important thing to take to the playing field with you?

1. a magic ___
2. ___ or twice
3. the front of your head
4. a ___ to earn money
5. a short coat
6. between your head and shoulders
7. where some people live

1. _ _ _ _ _
2. _ _ _ _ _ _
3. _ _ _ _ _
    m
    m
4. _ _ _ _ _ _
5. _ _ _ _ _
6. _ _ _ _
7. _ _ _ _ _ _

Using a *Dictionary*

PRONUNCIATION   Most dictionaries have a **pronunciation key** on every other page. It might look something like this:

a	hat	i	ice	u̇	put	**ə stands for**	
ā	age	o	hot	ü	rule	a	in about
ä	far, calm	ō	open	ch	child	e	in taken
âr	care	ȯ	saw	ng	long	i	in pencil
e	let	ô	order	sh	she	o	in lemon
ē	equal	oi	oil	th	thin	u	in circus
ėr	term	ou	out	ᴛʜ	then	<= derived from	
i	it	u	cup	zh	measure		

Look at the pronunciation in the entry **knee.** It tells how to say *knee.* It tells you that the **k** is silent and that the **ee** is pronounced like the **e** in **equal.**

knee (nē) **1** the joint between the thigh and the lower leg. **2** anything like a bent knee in shape or position *noun.*

Read the pronunciations below. Write the words that the pronunciation symbols stand for.

1. shu̇r   2. wôrm   3. drī   4. smash

77

Words with kn, wr, and st

■ **STUDY** Say each word. Read the sentence.

1.	knife	Use your **knife** and fork.
2.	know ✳	I **know** the answer.
3.	wrong	It is **wrong** to cheat.
4.	write	Dad will **write** me a letter.
5.	wrote	Mom **wrote** a note to her.
6.	listen	Just **listen** to that music!
7.	Christmas ✳	Enjoy the **Christmas** tree.

WATCH OUT FOR FREQUENTLY MISSPELLED WORDS!

8.	knee	Bend your right **knee.**
9.	knight	The **knight** wore armor.
10.	knock	I heard a loud **knock.**
11.	wrap	Did you **wrap** the gift?
12.	wrestle	They **wrestle** on a mat.
13.	castle	The king built a **castle.**
14.	whistle	The coach blew her **whistle.**

■ **PRACTICE** Sort the words by writing
- one word with both **wr** and **st**
- four other words with **wr**
- four other words with **st**
- five words with **kn**

■ **WRITE** Use two sentences in a paragraph.

CHALLENGE!

doorknob
knowledge
wristwatch
hustle

knee	know	knife	wrong	wrap
wrote	Christmas	listen	knock	wrestle
castle	write	knight	whistle	

PATTERNS Decide which letters would make list words. Write each word.

1. _ _ ite
2. _ _ ight
3. _ _ istle

4. _ _ _ ten
5. _ _ _ tle
6. _ _ ife

SEEING RELATIONSHIPS Complete each sentence with a list word.

7. An incorrect answer is a ___ answer.
8. If you sent a letter to your dad, you ___ to him.
9. Some cultures celebrate Hanukkah, some celebrate Kwanzaa, and some celebrate ___.
10. The ankle, wrist, and ___ all bend.
11. If you are good in math, you ___ the subject.

Strategic Spelling

Building New Words

12–14. Write *knock*, *wrestle*, and *wrap*. Write the forms of these words that complete the chart.
Remember: Make spelling changes when you need to.

Base Word	Add -ed	Add -ing
___	___	___
___	___	___
___	___	___

☰	Make a capital.
/	Make a small letter.
∧	Add something.
ℯ	Take out something.
⊙	Add a period.
¶	New paragraph

PROOFREAD A SIGN Find the misspelled word in the photograph below. Why do you think it was misspelled in this way? Write the word correctly.

MERRY
CHRITSMAS

PROOFREADING TIP
Some people make a hobby of finding mistakes in signs. Proofread your sign before it becomes part of someone's collection.

MAKE A SIGN Now it's your turn to make a sign. If you do a sign announcing an upcoming event, choose your words to make everyone want to attend. Use your spelling words and at least one personal word.

Word List

knee	write	knock
wrote	knife	whistle
castle	listen	wrap
know	knight	wrestle
Christmas	wrong	

Personal Words 1.___ 2.___

Review

CROSSWORD PUZZLE Fill in the puzzle by writing a word from the box for each clue.

knife
know
wrong
write
wrote
listen
Christmas

Across

1. answered a letter
3. a sharp tool
5. pay attention

Down

1. make words with a pencil
2. a holiday
3. understand
4. not right

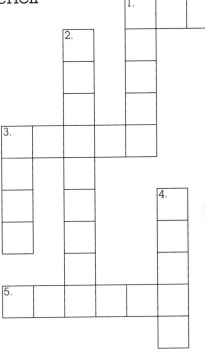

Word *Study*

HOMOPHONES Homophones are words that sound alike, but have different meanings and histories. *Ate* and *eight* are homophones.

Write the right homophones from the box to complete each sentence.

no/know
wrap/rap
write/right
night/knight

1. Last ___ a ___ rode up on a white horse.
2. Please ___ your name on the ___ line.
3. You can ___ the gift when I ___ on the door.
4. Say ___ if you don't ___ the answer.

Homophones

SPELLING FOCUS

Homophones are words that sound alike but have different spellings and meanings, such as **too, to,** and **two.**

■ **STUDY** Say each word. Read the sentence.

WATCH OUT FOR FREQUENTLY MISSPELLED WORDS!

1. there ✳	The ball rolled over **there.**
2. their ✳	They painted **their** house.
3. they're ✳	Finally, **they're** ready.
4. hour	The show lasts an **hour.**
5. our ✳	We went to visit **our** relatives.
6. to	She is going **to** a movie.
7. too ✳	I will go **too.**
8. two ✳	We invited **two** friends.

9. tail	The dog's **tail** drooped.
10. tale	A tall **tale** is funny.
11. hole	Dig a big **hole** for the tree.
12. whole ✳	He ate a **whole** melon.
13. weak	The sick girl felt **weak.**
14. week	One **week** is seven days.

CHALLENGE!

boarder
border
soar
sore

■ **PRACTICE** First, write the homophone groups that are hardest for you. Then write the rest of the homophone groups.

■ **WRITE** Choose six words. Write a sentence for each word.

tail	*their*	*hour*	*two*	*weak*
tale	*they're*	*to*	*hole*	*week*
there	*our*	*too*	*whole*	

MEANING CONNECTIONS Write the correct homophones to complete the sentences.

You (1) girls can go (2) the movies (3).
If (4) sitting over (5), then (6) books are with them.
Will (7) train be an (8) late?

RHYME TIME Complete the silly sentences with list words that rhyme with the underlined words.

In today's junk <u>mail</u> I read a <u>stale</u> (9) of a <u>snail's</u> (10).
A (11) <u>mole</u> went down a <u>mole</u> (12) and never paid a single <u>toll</u>.
If I could <u>sneak</u> a <u>peek</u> for just a (13) at a bird whose <u>beak</u> was very (14), I'd <u>squeak</u>!

Strategic Spelling

Seeing Meaning Connections

Words with *week*

weekend
weekly
weekday

Write the words from the box that fit the definitions.

15. any day of the week except Saturday and Sunday
16. Saturday and Sunday
17. happening each week

═	Make a capital.
/	Make a small letter.
∧	Add something.
ℰ	Take out something.
⊙	Add a period.
¶	New paragraph

PROOFREAD A NOTE Betsy left a note for her mother in the kitchen. She made three spelling errors and one careless error. Fix them.

Mom,

    Sue called to say she can go whith us us to the basball game next weak. She asked if we can get there early.

                 Betsy

PROOFREADING TIP
Can you tell where Betsy stopped to think about what she wanted to say? It's where she repeated a word. Fix this kind of error when you proofread.

WRITE A NOTE Write a note to a friend or a relative reminding that person of an event that is coming up. Use some of your spelling words and one or two personal words.

Word List

tail	our	hole
tale	hour	whole
there	to	weak
their	too	week
they're	two	

Personal Words 1.___ 2.___

Review

DEFINITIONS Write the word from the box that means the same as the phrase.

1. belonging to us
2. in that place
3. in the direction of
4. one plus one
5. they are
6. sixty minutes
7. belonging to them
8. also

there
their
they're
hour
our
to
too
two

Word *Study*

ANAGRAMS Anagrams are words or phrases formed by rearranging the letters of other words or phrases. The word *late* is an anagram of *tale.*

Write an anagram for each of these words. See if you can think of each anagram before looking at the words in the box for help.

1. wake
2. wrong
3. ate
4. grate
5. mane
6. den

grown
end
weak
eat
name
great

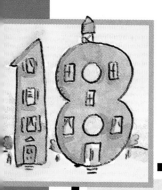

Review

REVIEW WORD LIST

1. alone	10. wear	19. neck	28. write
2. always	11. went	20. since	29. wrote
3. couldn't	12. when	21. ticket	30. hour
4. hadn't	13. while	22. castle	31. our
5. hasn't	14. chance	23. knee	32. they're
6. one	15. chase	24. listen	33. to
7. until	16. house	25. whistle	34. too
8. warm	17. jacket	26. wrap	35. week
9. watched	18. locker	27. wrestle	

Jalen put his poem into a get-well card for Gratia.
Complete his poem with list words. Use each word once.

wrap   knee   whistle   listen   too

Get Well Soon

Feeling awful? Can't even (1)?

Banged your (2)? Head like a missile?

Give a (3). Better (4) your head.

Take your pills (5), and off to bed.

86

The CASE of the missing jacket

locker neck wrestle jacket chase while

Leon always brainstorms before writing a story. These are his notes for a detective story. Use the list words to complete his ideas.

▶ We watch two athletes (1) in a match.
▶ A robbery takes place (2) everyone is in the gym.
▶ A (3) in the dressing room has been opened.
▶ A blue and white (4) is missing.
▶ It belongs to the athlete with the scar on his (5).
▶ Police officers (6) a person running from the gym.

My New Home

wear always warm watched since went

Mai made notes in her journal during her first days in California. She and her family came from Vietnam. Complete the journal entries with list words. Use each one once.

Jan. 19 Today we (1) a parade that (2) down the main street of town.
Jan. 20 It's (3) sunny and (4) here in California.
Jan. 21 We will celebrate Tet next week. I will (5) my best dress for the New Year's celebration. I have not worn it (6) we came to California.

Say It Again, Sam

they're	hasn't
couldn't	hadn't

Sam wrote these sentences and underlined the words that can be changed without changing the meaning.

Write the contraction for each underlined phrase below.

1. Don <u>had not</u> remembered his notebook.

2. Allison <u>could not</u> find her shoes.

3. I think <u>they are</u> ready to go now.

4. I hope Jordan <u>has not</u> left anything behind.

Complete the ad from the Entertainment section of the newspaper. Use each list word once.

ticket   hour   chance   castle   when   one

A Night of Mystery and Fun!

Win a (1) for a night of mystery and fun! Take a three- (2) tour through an old (3), and solve a make-believe crime!

Each person will have a (4) to find clues. The first (5) to solve the mystery will win a prize. Dinner will be served (6) everyone comes to the dining room.

88

A hearing (((**ear**))) dog

house	wrote	week	write
alone	until	our	to

Jolene's mother cannot hear. Jolene wrote to an organization that trains dogs to help people. She received a letter back almost immediately.

Use each list word once to complete the letter.

A   H E L P I N G   P A W

Dear Jolene,

We're glad you (1) (2) us last (3) asking about a dog for your hearing-impaired mother. Because your mother is (4) in the (5) (6) you come home from school, we feel that we may be of some help.

We will (7) your mother and send her information about (8) dogs.

Sincerely,

Don Stearns
President
A Helping Paw, Inc.

STRATEGY WORKSHOP

Dividing Long Words

DISCOVER THE STRATEGY First, read these facts about syllables.

A **syllable** is a word or part of a word that you say as a unit. For example, *pan* has one syllable and *panda* (pan • da) has two.

A **syllable** is usually made up of a vowel and one or more consonants or a vowel alone. For example, in *crocodile* the second syllable (croc • o • dile) is a vowel alone.

Here's how you can use syllables to make long words easier to study.

Step 1 Say the word slowly and **listen** for the syllables. **to geth er**

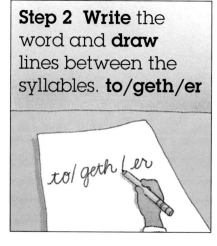

to geth er

Step 2 Write the word and **draw** lines between the syllables. **to/geth/er**

to/geth/er

Step 3 Study the word syllable by syllable. **to/geth/er**

TRY IT OUT Now practice this dividing-long-words strategy.

Write these two-syllable words: *zebra, tiger, monkey.* Listen to the syllables as you say each word. Then draw lines between the syllables. Compare with a partner how you divided the words. Check a dictionary if you need help.

Write these three-syllable words: *flamingo, chimpanzee, elephant.* Listen to the syllables as you say each word. Then draw lines between the syllables. Check your divided words with your partner's. Go to a dictionary if you need help.

LOOK AHEAD Look ahead at the next five lessons. Write four list words that are long and look hard to spell. Then divide each word by syllables to make it easier to study.

Words with Double Consonants

SPELLING FOCUS

Many words have double consonants that stand for only one sound: o**ff**, pre**tt**y.

■ **STUDY** Say each word. Read the sentence.

1.	*happen*	What will **happen** next?
2.	*pretty* ✳	She wrote a **pretty** poem.
3.	*letter*	A **letter** came in the mail.
4.	*little* ✳	The baby bear was **little.**
5.	*rabbit*	The **rabbit** eats carrots.
6.	*off* ✳	He fell **off** his bike.
7.	*hurry*	We were in a **hurry** to go.

✳
WATCH OUT FOR FREQUENTLY MISSPELLED WORDS!

8.	*million*	They won a **million** dollars.
9.	*balloon*	The **balloon** floated away.
10.	*ladder*	Climb down the **ladder.**
11.	*puddle*	I saw a **puddle** of water.
12.	*middle*	Drive in the **middle** lane.
13.	*hammer*	A builder uses a **hammer.**
14.	*lesson*	She has a piano **lesson.**

■ **PRACTICE** First write the words you think are easy to spell. Then write the words you think are hard to spell.

■ **WRITE** Choose two sentences to use in riddles or rhymes.

CHALLENGE!

intelligent
marshmallow
pepperoni
supposed

rabbit	middle	million	hurry	letter
ladder	off	hammer	lesson	little
puddle	balloon	happen	pretty	

MAKING COMPARISONS Complete each comparison using a list word.

1. The flower was as ___ as a picture.
2. Alan hops as fast as a ___.
3. Kendra is as tall and straight as a ___.
4. His swollen arm seemed as heavy as a ___.
5. The ___ seemed as big as a lake to the duck.

SYLLABLES Each group of letters is a syllable of a two-syllable word. Match the first to the second syllable to make list words. Write the two-syllable words.

6. mid   ry
7. hur   dle
8. lit   son
9. les   tle

10. Write the only one-syllable list word.

STRATEGIC SPELLING
The Dividing Long Words Strategy

11–14. Sometimes it helps to study long words piece by piece. Write *million, balloon, letter,* and *happen.* Draw lines between the syllables. Then study each word syllable by syllable. Check a dictionary if you need help.

> **Did You Know?**
> If you stacked up a million dollars in pennies, your stack would be almost 93 miles high.

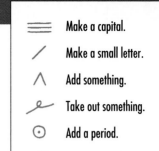

☰	Make a capital.
/	Make a small letter.
∧	Add something.
ℓ	Take out something.
⊙	Add a period.
¶	New paragraph

PROOFREAD A REPORT Blanca wrote a report on the wind damage to her school playground. Fix three misspelled words and the spacing of her handwriting.

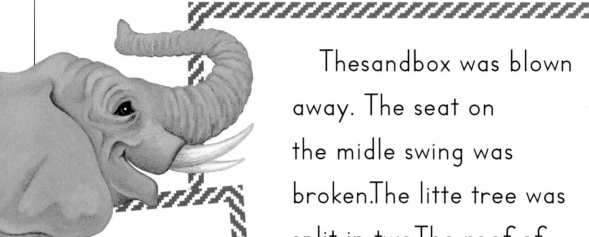

Thesandbox was blown away. The seat on the midle swing was broken.The litte tree was split in two.The roof of the playhouse was blown of too.

PROOFREADING TIP
An elephant never forgets. You must never forget to leave a little space between each word in a sentence, and then double that space between sentences.

WRITE A REPORT Pretend you were asked to write a report about the damage caused to a park or a zoo by a bad storm. Use some list words and a personal word.

Word List

rabbit	balloon	lesson
ladder	million	pretty
puddle	hammer	letter
middle	happen	little
off	hurry	

Personal Words 1.___ 2.___

94

Review

CONTEXT CLUES Choose a word from the box to replace each underlined word in the story.

There is a cute, (1) <u>small</u> (2) <u>bunny</u> in our garden. It likes to eat our carrots. If we (3) <u>chance</u> to see it, we will go outside to chase it (4) <u>away</u>. Then it will (5) <u>run</u> under the hedge where we can't see it. Then it will come back into the garden as soon as we go inside. I think I'll write a (6) <u>note</u> to Aunt Natalie to tell her about our (7) <u>beautiful</u> garden pest.

happen
pretty
letter
little
rabbit
off
hurry

Using a *Dictionary*

PARTS OF AN ENTRY An **entry** in a dictionary tells about the **entry word.** The **pronunciation** tells you how to say the word. The **definitions** tell you what the word means. If the entry word is more than one syllable, a dot is shown between the syllables.

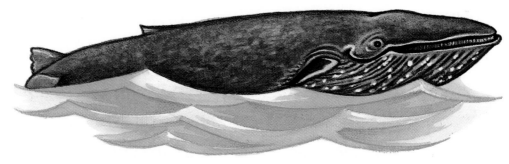

entry word · pronunciation · definitions

entry —

les•son (les′ n) **1** something to be learned or taught; something that has been learned or taught: *Children study many different lessons in school.* **2** a unit of teaching or learning; what is to be studied or taught at one time: *Tomorrow we study the tenth lesson.* *noun.*

Look at the entry for *lesson.* Then answer the questions.

1. How many definitions are given?
2. How many syllables does *lesson* have?
3. What part of the entry comes right after the entry word?

Vowel Sounds in *book* and *boy*

The vowel sound /u̇/ can be spelled **oo** and **u: t**oo**k, p**u**t**. The vowel sound /oi/ can be spelled **oy** and **oi: enj**oy**, p**oi**nt**.

■ **STUDY** Say each word. Read the sentence.

WATCH OUT FOR
FREQUENTLY
MISSPELLED
WORDS!

1.	*good*	Wish us **good** luck!
2.	*took* ✳	She **took** a hall pass.
3.	*cookie*	He ate an oatmeal **cookie.**
4.	*put*	We **put** our books down.
5.	*enjoy*	I hope you **enjoy** the play.
6.	*point*	The pencil **point** broke.
7.	*voice*	Speak in a clear **voice.**

8.	*shook*	I **shook** apples from a tree.
9.	*foot*	I can balance on one **foot.**
10.	*pull*	Let a pony **pull** the wagon.
11.	*toys*	It's fun to play with **toys.**
12.	*royal*	The **royal** palace was grand.
13.	*noise*	The crowd **noise** was loud.
14.	*oil*	Please **oil** that squeaky door.

■ **PRACTICE** Sort the words by writing
- seven words with a vowel sound spelled **oi** or **oy**
- seven words with the vowel sound spelled **oo** or **u**

■ **WRITE** Use two sentences to write about something you like to do.

CHALLENGE!

understood
plural
destroy
disappointed

shook	good	cookie	royal	enjoy
pull	put	toys	noise	point
took	foot	voice	oil	

DEFINITIONS Write the list word that means the same as each phrase. Use the Spelling Dictionary.

1. about kings and queens
2. a sound that is not pleasant
3. things for children to play with
4. a sharp end
5. small, flat, sweet cake
6. kind and nice
7. liquid for cooking
8. to place, lay, or set
9. held onto
10. move something toward yourself
11. twelve inches

TWO MEANINGS Write the list word that completes both phrases.

12. ___ the movie

___ good health

13. a nice singing ___

___ your opinion

14. ___ hands with me

___ from the cold

STRATEGIC SPELLING

Seeing Meaning Connections

Words with *foot*
foothill
footprint
barefoot

Complete the sentence with words from the box.

If you ever walk (15) on a (16) of a mountain, you might leave a (17) in the dirt.

═	Make a capital.
/	Make a small letter.
∧	Add something.
ℓ	Take out something.
⊙	Add a period.
⊬	New paragraph

PROOFREAD AN EXPLANATION

Ben wrote a paragraph explaining how to bowl. Fix three misspelled words and one incorrect adjective.

> First, put your fingers in the holes. Next, swing the ball back and then pool it forward as you walk toward the pins. Let go of it wen your fut reaches the line. This is the harder part of all.

PROOFREADING TIP

Is the penguin the *cuter* or *cutest* animal in the zoo? Remember to use **-est** when you compare three or more things.

WRITE AN EXPLANATION Write a paragraph explaining how to do something in steps. Use some spelling words and at least one personal word.

Word List

shook	foot	noise
pull	cookie	oil
took	toys	enjoy
good	voice	point
put	royal	

Personal Words 1.___ 2.___

Review

RHYMES Choose a word from the box to finish each silly rhyme.

good
took
cookie
put
enjoy
point
voice

1. Give the name of a joint
   You use when you ___.
2. Some toys really look ___
   When they're made out of wood.
3. Try to ___ it
   Before you destroy it.
4. Ask the rookie
   If she wants a ___.
5. Watch where you ___
   Your mud-covered foot.
6. There isn't a choice;
   You sing with your ___.
7. Somebody ___
   My history book.

Word *Study*

CLASSIFYING You can put words together into groups if they are alike in some way. Grouping them together is called **classifying.** The words *foot, hand,* and *arm* can be grouped together under the topic **Parts of the Body.**

Write two words that can be grouped under each topic.

1. Toys   **2. Animals**   **3. Desserts**

Vowel Sounds in *uncle* and *moon*

Short u is often spelled **u: study**. The vowel sound in **moon** can be spelled **ue** and **o: true, who**.

■ **STUDY** Say each word. Read the sentence.

1. study		I did **study** for the quiz.
2. summer		Students love **summer** vacation.
3. such		This is **such** a good book.
4. true		The answer is **true** or false.
5. due		The library book is **due** today.
6. who ✳		I know **who** you are.
7. move		Don't **move** a muscle!

✳
WATCH OUT FOR FREQUENTLY MISSPELLED WORDS!

8. truck		She drives a big **truck.**
9. uncle		Dad's brother is my **uncle.**
10. Sunday		We eat **Sunday** dinner together.
11. glue		Use **glue** to fix the vase.
12. clue		A **clue** helped me guess.
13. lose		Don't **lose** your balance.
14. movie		We saw a horror **movie.**

CHALLENGE!

dumped
clumsy
gruesome
whoever

■ **PRACTICE** Sort the words by writing
• four words with a vowel sound spelled **ue**
• four words with a vowel sound spelled **o**
• six words with a vowel sound spelled **u**

■ **WRITE** Choose six words. Write a sentence for each word.

uncle	lose	such	true	summer
glue	Sunday	movie	study	due
who	clue	truck	move	

OPPOSITES Write the list word that is the opposite of each word below.

1. win   2. aunt   3. winter   4. false

CLASSIFYING Write the word that fits each group.

5. car, van, ___
6. Friday, Saturday, ___
7. what, when, ___
8. TV program, play, ___
9. think, practice, ___

RHYMING Follow the directions below.

10–12. Write three list words that end like and rhyme with *true.*
13. Write the list word that rhymes with *much.*
14. Write the list word that rhymes with *groove.*

STRATEGIC SPELLING
Seeing Meaning Connections

Words with *move*
movable
mover
moving van

Match the words in the box with the definitions.
15. a covered truck used for moving
16. a person or company whose business is moving furniture
17. able to be moved or carried from place to place

Take a Hint
The words *lose* and *loose* are often confused. Don't *lose* the spelling bee by spelling *loose* with only one **o.**

☰	Make a capital.
/	Make a small letter.
∧	Add something.
℮	Take out something.
⊙	Add a period.
¶	New paragraph

PROOFREAD A LIST Marisa wrote a list of people and things she is grateful for. Fix three spelling errors and one careless error.

1. I'm grateful for my unkl because he takes me to the zoo.
2. I'm grateful for my freinds. They help my have fun.
3. I'm grateful for Sundy evenings. Hooray, we have ice cream.

PROOFREADING TIP
Marisa wrote *my*, but she meant to write *me*. When you proofread, check for words that are spelled correctly but have the wrong meaning.

MAKE A LIST Make a list of people you like. Tell why you are grateful that they are part of your life. Try to use list words and a personal word.

Word List

uncle	clue	study
glue	such	move
who	movie	summer
lose	truck	due
Sunday	true	

Personal Words 1.___ 2.___

Review

CROSSWORD PUZZLE Use the clues for words in the box to fill in the puzzle.

study
summer
such
true
due
who
move

Across

2. rhymes with *much*
4. go from one place to another
5. not false
6. When is the report ___?

Down

1. ___, whom, whose
2. a season
3. work at learning

Using a *Thesaurus*

PARTS OF AN ENTRY A thesaurus entry begins with the **entry word.** For each entry word there is a **definition** (telling the meaning) and an **example sentence** (showing the use). After these parts come the **synonyms** with definitions and examples. Some entries give **antonyms** for the entry word.

Look up the word *move* in your Writer's Thesaurus and answer these questions.

1. How many synonyms are given for *move?*
2. Write a sentence using one of the synonyms for *move.*

Entry Word   Definition   Example Sentence

Afraid

Afraid means feeling fear. *Katie and I are afraid of snakes.*

Synonyms— **Frightened** means afraid. *The frightened deer leaped over the fence and ran away.*

Scared means the same as afraid but is less formal. *Levar is never scared of the dark.*

Alarmed means fearful and aware of danger. *We were all alarmed when we heard the explosion.*

ANTONYM: fearless

Antonyms

Vowel Sound in *ball*

The vowel sound in **ball** can be spelled **al**, **aw**, and **au**: t**al**k, dr**aw**ing, bec**au**se.

■ **STUDY** Say each word. Read the sentence.

1. *walking*   We are **walking** to school.
2. *talk*   The principal gave a **talk.**
3. *drawing*   His **drawing** looks real.
4. *straw*   He wore a **straw** hat.
5. *claws*   A cat's **claws** are sharp.
6. *because* ✳   We left **because** it rained.
7. *fault*   The mistake was my **fault.**

8. *chalk*   She drew a cat with **chalk.**
9. *stalk*   I picked a **stalk** of wheat.
10. *lawn*   He mowed the **lawn.**
11. *thaw*   First, **thaw** out the frozen meat.
12. *sauce*   Brush on barbecue **sauce.**
13. *haunted*   The old house was **haunted.**
14. *cause*   What was the **cause** of the fire?

✳
**WATCH OUT FOR
FREQUENTLY
MISSPELLED
WORDS!**

■ **PRACTICE** Sort the words by writing
- five words with a vowel sound spelled **aw**
- five words with a vowel sound spelled **au**
- four words with a vowel sound spelled **al**

■ **WRITE** Use two sentences in a paragraph about safety.

CHALLENGE!

sidewalk
lawyer
laundry
faucet

because	lawn	stalk	drawing	thaw
chalk	walking	talk	straw	claws
sauce	haunted	fault	cause	

RHYMES Write the list word that rhymes with the underlined word and makes sense in the verse.

1. At the zoo where lunch is <u>raw</u>,
   Is it frozen; does it need to ___?
2. Don't be frightened (or do you say *daunted?*),
   The house is old, but it isn't ___.
3. We really must obey the <u>laws</u>,
   Don't ask why; it's just ___.
4. In the soup there's too much <u>salt</u>.
   We can't eat it, and it's all your ___.
5. They work so hard without a <u>pause</u>,
   No doubt they think it's for a good ___.

SEEING CONNECTIONS Write the list word that tells what each person might work with.

6. a teacher
7. a gardener
8. a veterinarian
9. a farmer
10. a basket maker
11. a cook
12. a speechwriter
13. an artist

STRATEGIC SPELLING

Seeing Meaning Connections

| sidewalk |
| walkie-talkie |

14. Write the list word that is related in spelling and meaning to the words in the box.

Then write the words from the box that fit the clues.

15. I'm not a garden path. I'm paved and at the side of a street.
16. You can't get the top forty songs on me, but I am a radio.

☰	Make a capital.
/	Make a small letter.
∧	Add something.
ℓ	Take out something.
⊙	Add a period.
¶	New paragraph

PROOFREAD A PROBLEM Jeremy wrote a letter asking for advice. He misspelled two words and used a proper noun three times when a pronoun would have been better. Fix his mistakes.

PROOFREADING TIP
Don't repeat someone's name over and over again. Use the correct pronoun every once in a while when you refer to that person.

Dear Kid Adviser,
    It was all Pete's falt. Pete promised to meet me at the Reptile House. Pete never showed up. I can't depend on him becase he doesn't keep Pete's promises. What should I do?

WRITE A SOLUTION Pretend you are Kid Adviser. Write a solution to Jeremy's problem. Use some spelling words and at least one personal word.

Word List

because	haunted	straw
chalk	stalk	cause
sauce	talk	thaw
lawn	fault	claws
walking	drawing	

Personal Words 1.___ 2.___

Review

CLASSIFYING Write the word from the box that finishes each set.

1. dry grass, hay, ___
2. painting, sketching, ___
3. mistake, error, ___
4. since, as, ___
5. horns, teeth, ___
6. speak, say, ___
7. running, strolling, ___

> walking
> talk
> drawing
> straw
> claws
> because
> fault

Multicultural *Connection*

NO WORDS People don't always use spoken or written words to communicate. We can talk with our faces and bodies. We can even use sign language. Write a word or phrase from the box that fits each picture.

> **So sad**
> **Sleepy**
> **OK**
> **Cold**
> **Don't know**
> **Happy**

1. 3. 5.

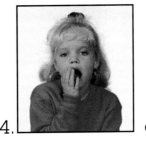

2. 4. 6.

Getting Letters in Correct Order

SPELLING FOCUS

Watch for letter combinations that are hard to keep in order and pay special attention to those parts: **fri̲end, ni̲ght, peopl̲e.**

■ **STUDY** Say each word. Read the sentence.

WATCH OUT FOR FREQUENTLY MISSPELLED WORDS!

1. *friend* ✳	You are my best **friend.**
2. *night*	A full moon lit the **night.**
3. *thought* ✳	He **thought** of a plan.
4. *does*	The cook **does** a good job.
5. *again* ✳	We sang the song **again.**
6. *said* ✳	Ann **said** she'll be late.
7. *people* ✳	All **people** need love.

8. *believe* ✳	I **believe** your story.
9. *tried*	He **tried** to win the race.
10. *died*	In fall the flowers **died.**
11. *eight*	He bought **eight** oranges.
12. *tired*	The **tired** runners rested.
13. *Friday*	Camp ended **Friday** afternoon.
14. *Saturday*	We left **Saturday** morning.

CHALLENGE!

pierced
horrible
jewelry
guard

■ **PRACTICE** Write the words that are easier for you first. Then write the words that are harder for you.

■ **WRITE** Use ideas from at least two sentences to write an invitation.

friend	eight	Friday	died	does
believe	thought	Saturday	again	people
night	tired	tried	said	

TONGUE TWISTERS Write the list word that best completes each sentence. Hint: The list word should start with the same letter as the first word in each sentence.

1. Five fish are free for Flora on ___.
2. Save six sailboats for ___.
3. Add all apples and apricots___.
4. Every evening at ___ everyone eats.
5. Troy ___ on ten T-shirts today.
6. Theodore ___ their theater tickets were there.
7. Paula pointed a pinkie at ___ parading.
8. Debby dreaded the day the daffodils ___.
9. Don's dog ___ drink from a dark, deep dish.

SYNONYMS Write a list word that means the same as the underlined word.

10. I think it is all right to clap.
11. Kinuke stated her name clearly.
12. Lupe is a pal of mine.
13. Playing all day made her weary.
14. What evening are you free to go?

STRATEGIC SPELLING
Using the Problem Parts Strategy

15–17. Study the problem parts of words. Write three list words that are hard for you. Mark the part of each word that gives you problems and study it extra hard.

Take a Hint
Tired and *tried* are confused easily because they look so much alike. Remember that a **tired** tomato is red.

≡	Make a capital.
/	Make a small letter.
∧	Add something.
ℰ	Take out something.
⊙	Add a period.
¶	New paragraph

PROOFREAD A SIGN Find the spelling mistake in the sign. Write the word correctly.

CLOTHING
EN "ALL TYPES AND SIZES"
YOU WON'T BELEIVE IT'S A...
RESALE SHOP

PROOFREADING TIP
You don't have to be as tall as a giraffe to see a mistake on a billboard. Be careful when you copy your message from a small paper to a large one.

CREATE A SIGN Pretend you own a billboard beside an expressway. Try to make a sign that will get the drivers' attention as they whiz by.

Word List

friend	tired	again
believe	Friday	said
night	Saturday	does
eight	tried	people
thought	died	

Personal Words 1.___ 2.___

Review

PUZZLE Use words from the box to fill in the puzzle. The puzzle answers the riddle.

friend
night
thought
does
again
said
people

Who is the grandest man in the family?

1. used your head
2. a pal
3. spoke
4. opposite of day
5. How ___ she do it?
6. human beings
7. one more time

Word *Study*

WORDS WITH MORE THAN ONE MEANING

Many words have more than one meaning. Read the sentences below. Look in your Spelling Dictionary for the words *try* and *study*. Write the number of the correct definition for each sentence.

1. My father likes to try new recipes for cookouts.
2. She began to try the case in court on Monday.
3. Each week I study a new wild animal.
4. My aunt has a study in her house.

Review

Lesson 19: Words with Double Consonants   **Lesson 22:** Vowel Sound in ball
Lesson 20: Vowel Sounds in book and boy   **Lesson 23:** Getting Letters in Correct Order
Lesson 21: Vowel Sounds in uncle and moon

REVIEW WORD LIST

1. hammer	10. rabbit	19. clue	28. walking
2. happen	11. good	20. glue	29. again
3. ladder	12. noise	21. move	30. believe
4. lesson	13. oil	22. movie	31. night
5. letter	14. point	23. study	32. people
6. little	15. pull	24. summer	33. said
7. middle	16. put	25. true	34. thought
8. million	17. royal	26. chalk	35. tried
9. puddle	18. voice	27. lawn	

Hardware JUMBLE

Find the hidden list words in the silly words. The words will be things in a hardware store.

glue
ladder
hammer
oil

shammers

unladdered

misglueing

spoils

Vacation Calendar

Help Sam by writing list words to complete
one week of his summer schedule.

walking   put   rabbit   lawn   study   move   pull

Sun.	Mon.	Tues.	Wed.	Thurs.	Fri.	Sat.
1	**2**	**3**	**4**	**5**	**6**	**7**
___ for piano recital	___ up weeds in the garden	clean ___ cage	mow the front ___	___ new plants in the garden	___ grill from basement to backyard	begin dog-___ job

Around School with Anne Celene

Anne Celene writes a newsy column for the school paper. She wrote one about the last day of school. Finish her column with the list words below.

chalk   noise   summer   said
voice   lesson   happen

From the Office. "Best Wishes for a great (1)," (2) Mrs. Perkins.

In the Gym. "Keep the (3) down," the coach said at the top of her (4).

Mr. Taylor's Third Grade. "We worked hard," shouted the third graders, "and learned our (5)."

The Last Question. What will (6) to all that extra (7)?

Flicks From Fred

Fred also writes for the school newspaper. He writes movie reviews. Complete his comments with the list words.

movie
good
thought
people
again
night

The animated **1** I saw last **2** was very **3**. The **4** in the audience clapped a lot.

I'd like to see it **5**.

I **6** the music was great.

Once Upon a Time

Ian wrote a short bedtime story for his baby sister. Write the list words to finish his tale.

tried **believe** **puddle** **true** **royal** **little**

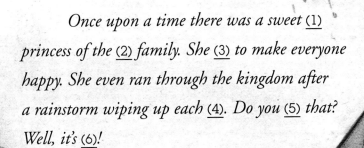

*Once upon a time there was a sweet (1)
princess of the (2) family. She (3) to make everyone
happy. She even ran through the kingdom after
a rainstorm wiping up each (4). Do you (5) that?
Well, it's (6)!*

Buy a Vowel

See if you can solve the puzzle without looking at the list words. Write each list word once.

Look at each (1) **cl__** carefully. Now for a

(2) **m_ll__n** points, what (3) **l_tt_r** comes in

the (4) **m_ddl_** of the word (5) **p__nt**? You do?

middle
million
letter
point
clue

115

STRATEGY WORKSHOP

Pronouncing for Spelling

DISCOVER THE STRATEGY We spell some words wrong because we say them wrong. If we say *They began to chair*, we probably will spell the word *cheer* wrong. Here's how to correct these kinds of mistakes.

1 **Say** the word correctly. **Listen** to the sound of each letter.

cheer

2 **Say** the word again as you **write** it.

cheer

They began to chair cheer

TRY IT OUT Now practice this correct-pronunciation strategy. Do the exercises on the next page.

Say each word in dark type correctly. Pay close attention to the sounds of the underlined letters. Say each word again as you write it.

1. Say **<u>are</u>,** not "ore."

2. Say **dif<u>fe</u>rent,** not "diffrent."

3. Say **hun<u>gr</u>y,** not "hungery."

4. Say **<u>sure</u>,** not "shore."

5. Say **<u>and</u>,** not "in."

6. Say **on<u>ce</u>,** not "ones."

LOOK AHEAD Look ahead at the next five lessons. Write three words you could use this strategy with. Mark the part of each word that you'll pay close attention to when you say it.

Including All the Letters

SPELLING FOCUS

Some words have more letters than you might expect. To spell these words, say each syllable carefully.

■ **STUDY** Say each word. Read the sentence.

WATCH OUT FOR
FREQUENTLY
MISSPELLED
WORDS!

1. easy		They do the **easy** jobs.
2. picture		Mom put my **picture** up.
3. through	✷	Go **through** the hallway.
4. guess		My **guess** was right.
5. caught	✷	He **caught** a bad cold.
6. kept		She **kept** her promise.
7. different	✷	Wear a **different** shirt.

8. surprise		I had a **surprise** party for her.
9. favorite	✷	Apples are my **favorite** fruit.
10. Tuesday		Practice is **Tuesday** night.
11. swimming	✷	Fish are **swimming** by.
12. Monday		I have a test on **Monday.**
13. fifth		A **fifth** grader showed me.
14. presents	✷	They can open the **presents.**

CHALLENGE!

answered
Hawaii
valuable
library

■ **PRACTICE** Think about the words you use most often when you write. Then write the words in order from the ones you use most often to the ones you may use least often.

■ **WRITE** Choose six words. Write a sentence for each word.

surprise	favorite	Tuesday	picture	through
guess	kept	different	presents	Monday
caught	swimming	easy	fifth	

ALPHABETICAL ORDER Write the letter of the alphabet that comes before each letter in the underlined code.

1. Do you hang a *pitcher* or a q j d u v s f?
2. Did he go *threw* or u i s p v h i the window?
3. Who can *guest* or h v f t t the answer?
4. Would you say *catched* or d b v h i u the ball?
5. Is it your *flavorite* or g b w p s j u f ice cream?
6. Is the second day of school *Twosday* or U v f t e b z?

PUZZLE Write the list word that matches the clue. The word in the box answers the riddle "What did the farmer put on his sick pig to cure it?"

7. after *Sunday*
8. a kind of party
9. not the same, but ___
10. a form of *keep*
11. a water sport
12. not hard, but ___
13. another word for *gifts*
14. comes after *fourth*

7. __ [ ] __ __ __ __

8. __ __ __ __ __ [ ] __ __

9. __ __ __ __ __ __ __ [ ] __

10. [ ] __ __ __

11. __ __ __ [ ] __ __ __

12. [ ] __ __ __

13. __ __ __ __ __ [ ] __ __

14. __ __ __ [ ] __

STRATEGIC SPELLING

Pronouncing for Spelling

15–16. We sometimes spell words wrong because we say them wrong. Write *surprise* and *different*. Be sure to say the sounds of the underlined letters.

119

≡	Make a capital.
/	Make a small letter.
∧	Add something.
ℓ	Take out something.
⊙	Add a period.
¶	New paragraph

PROOFREAD A DESCRIPTION

Judy wrote a description of an imaginary animal seen on an imaginary safari. Her friend will try to draw it from the description. Fix Judy's three misspelled words and wrong use of a word.

PROOFREADING TIP
If you add an apostrophe to **its**, you have a contraction that means "it is." Don't write **it's** when you mean "belonging to."

It has the head of an alligator and the body of a camel. It's legs are all most as long as a giraffe's. The real surprize is that it's green. Can you gess what it's called? It's an alcamaffe!

WRITE A DESCRIPTION Describe an imaginary animal that a friend might draw. Use one spelling word and one personal word.

Word List

surprise	swimming	presents
guess	Tuesday	fifth
caught	different	through
favorite	easy	Monday
kept	picture	

Personal Words 1.___ 2.___

Review

CONTEXT CLUES Use words from the box to finish the letter.

Dear Hassan,

It is very (1) here from the city. Uncle Bud and I went fishing yesterday. To get to his favorite fishing hole, we had to go (2) some wild country. It would be so (3) to get lost in those woods! I (4) I saw just about every wild animal there is! We (5) several fish, but we only (6) the biggest ones. When I get home, I'll show you a (7) of Uncle Bud and me with our fish. See you.

Your pal,
Mitch

easy
picture
through
guess
caught
kept
different

Using a *Dictionary*

FINDING THE RIGHT MEANING A dictionary gives more than one meaning for many words. A sentence or phrase often follows a definition. The sentence may help you figure out whether the definition is the one you want.

Read the definitions for *picture.* Then write the number of the definition that fits each sentence.

1. I can't *picture* you with short hair.
2. Can you adjust the *picture* on the television?
3. We have a *picture* of you in our album.

pic•ture (pik′chər). **1** a drawing, painting, portrait, or photograph; printed copy of any of these: *The book contains a good picture of a tiger.* **2** a likeness: *He is the picture of his father.* **3** to form a picture of in the mind: *It is hard to picture life a hundred years ago.* **4** a motion picture. **5** an image on a television set. 1, 2, 4, 5 *noun,* 3 *verb,* **pic•tures, pic•tured, pic•tur•ing.**

Prefixes un- and re-

When the prefixes **un-** and **re-** are added to words, make no change in the spelling of the base word: **un + happy = unhappy.**

■ **STUDY** Say each word. Notice what happens when the prefix is added.

un + happy	=	1.	*unhappy*
un + safe	=	2.	*unsafe*
un + lucky	=	3.	*unlucky*
re + start	=	4.	*restart*
re + write	=	5.	*rewrite*
re + play	=	6.	*replay*
re + read	=	7.	*reread*

un + tie	=	8.	*untie*
un + fold	=	9.	*unfold*
un + wrap	=	10.	*unwrap*
un + pack	=	11.	*unpack*
re + pay	=	12.	*repay*
re + fill	=	13.	*refill*
re + paint	=	14.	*repaint*

CHALLENGE!

unconscious
undefeated
remodel
rebound

■ **PRACTICE** Sort the words by writing
- seven words with **re-** in alphabetical order
- seven words with **un-** in alphabetical order

■ **WRITE** Use three words in sentences about coming home from summer camp.

unlucky	unwrap	unsafe	refill	reread
untie	unhappy	repay	restart	repaint
unfold	unpack	rewrite	replay	

WORD FORMS Write the list word that is formed by changing the underlined prefix to **un-** or **re-**.

1. <u>pre</u>pay

3. <u>re</u>pack

5. <u>re</u>tie

2. <u>mis</u>read

4. <u>pre</u>write

6. <u>re</u>fold

CONTEXT CLUES Write the list word that best fits in each sentence.

7. After the engine stopped, I had to ___ it.
8. Sonia had only one more package to ___.
9. We'll ___ the room another color right away.
10. Joachim was ___ after losing his baseball mitt.
11. It's ___ to ride your bike in heavy traffic.
12. I watched the instant ___ on TV.
13. After Shawna swallowed her lemonade, she asked for a ___.
14. Ali was the ___ person who did not get a ticket to the game.

STRATEGIC SPELLING

Building New Words

Add the prefix **un-** or **re-** to each word to make a new word. Remember what you learned.

15. run

16. even

Did You Know?
Ants feed on the sweet liquid of peony plants as the flowers **unfold.**

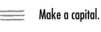

☰	Make a capital.
/	Make a small letter.
∧	Add something.
ℯ	Take out something.
⊙	Add a period.
⸿	New paragraph

PROOFREAD A LIST A.J. made a list to help him pack for vacation. He misspelled three words and used an incorrect pronoun. Fix his mistakes.

PROOFREADING TIP
If you want to use a pronoun to refer back to something earlier in the sentence, be sure it is the correct one. *Them* refers to two or more things. *It* refers to one thing—*tent.*

1. Carefully unfole the tent and check them.
2. Fix the knapsack so that it will be easy to unpake.
3. Be sure to rerede your list.

WRITE A LIST Pretend you are going on vacation. Make a list of the things you'll need to take along. Use some of your spelling words and at least one personal word.

Word List

unlucky	unpack	restart
untie	unsafe	replay
unfold	repay	reread
unwrap	rewrite	repaint
unhappy	refill	

Personal Words 1.___ 2.___

Review

PUZZLE Find a word from the box for each clue.
Fill in the puzzle to answer the riddle:

What covers an alligator's kitchen floor?

1. play again
2. dangerous
3. sad
4. begin again
5. write it over
6. not lucky
7. read again

unhappy
unsafe
unlucky
restart
rewrite
replay
reread

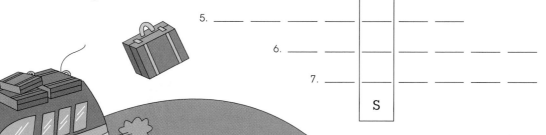

1. ____ ____ ____ ____ ____ ____
2. ____ ____ ____ ____ ____ ____
3. ____ ____ ____ ____ ____
4. ____ ____ ____ ____ ____
5. ____ ____ ____ ____ ____
6. ____ ____ ____ ____ ____ ____
7. ____ ____ ____ ____ ____ ____

S

Word *Study*

ANTONYMS Words that have opposite
meanings are called **antonyms.** Here are two
ways to write them. You can add the prefix
un- to a word, or you can use a different word.

happy/unhappy   happy/sad

Write two antonyms for each word below.
Use the prefix **un-** to form one of the antonyms.
The other antonym should be a different word.

1. button   2. true   3. safe

Suffixes -ful, -ly, -ness

When suffixes are added to most words, the base word stays the same. If the base word ends **consonant** and **y, y** is changed to **i** before the suffix is added: **happy + -ness = happiness.**

■ **STUDY** Notice what happens when a suffix is added.

care + ful	=	1. *careful*
beauty + ful	=	2. *beautiful* ✳
wonder + ful	=	3. *wonderful*
real + ly	=	4. *really* ✳
final + ly	=	5. *finally* ✳
sad + ness	=	6. *sadness*
happy + ness	=	7. *happiness*

✳
WATCH OUT FOR FREQUENTLY MISSPELLED WORDS!

help + ful	=	8. *helpful*
grace + ful	=	9. *graceful*
sad + ly	=	10. *sadly*
live + ly	=	11. *lively*
happy + ly	=	12. *happily*
kind + ness	=	13. *kindness*
sick + ness	=	14. *sickness*

CHALLENGE!

forgetful
lonely
easily
greediness

■ **PRACTICE** Sort the words by writing
■ five words with **-ly**   ■ four words with **-ness**
■ five words with **-ful**

■ **WRITE** Use four words in sentences about people you know.

126

careful	wonderful	finally	happily	sadness
helpful	beautiful	sadly	kindness	happiness
graceful	really	lively	sickness	

SYLLABLES Write each list word and draw lines between the syllables. Use the Spelling Dictionary.

1. wonderful   3. lively   5. graceful

2. sadness   4. happily   6. finally

CONTEXT Add a suffix to each word in parentheses to form a list word and complete each sentence.

7. She was (real) trying to help her brother.
8. Grandpa was crying softly and (sad).
9. Our veterinarian is (care) with her patients.
10. The local police are (help) in many ways.
11. You should be rewarded for your (kind).
12. Your (happy) shows in your face.
13. That was a (beauty) birthday card.
14. We're happy that Pedro's (sick) is over.

STRATEGIC SPELLING
Building New Words

15–16. Write the base words *play* and *tight*. Add the suffix. Make a new word. Remember what you learned.

Base Word	Suffix	New Word
	-ful	
	-ness	

≡	Make a capital.
/	Make a small letter.
∧	Add something.
ℓ	Take out something.
⊙	Add a period.
¶	New paragraph

PROOFREAD A PARAGRAPH

Shanna wrote a paragraph explaining who she thought was at fault when Jacqui was hurt. She misspelled three words, and her handwriting wasn't her best. Fix her mistakes.

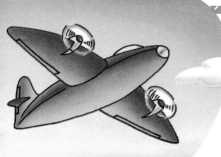

PROOFREADING TIP
If you don't form **b, o, w,** or **v** carefully, the letter might look like two letters. Be careful.

It might not have happened if Jacqui had been carful. The equipment was not unsave. She just started too quickly. Everyone at the airport showed kindnes.

WRITE A PARAGRAPH
Write a paragraph from Jacqui's point of view. She feels that she was careful and the airport equipment was not safe. Use some spelling words and one personal word.

Word List

careful	really	kindness
helpful	finally	sickness
graceful	sadly	sadness
wonderful	lively	happiness
beautiful	happily	

Personal Words 1.___ 2.___

Review

PUZZLE Write each letter of your answer on a separate line. Then use the numbered letters to solve the riddle.

careful	finally
beautiful	sadness
wonderful	happiness
really	

1. opposite of ugly
   — — — — — — — — —
   9   6 1

2. at last
   — — — — — — —
                  12

3. opposite of careless
   — — — — — —
      10   3

4. opposite of happiness
   — — — — — — —
      2   14

5. truly
   — — — — —
      8   11

6. amazing
   — — — — — — —
      5   4

7. opposite of sadness
   — — — — — — — — —
   7 13

What did the umpire who needed a ride say?

1	2	3		4		5	6	1		1	5		1	7	8		9	10	11	12		13	14
	K			M																		G		M	

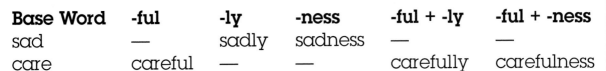

Word *Study*

SUFFIXES You can build new words easily by adding suffixes to base words. Read the chart.

Base Word	-ful	-ly	-ness	-ful + -ly	-ful + -ness
sad	—	sadly	sadness	—	—
care	careful	—	—	carefully	carefulness

Write four words by adding suffixes to these base words. Remember what you've learned about spelling changes when adding suffixes.

1. kind + ly + ness
2. happy + ness
3. thank + ful + ness
4. thought + ful + ness

129

Vowels with r

The vowel sound /ėr/ can be spelled **ear**, **ere**, **ir**, **ur**, and **or**: <u>ear</u>ly, w<u>ere</u>, th<u>ir</u>d, f<u>ur</u>, w<u>or</u>d.

■ **STUDY** Say each word. Read the sentence.

WATCH OUT FOR FREQUENTLY MISSPELLED WORDS!

1.	*early*	I take an **early** bus.
2.	*heard* ✳	Everyone **heard** the news.
3.	*were* ✳	We **were** home last night.
4.	*third*	My story won **third** place.
5.	*fur*	The rabbit has soft **fur**.
6.	*work*	He has to **work** at his job.
7.	*word*	That **word** has ten letters.

8.	*search*	The **search** for a cure goes on.
9.	*earth*	They farm the rich **earth**.
10.	*dirt*	We cleaned out the **dirt**.
11.	*nurse*	The **nurse** gave me a shot.
12.	*turkey*	We had a **turkey** dinner.
13.	*Thursday*	Her birthday is on **Thursday**.
14.	*world*	Look at a map of the **world**.

CHALLENGE!

rehearsal
twirl
furniture
worst

■ **PRACTICE** Sort the words by writing
- six words with **ir** or **ur**
- three words with **or**
- five words with **ear** or **ere**

■ **WRITE** Use two sentences in a paragraph about a family celebration.

were	work	Thursday	world	word
nurse	turkey	early	search	fur
earth	dirt	heard	third	

LETTER TRADE Write the list word that begins and ends with the same letters as each word below.

1. weak   4. hard   7. tried

2. Tuesday   5. speech   8. far

3. would   6. wore   9. weed

RHYMES Write the list word that rhymes with each word below.

10. hurt   11. purse   12. jerky   13. curly

STRATEGIC SPELLING
Seeing Meaning Connections

earthshaking
earthworm
earthquake

14. Write the list word that is related in spelling and meaning to the words in the box.

Then complete the sentence with words from the box.

An (15) is really an (16) event for an animal like the (17).

FREQUENTLY MISSPELLED WORDS * FREQUENTLY MISSPELLED WORDS * FREQUENTLY MISSPELLED WORDS

Remember: We were here! Yes, we were!

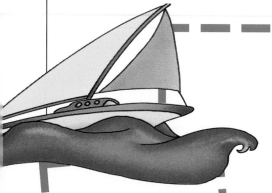

≡	Make a capital.
/	Make a small letter.
∧	Add something.
ℓ	Take out something.
⊙	Add a period.
⁋	New paragraph

PROOFREAD A POST CARD
Annie wrote a post card to Felipe.
She misspelled three words and
forgot to capitalize important words
in the greeting and closing. Fix her mistakes.

PROOFREADING TIP
In writing letters and notes, be sure to capitalize the first word of your greeting. Where else must you use a capital letter?

August 25, 20_ _

dear Felipe,

    We did serch for a perfect
spot, and we found it. No
wrok for the famly here.
We're having fun!

    your friend,
    Annie

WRITE A POST CARD Pretend you're on a trip.
Write a post card to a friend. Use a spelling word
and a personal word.

Word List

were	dirt	search
nurse	Thursday	third
earth	early	word
work	heard	fur
turkey	world	

Personal Words 1.___ 2.___

Review

early
heard
were
third
fur
work
word

SEEING RELATIONSHIPS Write a word from the box to finish each relationship.

1. *Saw* is to *eyes* as ___ is to *ears.*
2. *Play* is to *game* as ___ is to *job.*
3. *Sentence* is to *paragraph* as ___ is to *sentence.*
4. *Is* is to *are* as *was* is to ___ .
5. *First* is to *second* as ___ is to *fourth.*
6. *Morning* is to *evening* as ___ is to *late.*
7. *Coat* is to *person* as ___ is to *dog.*

Word *Study*

WORD PYRAMIDS Try adding a letter to a word to get a new word. You can put the letter anywhere and change the order of the other letters. Then add another letter to the second word to get a third word. You don't have to stop at three words. What you get is called a **word pyramid.**

or
row
word
world

Add a spelling word to complete these pyramids.

ear	run	care
hear	runs	reach

More Vowels with r

SPELLING FOCUS

The vowel sound /âr/ can be spelled **er** or **air**: v**er**y, h**air**. The vowel sound /ir/ can be spelled **ear** or **eer**: n**ear**, d**eer**.

■ **STUDY** Say each word. Read the sentence.

WATCH OUT FOR FREQUENTLY MISSPELLED WORDS!

1.	*America*	Chile is in South **America.**
2.	*very* ✽	He is a **very** tall man.
3.	*pair*	I need a new **pair** of socks.
4.	*hair*	Shiny **hair** looks healthy.
5.	*near*	I live **near** the library.
6.	*year*	She is a **year** older than us.
7.	*deer*	A **deer** ran across the path.
8.	*stereo*	The **stereo** plays music.
9.	*fair*	They'll pay us a **fair** price.
10.	*stairs*	Let's run up the **stairs.**
11.	*fear*	Jim has a **fear** of heights.
12.	*clear*	The pilot liked a **clear** day.
13.	*cheer*	We ended with a loud **cheer.**
14.	*steer*	The bike is easy to **steer.**

CHALLENGE!

prairie
beard
appear
volunteer

■ **PRACTICE** Sort the words by writing
- three words with **eer**
- three words with **er**
- four words with **air**
- four words with **ear**

■ **WRITE** Choose six words. Write a sentence for each word.

fair	stereo	America	year	clear
very	pair	near	cheer	steer
stairs	hair	deer	fear	

TONGUE TWISTERS Write the list word that would best complete each tongue twister.

1. Amelia ambled about the area of ___.
2. Fiona felt it would be ___ if the first food after the flood were fish.
3. Helene had hoped for help with her ___.
4. Calvin Collie can ___ the counter completely.
5. Perry peered at the ___ of purple pants.
6. Vita viewed a ___ valuable violin.
7. Sam suddenly stopped by the ___ and started to sing.

DEFINITIONS Write the list word that matches each clue.

8. To control the direction of a car, you do this.
9. If you are frightened, you have this.
10. Fifty-two weeks make one of these.
11. A fawn is a baby of this kind of animal.
12. You might do this if your team wins a game.
13. This system uses two or more sets of speakers.
14. Where are you if you are close by someone?

STRATEGIC SPELLING

Building New Words

Add the suffix to each base word to make a new word. Remember what you learned.

15. cheer **-ful**

16. year **-ly**

17. near **-ness**

Did You Know?
The word *America* came from the name of the Italian explorer Amerigo Vespucci. North America and South America are known as the Americas.

135

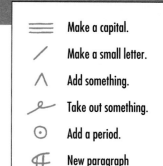

≡	Make a capital.
/	Make a small letter.
∧	Add something.
ℓ	Take out something.
⊙	Add a period.
¶	New paragraph

PROOFREAD DIRECTIONS Turia invited some friends to her house after school. She gave them directions, but she misspelled three words, and her handwriting wasn't her best. Correct her mistakes.

PROOFREADING TIP
Did Turia write *miclclle* or *middle*? Carelessly formed letters may look like other letters. Proofread for handwriting that is unreadable.

Turn right on Main St. to Walnut. Turn right again. Very nere the middle of the block is 3427. That's my house. You'll see some stars, and if you hear the sterio, come to the second floor.

WRITE DIRECTIONS Write directions to your house from school. Be sure to use some spelling words and one or two personal words.

Word List

fair	hair	cheer
very	America	fear
stairs	near	clear
stereo	deer	steer
pair	year	

Personal Words 1.___ 2.___

Review

CROSSWORD PUZZLE Fill in the puzzle by writing a word from the box for each clue.

America
very
pair
hair
near
year
deer

Across

2. close by
3. twelve months
5. Thank you ___ much.
6. something you comb
7. two things that match

Down

1. a forest animal
4. North and South ___

Multicultural *Connection*

CELEBRATIONS Everyone has a birthday. It's the date on which you were born. Every year on that date you become one year older.

People of different cultures celebrate birthdays in different ways. Write four words that describe or name important parts of your birthday celebration every year.

Review

Lesson 25: Including All the Letters
Lesson 26: Prefixes un- and re-
Lesson 27: Suffixes -ful, -ly, -ness

Lesson 28: Vowels with r
Lesson 29: More Vowels with r

REVIEW WORD LIST

1. caught	10. through	19. careful	28. word
2. different	11. replay	20. finally	29. America
3. easy	12. restart	21. happily	30. cheer
4. favorite	13. unfold	22. happiness	31. fair
5. guess	14. unlucky	23. lively	32. pair
6. kept	15. unpack	24. wonderful	33. steer
7. presents	16. unsafe	25. early	34. very
8. surprise	17. unwrap	26. search	35. year
9. swimming	18. beautiful	27. were	

A six-letter list word that begins with **un-** is hidden in each silly word. Write each hidden word once.

unfold   **unwrap**   **unpack**   **unsafe**

• **funfolder**   • **punpackage**
• **runwrapper**   • **sunsafety**

Going, going, gone

Marty organized a neighborhood sale for kids. He and a few friends had old collections they decided to put up for sale. Complete the sentences with list words.

were   kept   easy   beautiful
very   finally   different   careful

The first item sold was a set of five baseball cards— all (1) from one another. The owner was (2) not to bend them.

The second item was a collection of (3)-to-read books. There (4) three favorite stories.

We (5) sold two (6) nice dolls. These (7) dolls were (8) in a case as part of a collection.

Go fish

Terry wrote some things to remember when you go fishing. Write a list word to complete her tips.

restart   through
caught   early   steer

1. Everything's set;
   the worms are curly,
   To catch a fish, you get up ____.
2. If the boat is still and won't ____,
   Then the motor's dead;
   better get a part.
3. To cast your line straight and true,
   Bend your wrist and follow ____.
4. Remember how that last fish fought?
   It twisted and turned before it
   was ____.
5. Before night falls, point the boat
   and ____
   Toward the shore; come back here.

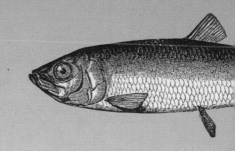

The BallOOn Lady

La Tisha wrote a story about a woman in her neighborhood who sold balloons and other things. Write the list words to complete her story.

cheer   wonderful   happiness
year   presents   surprise

The balloon lady has a small shop with (1) things in the window. There are toys and baskets and all sorts of great (2). She sends balloons to (3) up sick people. She fixes baskets of fruit and always puts a small box of candy in as a (4). She brings (5) to customers all (6) long. I like her balloons best of all.

Ricardo wrote clues that describe some of the games he and his friends like to play. Write the list words to complete the clues.

word   pair   search   guess   unlucky

1. Ask questions that can be answered yes or no before making a ___.
2. To get a matching ___ of cards, you ask another player for the card you need. If that player doesn't have the card you need, he or she tells you to do something.
3. One or more persons have to hide and whoever is "It" has to ___ for them.
4. Everyone walks around a line of chairs until the music stops. The ___ one can't find a chair to sit on and is out of the game.
5. Each player takes turns building a ___ with letters.

These were the winning entries in the Perfect Vacation Contest. Write the list words to complete each description.

replay
happily
swimming
favorite
America
fair
lively

1. My perfect vacation has to include ___ in the ocean every day.
2. Touring the United States of ___ is my idea of a great vacation.
3. I could spend my whole vacation at my ___ place in the world—my grandma's cottage.
4. Listening to some ___ music in a big park is a good way to spend part of a vacation.
5. I would like a ___ of last year's vacation in Washington, D.C.
6. As part of my vacation, I'd like to go to the state ___.
7. On my perfect vacation, I could sleep ___ for a week.

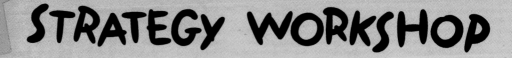

STRATEGY WORKSHOP

Dividing Long Words

DISCOVER THE STRATEGY In Unit 4 you used syllables to divide long words. In this workshop you'll learn two more ways to divide long words for study. First, work with words that are compounds.

1 Draw a line between the base words of the compound.
some/times

2 Study the compound one part at a time.
some/times

TRY IT OUT Now practice dividing long words for study with your partner or group.

Write *something, bathtub, sunshine, outside,* and *airplane.* Draw a line between the two base words in each compound.

Now look back at the five compounds. Notice that the spelling of the base words did not change when they were joined to make compounds.

DISCOVER THE STRATEGY Here's another way to divide long words for study. Work with words that have prefixes or suffixes.

1 Draw a line between the base word and the prefix or suffix. **un/luck/y beauti/ful**

2 Study the word one part at a time. **un/luck/y beauti/ful**

TRY IT OUT Practice this strategy with your partner or group.

Write *wonderful, unwrap, repaint,* and *happiness.* Draw a line between each base word and the prefix or suffix.

Now look back at the words with suffixes. The spelling of one base word changed when the suffix was added. Mark the letter that replaces the **y** before the suffix is added.

LOOK AHEAD Look ahead at the next five lessons. Write five list words that are long and look hard to spell. Then divide each word for study.

Compound Words

SPELLING FOCUS

A compound word is usually made of two smaller words. Keep all the letters when spelling compounds: **out + side = outside.**

■ **STUDY** Say each word. Read the sentence.

1. *himself* — He excused **himself** and left.
2. *afternoon* — The baby naps all **afternoon.**
3. *everything* ※ — I have **everything** I need.
4. *grandmother* — I sat with my **grandmother.**
5. *homework* — She started her **homework.**
6. *outside* ※ — They went **outside** to play.
7. *bedroom* — My **bedroom** rug is blue.

8. *butterfly* — A **butterfly** landed by me.
9. *grandfather* — Let's visit our **grandfather.**
10. *everybody* ※ — Tell **everybody** to come.
11. *backyard* — A **backyard** party is fun.
12. *popcorn* — The **popcorn** was salty.
13. *everyone* ※ — I knew **everyone** in the room.
14. *anyone* — If **anyone** can do it, you can.

CHALLENGE!

reindeer
lamppost
nowhere
nickname

■ **PRACTICE** Write the words you already know how to spell. Then write the words you are just learning to spell.

■ **WRITE** Use two of the sentences to write riddles.

everything outside   grandfather popcorn   himself
butterfly   grandmother everybody   homework   bedroom
afternoon   everyone   backyard   anyone

JOINING WORDS Find the two words in each
sentence that make up a compound word from the
list. Write the word.

1. She packed every coat but one.
2. The game will start after twelve o'clock noon.
3. We always pop the corn in a heavy pan.
4. Your bed is in the room at the end of the hall.
5. Take home the work you haven't finished.
6. Can any person be the one chosen to go?
7. The grand prize was won by my father.
8. That drawing of him is a self-portrait.
9. We looked at every map, but we couldn't find a
   body of water with that name.
10. In the back of our house the yard is fenced.

RIDDLES Write the list word for each set of clues.

11. It begins like *off.* It rhymes with *ride.*
12. It begins like *even.* It rhymes with *sting.*
13. It begins like *better.* It rhymes with *cry.*
14. It begins like *great.* It rhymes with *brother.*

STRATEGIC SPELLING
The Dividing Long Words Strategy

*FREQUENTLY MISSPELLED WORDS * FREQUENTLY MISSPELLED WORDS*

The **e** is the **very** thing
to help you spell
everything.

Study long words piece
by piece. Write two
hard list words. Draw
a line between the
base words in each
compound. Notice that
the compound has all
the letters from both
base words.

≡	Make a capital.
/	Make a small letter.
∧	Add something.
ℓ	Take out something.
⊙	Add a period.
¶	New paragraph

PROOFREAD AN INVITATION

Yoko wrote invitations to her dog's first birthday party. She misspelled three words and forgot two commas. Fix her mistakes.

July 6 20_ _

Dear Friends
    Please come to Dexter's party on Friday afternon in my bakyard. I hope evryone can come.

                    Yoko

PROOFREADING TIP
Remember to use a comma after a greeting in a letter or note and also between the date and year.

WRITE AN INVITATION Write an invitation to a party or a picnic. Use two spelling words and at least one personal word.

Word List

everything	everyone	homework
butterfly	grandfather	anyone
afternoon	everybody	himself
outside	backyard	bedroom
grandmother	popcorn	

Personal Words 1.___ 2.___

Review

CONTEXT CLUES Use words from the box to finish the paragraph.

On his way to school Josh reminded (1), "As soon as I get home this (2), I'll finish my (3) and other chores. Then I'm going to call my (4). I'll ask her what kind of bird I saw (5) my (6) window this morning. When I get to school I should write down (7) I remember about it."

himself
afternoon
everything
grandmother
homework
outside
bedroom

Using a Dictionary

SPECIAL FORMS To find the word *hurried* in the dictionary, you need to look up the base word *hurry*. *Hurried* is a special form of *hurry*. You'll find it at the end of the entry for *hurry*.

Usually the dictionary shows special forms for an entry word only if there are spelling changes to the base word when an ending is added. Use your Spelling Dictionary to answer these questions.

1. What are the special forms for *hurry*?
2. What word would you look up to find *butterflies*?
3. Why aren't the **-ed** and **-ing** forms shown in the entry for *fear*?

147

Contractions

SPELLING FOCUS

In contractions an apostrophe takes the place of letters that are left out: **I am** becomes **I'm.**

■ **STUDY** Say each word. Notice what happens when the contraction is formed.

❋
WATCH OUT FOR FREQUENTLY MISSPELLED WORDS!

I + am	=	1. *I'm* ❋
it + is	=	2. *it's* ❋
he + is	=	3. *he's*
that + is	=	4. *that's* ❋
did + not	=	5. *didn't* ❋
will + not	=	6. *won't*
let + us	=	7. *let's*

have + not	=	8. *haven't*
does + not	=	9. *doesn't*
are + not	=	10. *aren't*
I + have	=	11. *I've*
they + have	=	12. *they've*
we + are	=	13. *we're* ❋
you + will	=	14. *you'll*

CHALLENGE!

needn't
should've
you've
that'll

■ **PRACTICE** From the word list write the ten contractions you use most in your writing. Then write the other four.

■ **WRITE** Use six of the words in sentences.

that's	won't	aren't	they've	you'll
it's	haven't	didn't	I'm	let's
he's	doesn't	I've	we're	

CONTEXT CLUES Write the contraction that best fits in each sentence below.

1. ___ written all the invitations by myself.
2. Yes, ___ time to go to bed.
3. ___ going on a picnic with my dad.
4. We know ___ do well in the race.
5. I ___ be able to finish my chores in time.
6. The doctors ___ in the office today.
7. Call Max to see if ___ going with us.
8. We ___ seen her all day.

WORD PARTS Write the list word that contains each word below.

9. they   11. did   13. does

10. that   12. let   14. we

STRATEGIC SPELLING
Building New Words

Add the contraction for *not* to the base words. Remember what you learned.

Base Word	Contraction with -n't
15. was	___
16. would	___
17. were	___

FREQUENTLY MISSPELLED WORDS ✳ FREQUENTLY MISSPELLED WORDS ✳ FREQUENTLY MISSPELLED WORDS

Remember that **won't** means **will not.** There's a spelling change in the base word of this contraction.

≡	Make a capital.
/	Make a small letter.
∧	Add something.
ℰ	Take out something.
⊙	Add a period.
¶	New paragraph

PROOFREAD A PREDICTION For a Class Book of the Future, DeShawn wrote what he thought cars and bikes would be like. In his prediction he misspelled three words and forgot to use a capital in one place. Fix his mistakes.

In 2050, cars and bikes wont look the way they do now. You see, thats because new materials will be invented. New cars cud go faster and, i think, use less fuel. Bikes will be safer too.

PROOFREADING TIP
DeShawn refers to himself by using a pronoun. That pronoun should always be capitalized.

WRITE A PREDICTION Write a prediction about what houses and apartments will be like in the future. Use a spelling word and a personal word.

Word List

that's	doesn't	I'm
it's	aren't	we're
he's	didn't	you'll
won't	I've	let's
haven't	they've	

Personal Words 1.___ 2.___

Review

PUZZLE Use words from the box to fill in the puzzle. The puzzle answers the riddle.

Why does the dog come to the kitchen?
The teakettle—

I'm
it's
he's
that's
didn't
won't
let's

1. will not
2. that is
3. I am
4. it is
5. did not
6. let us
7. he is

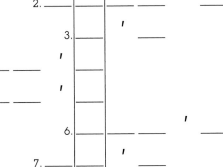

```
        ┌───┐
    1.  │   │___  ___  ___'
        │   │
    2. ___│   │___  ___  ___'
        │   │
    3.  │   │___  ___'
        │   │
  4. ___ ___'
        │   │
5. ___ ___ ___ ___
        │   │
    6.  │   │___  ___  ___'
        │   │
  7. ___│ S │___  ___'
        └───┘
```

Word *Study*

USING CONTRACTIONS Pronouns and verbs are often put together to make contractions. Here are some examples.

I am/I'm   we are/we're
she is/she's   you are/you're
he is/he's   they are/they're
it is/it's

People like to use contractions when they talk or write. Write a contraction to complete each sentence below.

1. Bonita thinks ___ going to join her team this year.
2. I think ___ one of the best ballplayers around.
3. I know ___ hoping to win every game this year.

Vowels in Final Syllables

SPELLING FOCUS

Vowels in final syllables often sound alike even when they are spelled differently: **wag<u>o</u>n, gard<u>e</u>n; sug<u>ar</u>, pap<u>er</u>; trav<u>e</u>l, anim<u>a</u>l.**

■ **STUDY** Say each word. Read the sentence.

1. *wagon* The boy pulled a red **wagon.**
2. *open* Please **open** the door for me.
3. *garden* Mom has a flower **garden.**
4. *sugar* Sweeten the tea with **sugar.**
5. *paper* Our class recycles **paper.**
6. *travel* We got to **travel** by camel.
7. *animal* Pat likes **animal** stories.

8. *lemon* The **lemon** tasted sour.
9. *dollar* Can I borrow a **dollar?**
10. *another* ✳ I'd like **another** sticker.
11. *brother* ✳ They are sister and **brother.**
12. *squirrel* A **squirrel** has a bushy tail.
13. *nickel* The change was a **nickel.**
14. *final* Read the **final** chapter.

WATCH OUT FOR FREQUENTLY MISSPELLED WORDS!

■ **PRACTICE** Sort the words by writing
- five words that end with **er** or **ar**
- four words that end with **on** or **en**
- five words that end with **el** or **al**

■ **WRITE** Choose six words. Write a sentence for each word.

CHALLENGE!

Oregon
calendar
character
cardinal

travel	wagon	sugar	animal	lemon
open	final	garden	nickel	brother
dollar	squirrel	paper	another	

SYLLABLES Write the list word that starts with the same letter and has the same number of syllables as each word below.

1. police   2. border   3. dreamer   4. nightlight

WORD SEARCH Find the ten list words in the puzzle. Write the words. They may be printed down or across.

```
o  c  m  w  a  g  o  n  w
g  s  a  b  f  i  n  a  l
t  q  u  g  j  o  e  b  n
s  u  g  a  r  i  s  b  o
o  i  t  r  a  v  e  l  i
p  r  o  d  o  l  l  a  d
e  r  l  e  m  o  n  y  p
n  e  a  n  o  t  h  e  r
a  l  e  a  n  i  m  a  l
```

STRATEGIC SPELLING
The Dividing Long Words Strategy

15–17. Sometimes it helps to study long words piece by piece. Write *holiday, because,* and *Saturday.* Draw lines between the syllables. Then study each word syllable by syllable. Check a dictionary if you need help.

Did You Know?
A squirrel can use its tail to make its own shady spot on a sunny day. The word *squirrel* means "shadow tail."

≡	Make a capital.
/	Make a small letter.
∧	Add something.
ℯ	Take out something.
⊙	Add a period.
⨍	New paragraph

PROOFREAD TIPS Tammy's mother is a travel agent, so Tammy thinks she can give vacation travel tips. Fix her three misspelled words.

PROOFREADING TIP
Tammy misspelled a word because she used an incorrect ending when she wrote a plural noun. Check all plural nouns as you proofread.

To get the most for your travle doller, make your plans early. Shop around for good train or airplane fares. Summer in your backyard can cost just pennys.

WRITE TIPS Pretend you have some experience in the travel business or another kind of business. Write some tips for people who will be using your services. Use some spelling words and at least one personal word.

Word List

travel	squirrel	nickel
open	sugar	another
dollar	garden	lemon
wagon	paper	brother
final	animal	

Personal Words 1.___ 2.___

Review

RHYMES Choose a word from the box to finish each silly rhyme. Hint: You should capitalize two words.

wagon
open
garden
sugar
paper
travel
animal

1. When he wants to see inside,
   The dentist says, "___ wide."
2. Our experiment today is with water vapor.
   For taking notes you'll need pencil and ___.
3. ___ that is sweet
   Can come from a beet.
4. I beg your pardon;
   You walked through my ___.
5. Before I decide what I should get,
   Tell me what ___ is the best pet?
6. The judge banged her gavel
   And said, "You can't ___."
7. That green plastic dragon
   Will fill up Su's ___.

Word *Study*

SOUND WORDS Can you think of a word that describes how a nickel sounds when you drop it on the sidewalk? Does it *plink* or *ting*? Words like *plink, ting, crash,* and *boom* are examples of **sound words.** The word imitates the sound you are trying to describe.

Say each word below. Write a word that tells what or who might make each sound.

1. growl
2. tweet tweet
3. tick-tock
4. roar
5. zoom

Suffixes -er, -or, -ist

Suffixes **-er, -or, -ist** change a word to show someone who does something: **read + er = reader, visit + or = visitor, art + ist = artist.**

■ **STUDY** Say each word. Then notice what happens when the suffix is added.

farm + er	=	1.	*farmer*
read + er	=	2.	*reader*
play + er	=	3.	*player*
visit + or	=	4.	*visitor*
sail + or	=	5.	*sailor*
art + ist	=	6.	*artist*
final + ist	=	7.	*finalist*
paint + er	=	8.	*painter*
wait + er	=	9.	*waiter*
hunt + er	=	10.	*hunter*
act + or	=	11.	*actor*
invent + or	=	12.	*inventor*
violin + ist	=	13.	*violinist*
tour + ist	=	14.	*tourist*

CHALLENGE!

announcer
manager
governor
scientist

■ **PRACTICE** Sort words by writing
- four words with **-ist**
- six words with **-er**
- four words with **-or**

■ **WRITE** Choose two of the words to write about careers.

painter	waiter	artist	finalist	sailor
reader	player	violinist	actor	inventor
farmer	hunter	tourist	visitor	

WORD FORMS Add **-er** or **-or** to each word below to form a list word.

1. read
2. paint
3. visit
4. hunt
5. invent
6. farm
7. play
8. sail

SEEING CONNECTIONS Write a list word that best matches each clue.

9. someone who works in a restaurant
10. someone who has a chance to win a contest
11. someone who travels for pleasure
12. someone who plays a musical instrument
13. someone who performs in a movie or play
14. someone who draws or paints pictures

STRATEGIC SPELLING
Building New Words

15–16. Write the base words *teach* and *dream*. Add the suffix **-er** to make new words.

Did You Know?
An average of 3,400,000 tourists visit the Statue of Liberty and Ellis Island yearly.

≡	Make a capital.
/	Make a small letter.
∧	Add something.
ℯ	Take out something.
⊙	Add a period.
¶	New paragraph

PROOFREAD A PROGRAM Neil wrote the program for Longfellow School's outdoor concert, but he misspelled three words and forgot to capitalize two letters. Fix his mistakes.

Mrs. Granger will introduce each finelist. Celia Alba, violinis, will play an original composition. Donato Perlas, piano artist, will play sum songs by george gershwin.

PROOFREADING TIP
Don't forget what you know about capitalizing proper nouns. Names of people, places, and things should begin with capital letters.

WRITE A PROGRAM Pretend you are the program chairperson for a school concert. Write a program for the audience. Use some spelling words and one or two personal words.

Word List

painter	hunter	actor
reader	artist	visitor
farmer	violinist	sailor
waiter	tourist	inventor
player	finalist	

Personal Words 1.___ 2.___

 Review

farmer	sailor
reader	artist
player	finalist
visitor	

PUZZLE Write each letter of your answer on a separate line. Then use the numbered letters to solve the riddle.

1. someone who goes to sea — — — — $\underset{2}{\quad}$ $\underset{7}{\quad}$

2. a guest — — — — $\underset{9}{\quad}$ $\underset{4}{\quad}$ —

3. someone who reads — — — — $\underset{3}{\quad}$

4. a painter — $\underset{5}{\quad}$ — — —

5. someone who raises food — — — — $\underset{1}{\quad}$

6. a possible winner — — — $\underset{8}{\quad}$ — — — —

7. someone who takes part in a game — — — $\underset{6}{\quad}$ — —

How can you get out of deep water?

1	2			3	4			5	2			6	2		7		2	8	9
		W	,			W	,			W			U			,	B		

Multicultural *Connection*

ARTISTIC EXPRESSION People all over the world have made our lives better because of their talents. We have special words for these people.

Garrett Morgan <u>invented</u> the traffic signal. He was a wonderful <u>inventor</u>.

Write the spelling word that completes the second sentence. The underlined word is a clue.

1. Itzak Perlman is a musical talent who plays the <u>violin</u>. He is a talented ___.
2. Maria Montoya Martinez created beautiful <u>art</u> with pottery. She was a famous ___.
3. Babe Ruth <u>played</u> for the New York Yankees. He was a famous baseball ___.

Words with No Sound Clues

SPELLING FOCUS

Some words have letters you don't hear when you say the word: **could.** In some words the vowel sound you hear gives no clue to its spelling: **special.**

■ **STUDY** Say each word. Read the sentence.

WATCH OUT FOR FREQUENTLY MISSPELLED WORDS!

1. *special*   We had a **special** dinner.
2. *real*   Mom's pearls are **real.**
3. *before* ✳   We were home **before** dark.
4. *every*   Look in **every** corner.
5. *being*   Nan likes **being** the tallest.
6. *laugh*   His giggle makes me **laugh.**
7. *could* ✳   You **could** be right this time.

8. *caterpillar*   A fuzzy **caterpillar** wiggled.
9. *cousin* ✳   My aunt and **cousin** stayed.
10. *chocolate*   Dad made a **chocolate** cake.
11. *dinosaur*   The **dinosaur** bone is huge.
12. *upon* ✳   I put it **upon** the shelf.
13. *Wednesday*   Art class is on **Wednesday.**
14. *clothes* ✳   Wear your new **clothes.**

CHALLENGE!

barbecue
scissors
somersault
cupboard

■ **PRACTICE** Write the four longest words in alphabetical order. Then write the rest of the words in any order you like.

■ **WRITE** Use two of the sentences to write riddles.

160

could	clothes	upon	cousin	being
laugh	Wednesday	every	dinosaur	caterpillar
real	chocolate	before	special	

RHYMES Write the list word that rhymes with each word below. Underline the list words that do not end like their rhyming partners.

1. skiing   3. should   5. staff

2. rose   4. steal   6. therefore

CLASSIFYING Write the list word that completes each group.

7. Sunday and Monday, Tuesday and ___
8. vanilla, strawberry, ___
9. aunt, uncle, ___
10. some, many, ___
11. silkworm, earthworm, ___
12. brontosaurus, stegosaurus, ___
13. up, on, ___
14. great, unusual, ___

STRATEGIC SPELLING
Using the Problem Parts Strategy

15–16. Vowels in some words have no sound clues. Those words may be hard to spell. Write two words from the spelling list that are hard for you to spell. Mark the problem parts.

Did You Know?
The word *dinosaur* means "terrible lizard," but a dinosaur wasn't a lizard. Some lizards look like little dinosaurs, but they aren't dinosaurs either.

≡	Make a capital.
/	Make a small letter.
∧	Add something.
ℓ	Take out something.
⊙	Add a period.
¶	New paragraph

PROOFREAD A SIGN As the Martinez family drove through the Southwest on their vacation, Pablo saw this sign. He found the spelling error. Can you? Write the word correctly.

PROOFREADING TIP
In making signs, many things are considered all right, such as writing in all capital letters. Misspelling a word is never all right. Be sure to proofread signs and posters carefully.

OPEN 11:00 AM

WENESDAY
2 FOR 1
EVERYTHING
8 TILL CLOSE

MAKE A SIGN Make a sign announcing a sale that seems too good to be true. Use some spelling words and one personal word.

Word List

could	chocolate	dinosaur
laugh	upon	special
real	every	being
clothes	before	caterpillar
Wednesday	cousin	

Personal Words 1.___ 2.___

Review

CROSSWORD PUZZLE Use the clues to fill in the puzzle.

special
real
before
every
being
laugh
could

Across

4. He likes ___ at home.
5. Eat breakfast ___ school.
6. You ___ win $1,000,000.
7. Her jokes make me ___.

Down

1. Grandma calls us ___ week.
2. Dad's barbecued ribs are a ___ treat.
3. They told the ___ story.

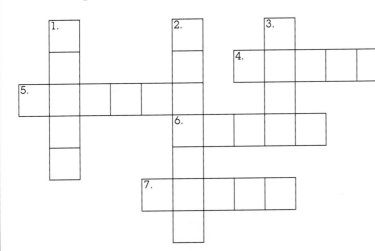

Word *Study*

COMPARISONS Often when you write you compare two things. Useful words for comparing things are **alike** (the same) and **different** (not the same).

Look at the picture of these two cousins. Tell how they are alike and how they are different.

1. Write one way in which the girls are alike.
2. Write one way in which the girls are different.

Review

Lesson 31: Compound Words
Lesson 32: Contractions
Lesson 33: Vowels in Final Syllables

Lesson 34: Suffixes -er, -or, -ist
Lesson 35: Words with No Sound Clues

REVIEW WORD LIST

1. afternoon
2. backyard
3. bedroom
4. butterfly
5. grandfather
6. grandmother
7. himself
8. outside
9. popcorn
10. didn't
11. I'm
12. it's
13. animal
14. another
15. brother
16. dollar
17. garden
18. lemon
19. squirrel
20. sugar
21. wagon
22. actor
23. farmer
24. hunter
25. painter
26. sailor
27. violinist
28. waiter
29. caterpillar
30. chocolate
31. clothes
32. could
33. cousin
34. upon
35. Wednesday

sugar   lemon   popcorn   chocolate

Write the list words hidden in the silly lunch menu.

1. Unpopcorned beef sandwich
2. Large prelemonade
3. Dischocolater cake
4. One sugarless candy cane

HELP WANTED

Write the occupation for each advertisement.

| actor | waiter | farmer |
| painter | violinist | sailor |

1. **Wanted:** A person to paint and decorate my apartment.

2. **Needed for the Concert Season:** An expert with a violin.

3. **Broadway Bound:** An amateur performer who acts like a professional is needed.

4. **Help Wanted:** An experienced person to take orders and serve meals.

5. **Help with the Harvest:** Farming experience necessary.

6. **Ahoy:** A second mate needed to sail across the ocean.

As Good As Money

Money was scarce during the time of the settlers. People traded goods and services for things they needed. Such trading is called "bartering."

| bedroom | wagon | squirrel |
| hunter | animal | clothes | himself |

Write list words to complete the information about bartering.

A good (1) might trade an (2) skin for food. A (3) skin could be made into a warm hat. The hunter (4) might have to trade his horse and (5) for a warm (6) and some homespun (7).

165

Family Tree

brother   grandfather   cousin   grandmother

When Gerard's teacher asked him to draw a family tree, he did. Help him by writing list words.

Slogans, Naturally

it's   outside   garden   caterpillar
backyard   afternoon   butterfly

The botanical garden in the city where Sheila lives had a contest. Who could write the best slogan to attract visitors? Help Sheila with her ideas. Write the list words to complete the slogans.

Spend the (1) with a beautiful (2) and a fuzzy (3). Come (4) and enjoy this city (5). Pretend (6) your own (7).

Who Said?
(Mother Goose, of Course!)

Wednesday   dollar   upon   another   could   I'm   didn't

Do you remember these children's rhymes from the time you were little? Complete the familiar rhymes with list words.

Ride a fast horse
To Banbury Cross
To see a fine lady (1) a white horse.

Here am I, little jumping Joan
When nobody's with me
(2) always alone.

A dillar, a (3),
A ten o'clock scholar . . .

Rain, rain, go away,
Come again (4) day.

How many days has my baby to play?
 Saturday, Sunday, Monday,
 Tuesday, (5), Thursday, Friday,
 Saturday, Sunday, Monday.

Tom he was a piper's son,
He learned to play when he was young;
But all the tunes that he (6) play,
Was "Over the hills and far away."

There was an old woman
who lived in a shoe,
She had so many children
she (7) know what to do.

Vocabulary, Writing, and Reference Resources

Cross-Curricular Lessons

Writer's Handbook

Spelling Dictionary

Writer's Thesaurus

English/Spanish Word List

Cross-Curricular Lessons

grid
locate
compass rose
cardinal
  directions
scale
miles
map key
symbol

Using a Map

How good are you at map talk? These words will help you read a map. Look up unknown words in the Spelling Dictionary. Add another word to the list that might help you find your way around a map.

■ GETTING AT MEANING

Labeling a Map Write list words to identify the different parts of a map. The NOT clues can help you. They tell the usual meanings of the words. The map shows the special meanings of the words.

4 NOT a red bird

1 NOT a flower to put in a vase

2 NOT for weighing people

3 NOT for locking a door

Following a Map Ms. Sip Sippy and her Outdoor Adventures class are looking at the map before they begin their hike. Use list words to complete the directions.

First find, or (5), where we are now. Use the map (6) to trace imaginary lines west of F and north of 3 until they cross. We are at F3, at Gumboville. We'll hike northwest along Pokey Creek for about two (7). To see where we'll stop for lunch, find the picture of a table. As you can see on the map key, the table is a (8) that shows where there is a picnic area.

How do you get there from here?

Find a good map of your town or neighborhood. Then trace the best route to school or to a friend's or relative's house that is at least one mile away.

■ **SPELL WELL**

Problem Parts Write two list words that are hard for you to spell. Mark the part of each word that gives you problems and study it extra hard.

Urban Communities

cities
urban
goods
services
shipped
police
firefighter
tourist

These list words are useful for talking about urban, or city, living. Look up unknown words in the Spelling Dictionary. Think of another word to add to the list.

■ GETTING AT MEANING

Writing Labels   Write three words from the list to name these people you might see in a big city.

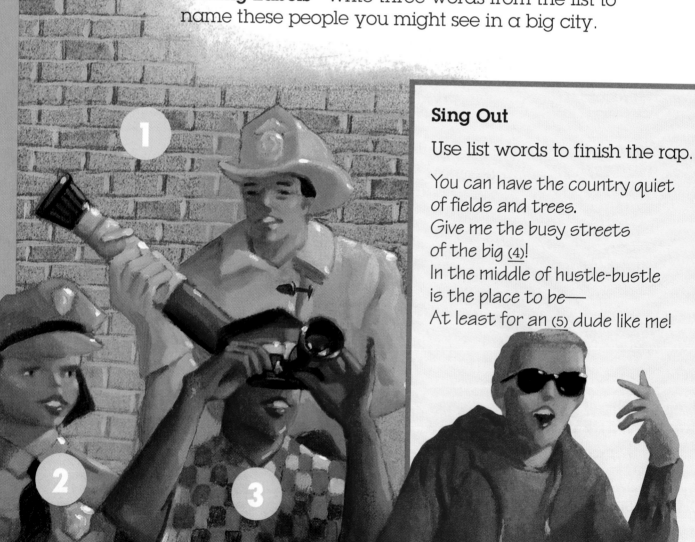

Sing Out

Use list words to finish the rap.

You can have the country quiet
of fields and trees.
Give me the busy streets
of the big (4)!
In the middle of hustle-bustle
is the place to be—
At least for an (5) dude like me!

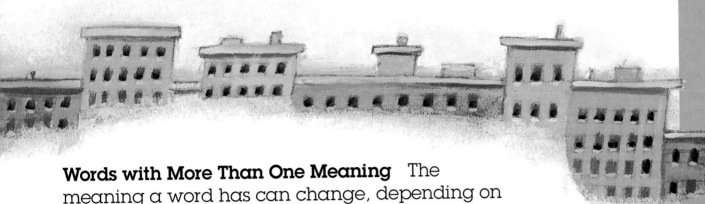

Words with More Than One Meaning The meaning a word has can change, depending on how it is used. Write the list word that completes the second sentence in each pair.

- A certain store is a **good** place to shop.
- The store had many (6) for sale.

- You went to a religious **service** last Sunday.
- The helpful and useful jobs done by police, firefighters, and other city workers are public (7).

- Your uncle won a cruise on a big **ship.**
- Your uncle (8) some things from one place to another by water, land, and air.

■ **SPELL WELL**

Adding Endings Add **-s** or **-es** to the words below. Remember: For words that end in a consonant and **y**, change **y** to **i**, and then add **-es.**

9. service

10. city

To the **Rescue!**

Which would you like to be: police officer, firefighter, or paramedic? Survey the class. Who would like to do each job? Break into three groups. Each group works together to list the duties of one of the jobs and presents the list to the class.

woods
farming
soil
coastlines
fishing
pasture
ranching
logging

Rural Communities

The list words tell about jobs in rural communities, or small communities that are away from cities. Look up unknown words in your Spelling Dictionary. Add another word to the list.

■ GETTING AT MEANING

Labeling Use list words to name each job in the pictures. Then write the list words that complete the sentences below the pictures.

1

2 These workers are found in the ___.

3

4 These workers sail on lakes or oceans along the ___.

174

■ SPELL WELL

Add -ing Add **-ing** to the words below. Remember: If a word is one syllable and ends with **consonant-vowel-consonant**, double the final consonant before adding **-ing**.

ranch
log

Rural Riches 🐛

Here is another kind of chart. Each picture stands for farming, ranching, fishing, or logging. Make your own chart. Think of something you eat or use that is supplied by each business. Draw a picture of each product in the correct section.

5

6 These workers plow and plant seeds in the rich ___.

7

8 These workers take care of cattle feeding in the ___.

175

culture
customs
beliefs
language
religion
festivals
heritage
traditions

Culture

These words tell what people from the same family, tribe, or country often share. Look up unfamiliar words in the Spelling Dictionary. Think of another word to add to the list.

■ GETTING AT MEANING

Puzzle Unscramble the letters and write the list word that fits each definition. Then unscramble the letters in the boxes to form a word that tells where you may learn about the list words.

1 **t h e r a g i e**
The beliefs, traditions, and customs passed down through generations

2 **t o m u s c s**
Special ways of doing things or celebrating that people hand down

3 **d i s t o n r a i t**
The handing down of beliefs, stories, and customs from adults to children

4 **t u l e c u r**
The customs, beliefs, traditions, and ways of doing things of a group of people

Making Connections Write the list word below
that fits with each group of words.

beliefs   **language**   **religion**   **festivals**

5. Christianity, Judaism, Hinduism
6. holidays, feasts, celebrations
7. what is believed, accepted truths, faiths
8. reading, talking, writing

■ SPELL WELL

Dividing Long Words The words below are
divided into syllables. Study them syllable by
syllable. Then cover them and write them.

9. tra • di • tions

10. re • li • gion

CALLING ALL CULTURES!

Do you have a special tradition
in your culture? Do you know someone who
celebrates the customs of another culture?
Write a paragraph about a special
tradition from your own culture
or someone else's.

Citizenship

government
democratic
vote
elections
rights
responsibilities
citizen
United States

Do you have the vocabulary of a good citizen? Look up list words that you do not know in the Spelling Dictionary. Add another word that talks about citizenship.

■ GETTING AT MEANING

In a Democracy   Write a list word for each picture.

Here in the we have a form

of that gives each the right

to for whomever he or she thinks would

do the best job of running the country.

Related Words Use the underlined word to help you write the list word that completes each explanation.

When it is time to **elect** people to run a government, an (5) is held.

It doesn't matter if you are a **Democrat** or a Republican. In a (6) society every adult citizen has a right to vote.

If you are **responsible**, you will carry out both the rights and the (7) of a good citizen.

People **rightly** treasure the (8) that a free country gives them.

Voting Rights
Make a survey form and ask at least five people over 18 about their right to vote. How do they feel about this right?

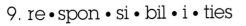

SPELL WELL

Dividing Long Words The words below are divided into syllables. Study them syllable by syllable. Then cover them and write them.

9. re • spon • si • bil • i • ties

10. dem • o • crat • ic

buffalo
roamed
tepees
cliff dwellers
Anasazi
mesa
pottery
kiva

Native Americans of the Past

The list words will help you talk about American Indians who lived in the Southwest and Plains. Look up unknown words in the Spelling Dictionary. Add to the word list a word you know about American Indians.

■ GETTING AT MEANING

Crossword Puzzle Use the clues and the word list to solve the crossword puzzle.

DOWN

1. Tents made of buffalo skin
2. Large animal of the American Plains

ACROSS

3. These two words describe Indians that live in homes on rocky slopes.
4. Proper name for ancient Indian tribes
5. Wandered

180

Labeling Pictures Use the information about each word at right to label each picture.

6.

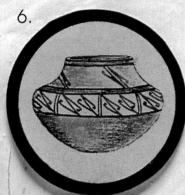

7.

8.

- The American Indian word *kiva* means "a large room, often underground, used for religious ceremonies."

- The word *mesa* came from the Latin word *mensa,* which means "table."

- The word *pottery* came from an Old French word that means "pot."

■ **SPELL WELL**

Double Consonants The double consonants in *buffalo, cliff dwellers,* and *pottery* have only one sound. To spell the words correctly, you must include both letters. Write these words and underline the double consonants.

What can you do with a

buffalo?

The Plains Indians didn't have stores like we do. They hunted buffalo. They used every part of the animal to provide themselves with food, clothing, shelter, and decorations. Work with a partner to list uses for buffalo parts. You may want to look for a book to check your ideas.

crown
enamel
plaque
floss
pulp
gum
root
dentist

Your Teeth

Look over these words that a dentist might use.
Find any unknown words in your Spelling
Dictionary. What other word could you add
to the list?

▪ GETTING AT MEANING

Labeling Write list words to identify the different
parts of a tooth. The NOT clues can help you. They
tell the usual meanings of the words. The diagram
shows the special meanings of the words.

enamel   crown   pulp   gum   root

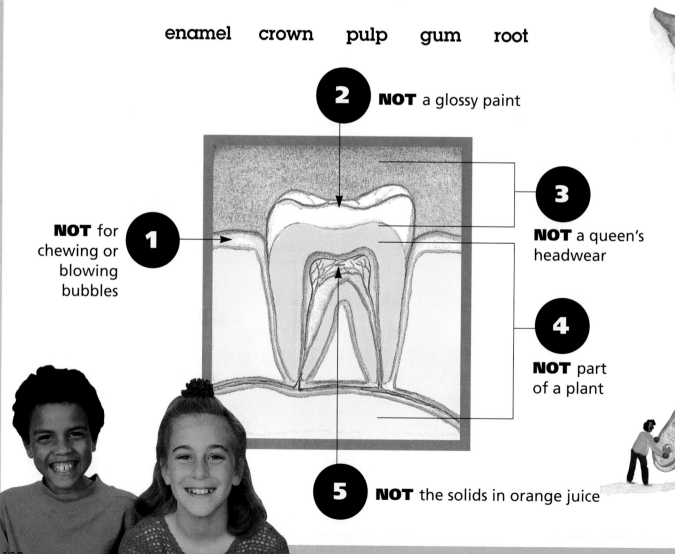

2 **NOT** a glossy paint

NOT for
chewing or
blowing
bubbles
1

3
NOT a queen's
headwear

4
NOT part
of a plant

5 **NOT** the solids in orange juice

182

Teeth Terms Use list words to complete these definitions.

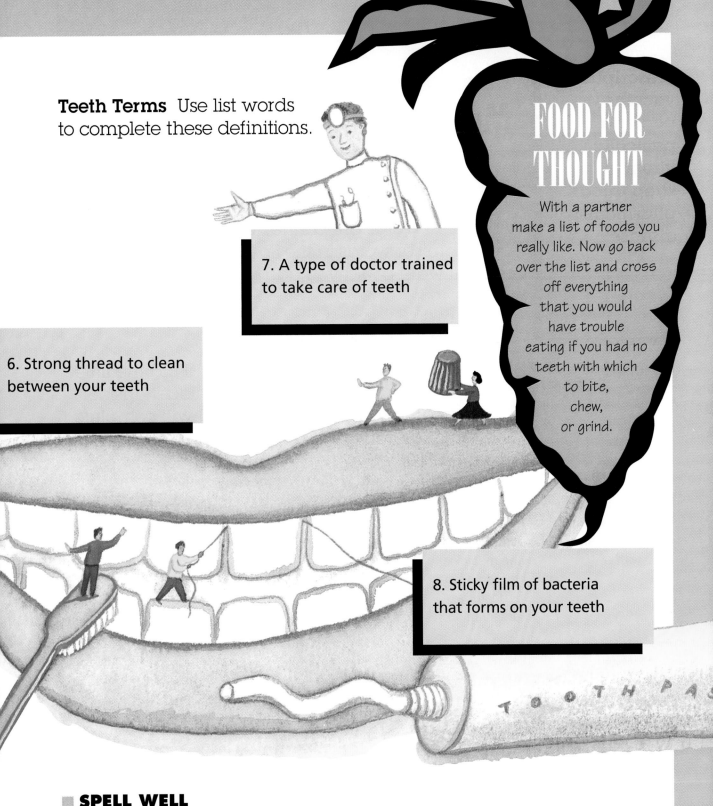

7. A type of doctor trained to take care of teeth

6. Strong thread to clean between your teeth

8. Sticky film of bacteria that forms on your teeth

FOOD FOR THOUGHT

With a partner make a list of foods you really like. Now go back over the list and cross off everything that you would have trouble eating if you had no teeth with which to bite, chew, or grind.

■ SPELL WELL

Memory Hints Look for little words inside bigger words to help you remember how to spell them correctly. Write the list words that these clues can help you spell.

9. Make sure you put a *dent* in ___.
10. Your *name* is on that ___.

Medicine

prescription
vaccine
bacteria
penicillin
virus
strep throat
pharmacist
disease

All the list words are connected to medicine. Look up unfamiliar words in the Spelling Dictionary. What related word could you add?

▦ GETTING AT MEANING

Hidden Words Read each sentence. Find the little word in dark type. Find that word hidden inside a list word below. That bigger word will complete the sentence correctly.

1
You feel hot and ill at **ease** when you are sick with a ___.

2
To keep you from **harm,** the ___ carefully prepares the medicine ordered by the doctor's prescription.

3
Try not to **rip** the paper on which your doctor wrote you a ___ for medicine.

4
Tiny one-celled creatures that **act** to cause infection and illness are called ___.

5
A nasty, tiny germ that can make **us** sick is called a ___.

bacteria

pharmacist

prescription

virus

disease

Using a Table Read the table about diseases and medicines. Use list words to complete the doctor's sentences.

Did you know?

Don't turn your nose up at a moldy slice of bread. Those little growths may be members of the penicillin family. Countless people are alive today because Alexander Fleming discovered how to use penicillin to kill many deadly bacteria.

Disease	Winter Flu	Bronchitis	Strep Throat
Symptoms	general aching, fever, upset stomach	cough, chest pain, and difficulty breathing	sore throat, swollen glands
Medicines that can help	vaccine before the flu season starts	cough medicine, penicillin	penicillin, throat lozenges

"When a patient has a very sore throat, I give a test to see if she has (6).

When a patient has bronchitis, I prescribe (7).

Before the flu season begins, I suggest that my patients get the (8) to prevent certain kinds of flu."

SPELL WELL

Problem Parts Some words have unusual letter combinations. Write each word below. Underline any letters you need to remember.

9. pharmacist

10. penicillin

clinic
sanitation
   workers
pollute
litter
recycle
community
landfill
sewage

A Healthy Community

Look at these words you could use to check out your community's health. Check unknown words in your Spelling Dictionary. What other word can you add to the list?

■ GETTING AT MEANING

Jobs Use the list words to complete the work assignments that the Community Pride Committee made for Keep Keaton Place Clean Day.

1. Dr. Santos and his staff will paint the ___ so we can get our health care in bright surroundings.

2. Cub Scouts and Brownies will pick up ___ carelessly thrown on the sidewalks and in the square.

3. Teen Action Teams will collect and sort bottles, cans, and paper so they can ___ them.

4. The mayor will provide clean-up bags printed with the slogan "Working together for a clean and healthy ___ ."

5. Garth's Junk Service will have a truck to take filled trash bags to the ___, or dump.

Related Words Complete each sentence with a list word that is related to the word in dark type.

Communities maintain underground pipes and drains called **sewers** to take away the liquid waste called ___.

Make stopping **pollution** your bag. Remember that paper bags and containers ___ less than plastic.

Removing garbage so that streets and alleys are **sanitary** is the job of ___.

■ SPELL WELL

Double Up Double letters can cause spelling problems. Write the list words with double letters in the middle of the words. Underline the double letters to help you remember them.

Count on Them

With your classmates, list workers in your school and community whose jobs are to keep places clean and healthy. Then each of you pick one job and make a button that shows why that job is important. Wear your button to class and tell your classmates about it.

mammals
reptiles
amphibians
gills
lungs
cold-blooded
warm-
    blooded
backbone

Animals with Backbones

These words are all about animals with backbones. Look up unknown words in your Spelling Dictionary. Which of these words describe your pet? Can you add another word to the list?

■ GETTING AT MEANING

Using a Chart Read the chart. Use the list words to tell about the animals on the next page.

Class	Mammal	Reptile	Amphibian
Outer Skin	Hairy or furry	Has scales	Moist skin without hair or scales
Breathing Organ	Breathes air with lungs	Breathes air with lungs	Young breathe water with gills, most adults breathe air with lungs
Body Temperature	Warm-blooded (keeps same body temperature when the surrounding air/water changes)	Cold-blooded (body temperature changes when the surrounding air/water temperature changes)	Cold-blooded (body temperature changes when the surrounding air/water temperature changes)

ANIMALS WITH BACKBONES

Which animal at the right belongs to which class?

mammal   **amphibian**   **reptile**

A snake, a dog, and a frog all have one thing in common, a ___.

snake

dog

frog

Label these animals cold-blooded or warm-blooded.

cat

alligator

Which baby uses gills and which uses lungs?

human

amphibian

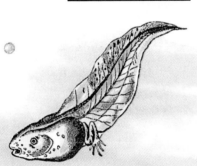

■ SPELL WELL

Unexpected Spellings The words *mammal* and *amphibian* are not spelled the way they are pronounced. Write them and underline any letters that might cause you problems.

STRAIGHTEN UP!

Imagine a giraffe without a backbone! What would it look like? How would it get around? Draw a picture of how you or your favorite animal would look without a backbone.

length
width
height
volume
meter
liter
weight
grams

Measuring Matter

You need to use these words when you measure things. Look up unknown words in the Spelling Dictionary. What other measuring word could you add to the list?

■ GETTING AT MEANING

Measure Up Star Captain Kylah is using this diagram to write a report on the ultralight planter boxes she has designed for a space garden project. Use the diagram to fill in her notes with list words.

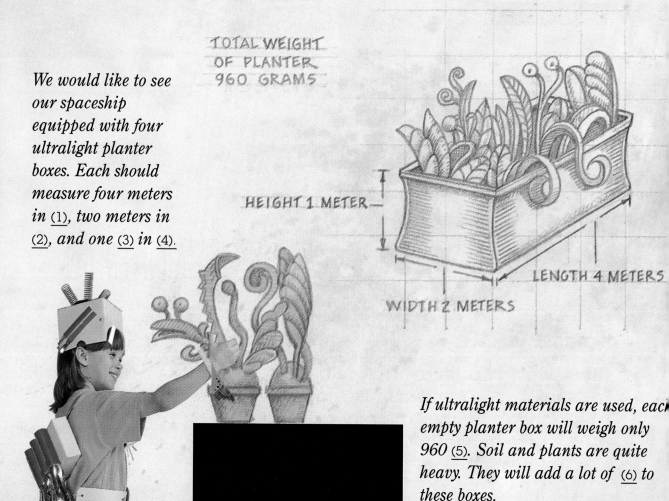

We would like to see our spaceship equipped with four ultralight planter boxes. Each should measure four meters in (1), two meters in (2), and one (3) in (4).

TOTAL WEIGHT OF PLANTER 960 GRAMS

HEIGHT 1 METER

LENGTH 4 METERS

WIDTH 2 METERS

If ultralight materials are used, each empty planter box will weigh only 960 (5). Soil and plants are quite heavy. They will add a lot of (6) to these boxes.

■ SPELL WELL

Spelling Measures Here's a riddle for you. *What's a good number to keep in mind when you spell measuring words?* To show you know the answer, write two list words whose last five letters spell the number between seven and nine.

Watering will be done by misting tanks hung above the ultralight boxes. Each tank will hold a (7) of 100 liters. The misting will be set for a light cycle. The tank will spray one (8) of water every 24 hours.

VOLUME 100 LITERS

MISTING CYCLE
1 LITER
EVERY 24 HOURS

How little can you get?

A nanosecond is a billionth of a second. A nanogram is a billionth of a gram. Would a nanoliter of water be enough to stop you from being thirsty?

$$\frac{1}{1,000,000,000}$$

lever
fulcrum
screw
pulley
load
inclined
plane
wheels and
axles
wedge

Simple Machines

Did you ever use a hammer? play on a teeter-totter? unscrew the lid of a jar? If you did, you were using a simple machine. Read the list words. Look up the unknown words in the Spelling Dictionary. Then add your own machine word to the list.

■ GETTING AT MEANING

Labeling Read the sentences below for clues. Then look at the pictures. Use the list words to label these simple machines. Two of the pictures show two of the list words.

- The twisted ridges on a **screw** help hold things together.
- Move the rope on a **pulley** to bring things up and down.
- A simple machine like a pulley can move a heavy **load**.
- A board placed at an angle is an **inclined plane**.
- Use a board and log as a **lever** to move a rock.
- Use the log as a **fulcrum** to support the board.
- Without **wheels and axles**, your cars and wagons wouldn't roll.
- Use a **wedge** to split something apart.

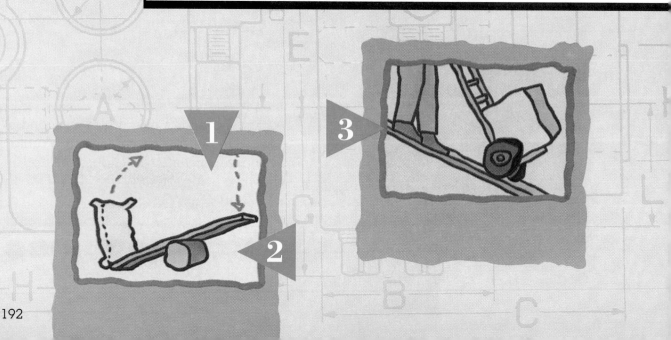

192

Rhyme Time Complete each sentence with the list word that rhymes with the underlined word.

Be <u>clever</u> and use a ___.

A 500-pound <u>toad</u> is really a ___.

How does it work?

They're everywhere! Look around your school and home. List all of the simple machines that you can find in the things we use every day. For example, a skateboard uses wheels and axles, and a wheelchair ramp is an inclined plane. Share your list with the class.

core
mantle
crust
earthquake
magma
erupt
volcano
lava

Earth's Layers

Do you know these terms used in talking about the earth? If not, look them up in the Spelling Dictionary. Add another word to the list.

■ GETTING AT MEANING

Earthly Definitions Use the diagram to help you match four of the list words with their definitions.

1. the top layer of the earth
2. a mountain with an opening from which lava may erupt
3. hot liquid which spills out from a volcano
4. the red-hot, melted rock, deep inside the earth

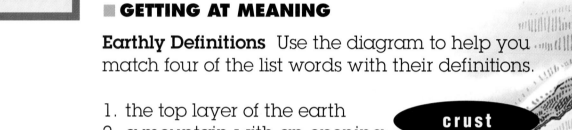

crust

mantle

magma

lava

volcano

Completing Sentences Use list words to complete these sentences.

5. A volcano is said to ___ when pressure forces magma, gases, and ash through the earth's crust.
6. Magma is the extremely hot rock that can be found in the earth's mantle and all the way down to the center, known as the earth's ___.
7. An ___ is another kind of violent movement of the earth's crust.
8. Magma rises from a layer of the earth below the crust called the ___.

■ **SPELL WELL**

Memory Hints Look for the little words inside bigger words to help you remember how to spell them correctly. Complete each memory hint with a list word.

9. You'll find a **can** in ___.
10. The direction **up** is within ___.

Hot
Rocks

Red-hot lava is plenty hot— it can reach 2012° F (1100° C). But if you want something that's even hotter, dig through the 4,000 miles from the earth's crust to the deepest core. The temperature of the magma there can reach 9000° F (4982° C).

solar system
planets
Mercury
Venus
Earth
Mars
Saturn
astronauts

The Solar System

These words will help you talk about our universe.
If you need help with a word, use your Spelling
Dictionary. Can you add another word about
outer space to the list?

■ GETTING AT MEANING

Complete Sentences Study the information
Nahiro included on his Science Fair Poster. Then
complete his notes for his oral report with the
correct list words.

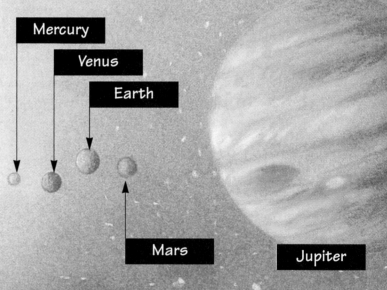

Mercury
Venus
Earth
Mars
Jupiter

- Begin by saying that the
(1) includes the sun and all
the planets.

- Count out the nine (2) that
revolve around the sun. Cheer
when you get to the third
planet — our home, (3).

THE plan

■ **SPELL WELL**

Dividing Long Words Sometimes it helps to study long words syllable by syllable. Study the words below. Then cover them and write them.

as • tro • nauts   so • lar sys • tem

• Point out that the closer you are to the sun, the hotter it is. (4) and (5) are very hot since they are the two planets closest to the sun.

Pluto

Saturn   Uranus   Neptune

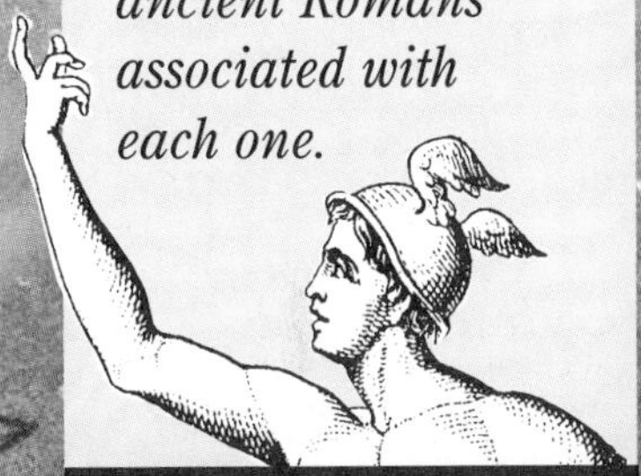

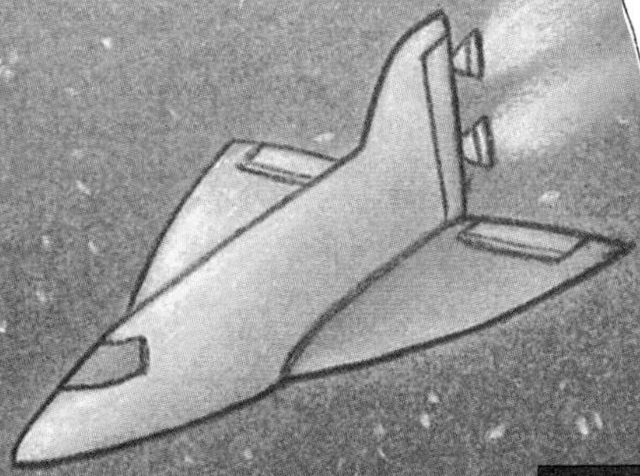

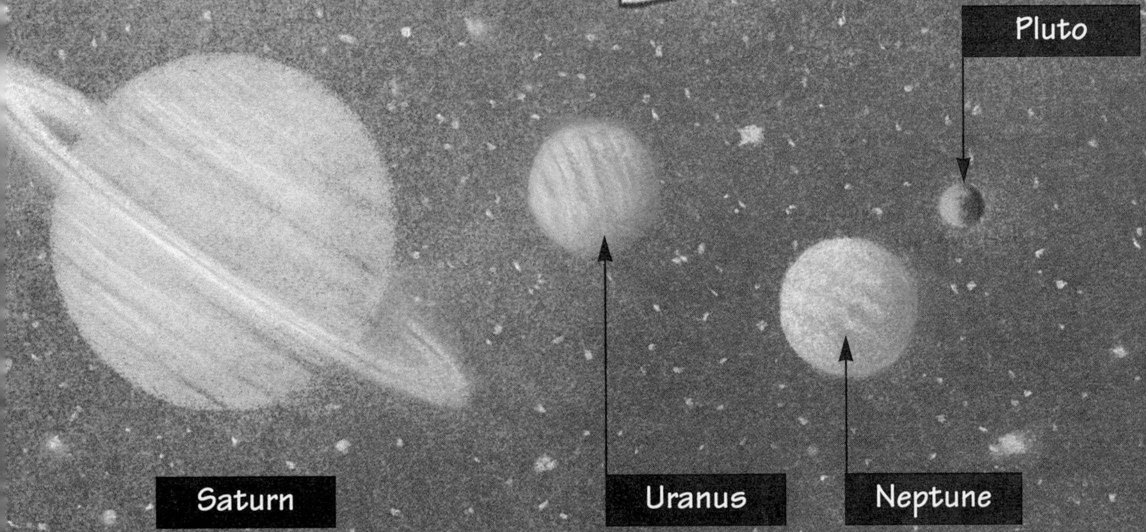

• Make a joke about how men from (6) would have to be cooler than Earthlings since this is the fourth planet from the sun.

• Tell the class that the name of the sixth planet from the sun is (7). This is also the name of a series of rocket ships that were flown by (8) who explored the moon.

197

backfired
discouraged
unidentified
misbehaving
mischievous
question
senseless
unpleasant

Stories That Twist

You may meet some of these words in stories that don't end the way you might expect. Look up unknown words in your Spelling Dictionary. Can you add another word to the list?

■ GETTING AT MEANING

Related Words Cheerful Charlie and Grouchy Gus don't always agree. The underlined words in Charlie's statements are related to the missing words in Gus's statements. Write the missing list words.

Charlie: I had a <u>pleasant</u> time at the Old-Timers–New Kids checkers competition!

> **Gus:** Humph! I thought it was most (1) to have a third grader beat me.

Charlie: It took <u>courage</u> for those young people to take on checkers champs like us.

> **Gus:** I wish the kid I was playing had been (2) enough to quit when I was ahead. Instead, she won!

Charlie: You lost because you thought you could <u>fire off</u> a few tricky jumps. It was <u>unquestionably</u> a bad strategy.

> **Gus:** Those moves certainly (3). You are right to (4) my strategy. I set up a triple jump for her.

■ **SPELL WELL**

Prefixes Add the prefix **un-** to each word below to make a list word.

pleasant
identified

Charlie: Stop complaining. Your opponent was <u>behaving</u> like a good sport.

    Gus: I still say she only won because those checker pieces of mine were <u>(5)</u>!

Charlie: Gus, be <u>sensible</u> and be a better sport.

    Gus: Now Charlie, you know I feel pretty <u>(6)</u>. I lost to an eight-year-old!

Charlie: I don't mean any <u>mischief</u>, but does it bother you that I <u>identified</u> that young person?

    Gus: What a <u>(7)</u> question, Charlie! You know I could get over losing to an <u>(8)</u> stranger. But to find out that I lost to your granddaughter! That's too much!

Did you know?

Checkers is played a little differently around the world. In France and Poland, the board has 100 squares and each player uses ten checkers. In the United States, the board has 64 squares and each player uses twelve checkers. However, the game ends in the same way; one player captures all of the other player's checkers.

satisfaction
boulders
chimney
ladder
ashamed
forest
shovel
treasure

Life's Challenges

How would you do if challenged to spell these words? Use your Spelling Dictionary to look up unknown words. Add one more word to the list.

■ GETTING AT MEANING

Decoding Picture Clues Javon is faced with a real challenge! If he can figure out the directions on this map, he will find a hidden treasure. Help him by writing the list words that fit each picture clue.

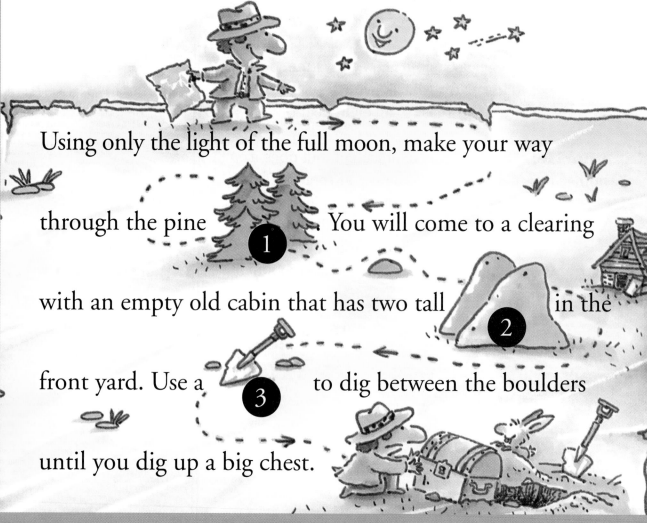

Using only the light of the full moon, make your way

through the pine ① You will come to a clearing

with an empty old cabin that has two tall ② in the

front yard. Use a ③ to dig between the boulders

until you dig up a big chest.

The key to this chest is in the cabin. To find the key, climb the [ladder] to the loft and look on the hook by the [chimney]. Once you have the key you can open up the chest and claim your [treasure].

Figuring Out Feelings Write the list words to explain the different feelings Javon might have, depending on how he faces his challenge.

If Javon hears a loud sound in the dark and gives up the hunt, he might feel (7) of himself.

If Javon keeps on trying even when he is afraid, he is likely to feel great (8) when he gets the treasure.

■ SPELL WELL

Silent Letters Some words have letters that you don't expect because you can't hear their sounds. Say the words and write them. Pay special attention to the underlined letters.

9. tre<u>a</u>sure

10. bo<u>u</u>lders

Did You Know?

Mel Fisher met a real-life challenge. He searched for the sunken treasure from the shipwreck of the *Nuestra Señora de Atocha* for twenty years, and he found it off the coast of Florida. You can see some of the treasure in a museum in Key West, Florida.

behavior
blushed
enemy
suggested
nervous
pretended
careless
threatening

Looking Beneath the Surface

Look in the Spelling Dictionary to help you understand these words that you might use to talk about how you really feel about things. Can you think of another word to add to the list?

■ GETTING AT MEANING

Get to the Point Ada is wordy! Help her rewrite this apology to her best friend. Write a list word to replace each underlined phrase.

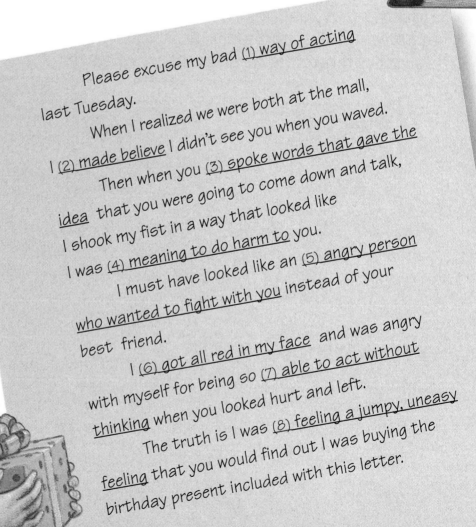

Please excuse my bad (1) way of acting last Tuesday.

When I realized we were both at the mall, I (2) made believe I didn't see you when you waved.

Then when you (3) spoke words that gave the idea that you were going to come down and talk, I shook my fist in a way that looked like I was (4) meaning to do harm to you.

I must have looked like an (5) angry person who wanted to fight with you instead of your best friend.

I (6) got all red in my face and was angry with myself for being so (7) able to act without thinking when you looked hurt and left.

The truth is I was (8) feeling a jumpy, uneasy feeling that you would find out I was buying the birthday present included with this letter.

202

Adding Endings Add **-ed** or **-ing** to each base word below to form a list word.

9. threaten
10. pretend

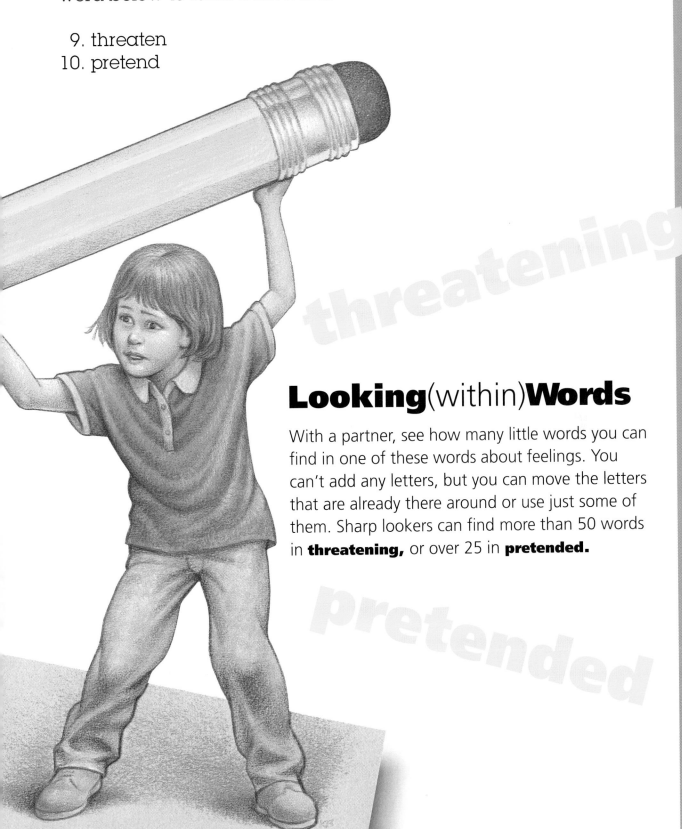

Looking(within)**Words**

With a partner, see how many little words you can find in one of these words about feelings. You can't add any letters, but you can move the letters that are already there around or use just some of them. Sharp lookers can find more than 50 words in **threatening,** or over 25 in **pretended.**

agreement
baffled
communicate
confused
conversation
embarrassed
frustrated
admiration

Understandings and Misunderstandings

Here are some words to help you talk about the way you understand or misunderstand things. Look up unknown words in your Spelling Dictionary. Can you think of another word to add to the list?

■ GETTING AT MEANING

Understanding Signs Test how good you are at understanding what someone else's facial expressions or actions might mean. Write a list word that fits each picture.

A few words have closely related meanings. Match them both with the same picture.

With a partner think of a conversation two people might have. For example, one friend might want to trade baseball cards with another. Then have a "silent conversation." Don't say a word aloud—let your facial expressions, gestures, and movements do all the talking.
Do your classmates understand your conversation?

■ SPELL WELL

Double Up Double letters can cause spelling problems. Write the list words that have double consonants.

►ff

rr...ss◄

►mm

flying saucer
invisible
foreigners
neighbor
spaceship
helmet
underground
vaporize

Unexpected Situations

These words can help describe something you won't expect to see in real life. If you need help with a word, use the Spelling Dictionary. Try to add another word to the list.

■ GETTING AT MEANING

Using a Catalog Help RU-KZ finish writing entries for the *Galaxy of Values Catalog*. Write the list words that complete these product descriptions.

Galaxy of Values

Fred's (1): specially designed for aliens; no one will be able to identify what galaxy you come from.

Breathe Easy (3): headgear with clear face mask—for aliens who need to filter out dangerous oxygen from Earth's atmosphere.

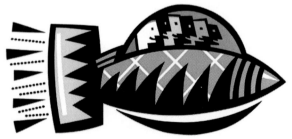

Uncle Sam's (2): Standard American design; holds six astronauts comfortably.

NEW

Fun Guide for (4): this tele-guide to all the hot spots in North America is a must for visitors from other countries and planets.

■ **SPELL WELL**

Getting Letters in Correct Order You may be tempted to change the order of the underlined letters in the words below. Write each word.

ne<u>i</u>ghbor   for<u>ei</u>gners

Let your brain go out in orbit! Think up another product for this catalog. Name it, write the catalog copy, and then draw a picture of it.

REDUCED

Spray-Away: this special cleaning agent will turn even moon rock into a mist that disappears. It can (5) solids in less than a minute.

High-Visibility Video: Capture (7) aliens on film! This camera films things you can't see but know are there.

FREE!

Desert Water Detector: laser-driven; finds water from hidden streams many hundreds of feet (6); works even on Mars.

sale

Space Phone: Extra sharp reception; makes a call from the next solar system as clear as a call from your next-door (8).

curious
faraway
rhythm
poetry
rhyme
creative
scenery
fantasy

Imagination at Work

How many of these words can you imagine spelling without any trouble? Use your Spelling Dictionary to look up words you do not know. Add another imaginative word to the list.

▉ GETTING AT MEANING

Writing Poems Trudy is working on a poem about her aunt. Test your imagination by using list words to finish this draft for her.

've got a great aunt — her name is Mary B.
She's a poet who writes great (1).

She'll take some words and make a picture with them.
She adds in a beat to give those words a (2).

She'll write and rewrite, time after time,
'Til she gets those words singing in a (3).

Some poems are funny; some are serious.
Some leave you happy; others leave you (4).

208

Some are set in the world of everyday reality.
Others are set in the magic land of (5).

One poem will talk about a place you pass every day.
Another will picture a land (6).

She's quite a poet, my aunt Mary B.
With words she paints beautiful (7).

She makes the lines on the paper seem to live–
I'm proud of Mary B. because she's so (8).

Imagine That!

What would your dream house look like? Draw a picture or write a plan for a home you would like to live in. Use your imagination! Your house can take any shape or have any special features you want, even if they haven't been invented yet.

■ SPELL WELL

Pronouncing Words Carefully We sometimes spell words wrong because we say them wrong. Say each word below carefully. Be sure to pronounce the sounds of the underlined letters. Then write the words.

9. scenery

10. faraway

clock
minutes
hour
day
week
calendar
month
year

Time

Do you know these words that keep track of time? You may want to look in the Spelling Dictionary to get the definition exactly right or to find another time word to add to the list.

■ GETTING AT MEANING

Time Machine Help Lupe and Kent figure out Professor Ella's instructions on how to set their time machine. Write list words to complete the sentences.

Time Machine Instructions

It's very easy to set the time machine to get you exactly where you want to be in the future.

A Dial A is a standard (1). When it shows 10:25, you know that the ten stands for the (2) of the day. The 25 shows how many (3) past the hour it is.

B Dial B lets you set the date on which you want the machine to stop. Right now it is set for the 9th (4) in the (5) of January in the (6) 2030. If you push the little red button, a small (7) will pop up. Use it to figure out whether you will be arriving on a Monday, Wednesday, or some other day of the (8).

When the dials are set, you will be ready for takeoff! Good luck!

■ SPELL WELL

Homophones Homophones are words that sound alike but are spelled differently. Complete each sentence with a list word that sounds like the underlined word.

9. <u>Our</u> grandfather clock chimes every ___.

10. When I was sick, I felt <u>weak</u> for a whole ___.

MATHEMATICS

Multiplication

Use your Spelling Dictionary to check the meanings of these words about multiplication. Can you add another word to the list?

■ GETTING AT MEANING

Understanding Math Terms   Multiplication is really a short way of adding the same number many times. A short way of solving the addition problem $2 + 2 + 2 + 2 + 2 = 10$ would be to **multiply** $5 \times 2 = 10$. The multiplication problem shows you that five groups of two are equal to 10.

In the problem $5 \times 2 = 10$, the numbers that you multiply are called the **factors,** and the answer is called the **product.** When you talk about this problem, you say, "Five **times** two equals ten."

You can show a multiplication problem by arranging objects into an **array** of rows and columns. The apples are arranged in an array. There are 5 apples in each **row** and 2 apples in each **column.**

Look through a catalog to find a T-shirt that your class might like. How much would it cost to buy a shirt for everyone in your class? Will you do the math in your head, use paper and pencil, or use a calculator to find the total cost?

Look at the array of plants. Complete these sentences using the list words.

1. There are twelve plants in the ___.
2. There are four plants in each ___.
3. There are three plants in each ___.
4. 3 x 4 = 12 is one of the ___ problems you could write about the plants.
5. You would say, "Three ___ four equals twelve."
6. The answer, or ___, is twelve.
7. Three and four are the ___.
8. When you ___ four times three, the product is twelve.

▪ SPELL WELL

Related Words Use related words to help spell hard words. Write the list word *multiply*. Then write the list word that is related in meaning and spelling.

cone
cube
sphere
cylinder
rectangular
  prism
faces
solid
edge

Geometry

Take a minute to look around you. How many of the shapes pictured below can you see in familiar objects? Write the names of other shapes you know on the list. Use your Spelling Dictionary if you need help.

cone	cylinder	cube	sphere	rectangular prism

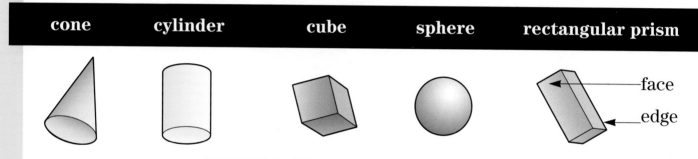

face

edge

▪ GETTING AT MEANING

Picture Clues Look at the pictures below and on the next page. Write the list word that names the shape of the object.

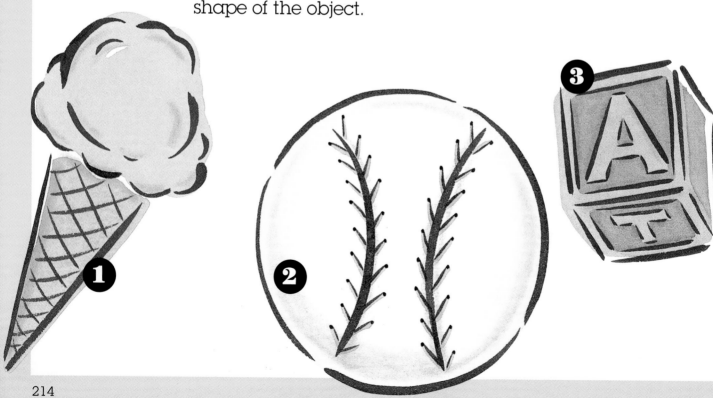

1

2

3

214

Sentence Completion Write the list word that correctly completes each sentence.

6. A cube has six surfaces, or ___, which are all the same size.
7. When two surfaces of a rectangular prism meet, they form an ___.
8. Figures that have three dimensions—length, width, and height—are called ___ figures.

Listen to This!

Get together with a friend. Describe one of the list words without naming it. Ask your friend to write the list word based on your description.

▪ SPELL WELL

Divide and Conquer Study the words below syllable by syllable. Then cover them and write them.

9. rec • tan • gu • lar prism
10. cyl • in • der

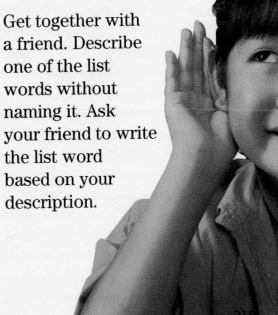

Measuring Capacity and Mass

Add another word to this list of terms that you use to measure how much. Use your Spelling Dictionary to check the unknown terms.

GETTING AT MEANING

Crossword Puzzler The pictures and clues should help you find the list words that will complete this crossword puzzle.

Across

2. Equal to 16 ounces
4. Equal to 4 quarts
5. Holds 8 ounces of liquid
8. Metric unit for measuring liquids; almost equal to one quart

Down

1. A metric unit for measuring mass
3. A slice of bread weighs about one ___.
6. Liquid measure equal to 2 cups
7. Liquid measure equal to 2 pints or 4 cups

SPELL WELL

Memory Tricks Use memory tricks to help you spell. Write a list word to complete each trick. Underline the matching letters.

9. D<u>on</u> bought a ___ of milk.
10. Drink a ___ of wat<u>er</u> a day.

Plan a Bake Sale

What would you bake if your class had a bake sale? Copy your favorite recipe on an index card. Be sure to copy the measurements carefully. Exchange recipes with your classmates or collect your recipes and make a cookbook.

whole
numerator
denominator
fifths
sixths
eighths
halves
fraction

Fractions

Do you know these words that will help you talk about fractions? Fractions name equal parts of a whole. You may want to look in the Spelling Dictionary to find the exact definition. Think of another word to add to the list.

■ GETTING AT MEANING

Pieces of the Pie Elmer, Hilda, Leona, and Milo each cut a pizza into equal portions. Use list words to describe the size of the pieces each person cut.

Elmer cut his pizza into 2 equal pieces. Elmer's pizza is divided into (1).

Hilda cut her pizza into 5 equal pieces. Hilda's pizza is divided into (2).

Leona cut her pizza into 6 equal pieces. Leona's pizza is divided into (3).

Milo cut his pizza into 8 equal pieces. Milo's pizza is divided into (4). If Milo eats all 8 pieces of his pizza, he will have eaten a (5) pizza.

What Do You Call It? Fractions are numbers used to describe parts of a **whole.** $\frac{2}{5}$, $\frac{1}{4}$, and $\frac{5}{6}$ are some common fractions. The top number of a **fraction** is called the **numerator.** The bottom number is called the **denominator.** Read the sentences. Then label each part of the number shown.

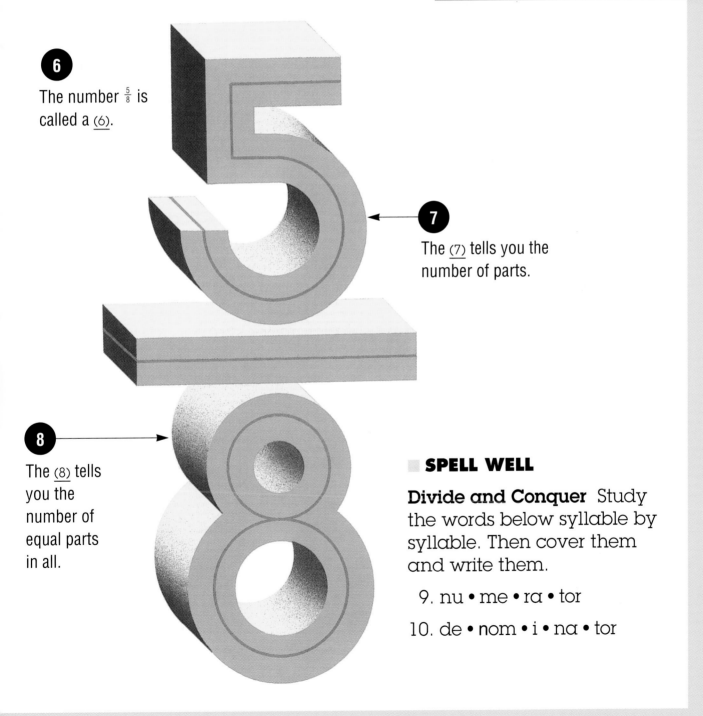

6

The number $\frac{5}{8}$ is called a (6).

7

The (7) tells you the number of parts.

8

The (8) tells you the number of equal parts in all.

■ **SPELL WELL**

Divide and Conquer Study the words below syllable by syllable. Then cover them and write them.

9. nu • me • ra • tor

10. de • nom • i • na • tor

data
tally chart
bar graph
pictograph
scale
tallies
labels
count

Graphs and Charts

Can you think of another word to add to this list of terms that you might use when talking about graphs? Use your Spelling Dictionary if you need help.

GETTING AT MEANING

Show Me Cara and Bob collected **data,** or information, about birthdays in their class. Here are three ways they showed their data. Label each type of chart or graph.

- Cara and Bob used a **tally chart** to record their classmates' birthdays. The marks, called **tallies**, are usually grouped by fives so they are easier to **count**.
- The **bar graph** has a **scale** to show the number of birthdays and **labels** to show which seasons are being shown.
- The **pictograph** uses pictures or symbols to stand for a specific number of items.

1

Classroom Birthdays

Season	Tally	Number
Spring	ЖЖ ЖЖ	10
Summer	||	2
Fall	ЖЖ |||	8
Winter	ЖЖ	5

2

Classroom Birthdays

Spring	🎁 🎁 🎁 🎁 🎁
Summer	🎁
Fall	🎁 🎁 🎁 🎁
Winter	🎁 🎁 🎁

Each 🎁 = 2 Students

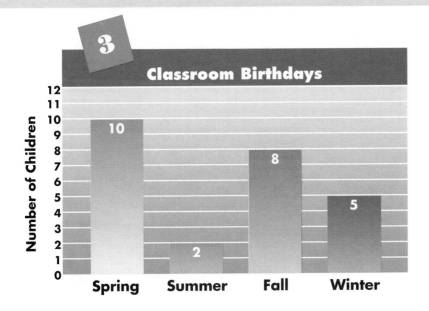

Classroom Birthdays

Number of Children

Spring	10
Summer	2
Fall	8
Winter	5

Reading Graphs and Charts Using Cara and Bob's graphs and charts, complete the following sentences.

4. The tally chart, the bar graph, and the pictograph all show information, or ___, about classroom birthdays.
5. Cara and Bob's tally chart shows ten ___ for spring birthdays.
6. The tallies are grouped by fives so they are easy to ___.
7. The ___ on the bar graph goes from 0 to 12.
8. The ___ on the bar graph and on the pictograph tell us that the number of birthdays that fall in each season are being compared.

■ **SPELL WELL**

Divide And Conquer Study the words below syllable by syllable. Then cover them and write them.

9. pic • to • graph

10. tal • lies

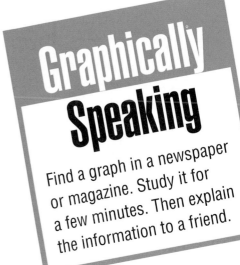

Graphically Speaking

Find a graph in a newspaper or magazine. Study it for a few minutes. Then explain the information to a friend.

pitcher
catcher
batter
infielders
outfielders
fly ball
line drive
pop-up

Baseball

Do you know what to say when you cheer the home team at a ball game? You may want to look in the Spelling Dictionary to get a definition exactly right or to find another word to add to the list.

■ **GETTING AT MEANING**

Places on a Diamond Look at the diagram. Then complete the sentences about the players with list words.

1. The ___ squats behind home plate.
2. The ___ gets ready to hit the ball at home plate.
3. The ___ cover the bases and the infield.
4. The ___ throws the ball to the batter.
5. The ___ field the balls that come to the outfield.

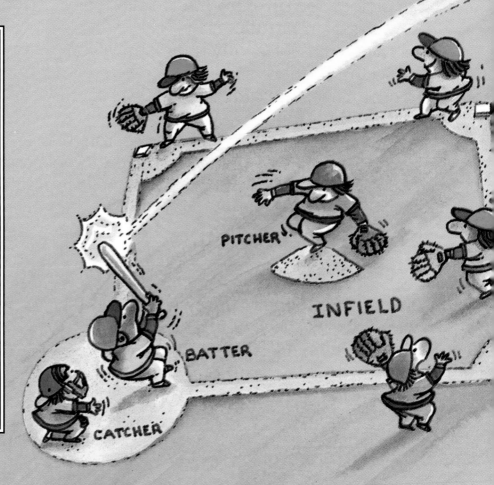

PITCHER

INFIELD

BATTER

CATCHER

Batter Up! Complete the sentences with list words that an announcer might use to describe a hit.

6. If the ball flies through the air in a straight *line*, low to the ground, it is called a ___.
7. If the ball goes *up up up*, high into the air, it is called a ___.
8. A ball that *flies* high, then curves down, and is caught is called a ___.

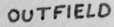
OUTFIELD

SPELL WELL

Adding Suffixes Add the suffix **-er** to each base word below to form a list word.

9. pitch
10. catch

Did You Know?

Being left-handed can affect the position you play on a baseball team. Catchers are almost never left-handed while first basemen often are. And all coaches like to have one or two "southpaws," or lefties, on their pitching staffs.

plans
cabinet
shelf
hammer
nail
saw
board
tape measure

Carpenter

Add another word to this list of terms that a carpenter uses. The Spelling Dictionary will help you understand any unfamiliar words.

■ GETTING AT MEANING

Labeling When Patrice's family came from Haiti, she helped her carpenter father learn English words by labeling the items in his shop. Name the list words that match these French words. Can you think of a reason why words 5 and 7 are the same in French?

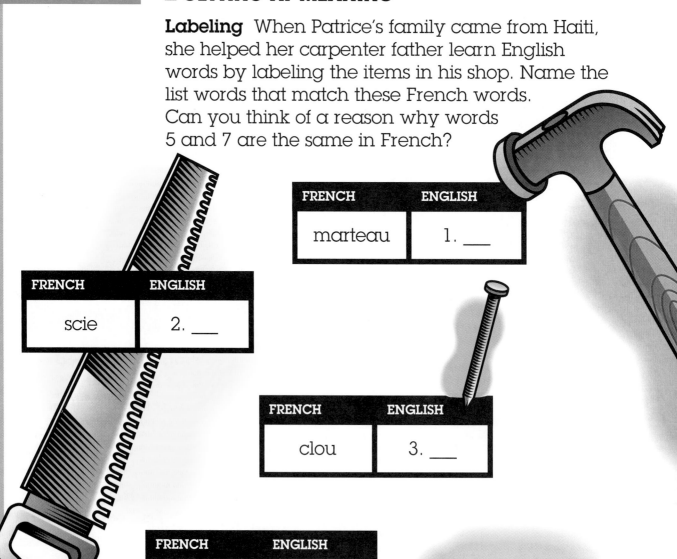

FRENCH	ENGLISH
marteau	1. ___

FRENCH	ENGLISH
scie	2. ___

FRENCH	ENGLISH
clou	3. ___

FRENCH	ENGLISH
mètre à ruban	4. ___

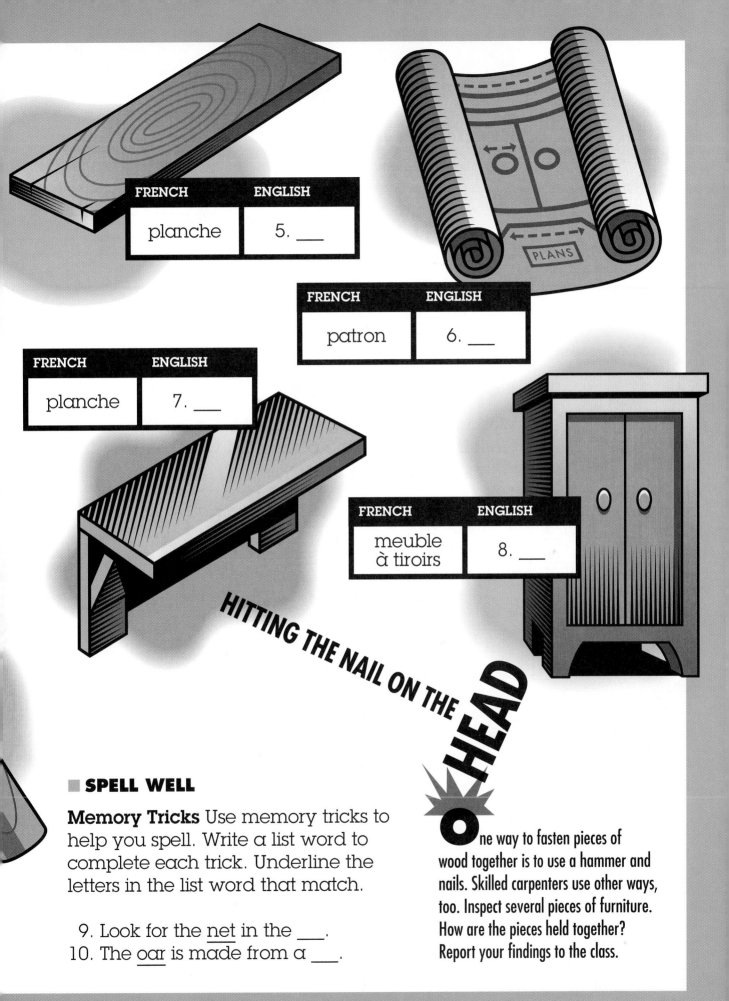

FRENCH	ENGLISH
planche	5. __

FRENCH	ENGLISH
patron	6. __

FRENCH	ENGLISH
planche	7. __

FRENCH	ENGLISH
meuble à tiroirs	8. __

HITTING THE NAIL ON THE **HEAD**

■ SPELL WELL

Memory Tricks Use memory tricks to help you spell. Write a list word to complete each trick. Underline the letters in the list word that match.

9. Look for the <u>net</u> in the ___.
10. The <u>oar</u> is made from a ___.

One way to fasten pieces of wood together is to use a hammer and nails. Skilled carpenters use other ways, too. Inspect several pieces of furniture. How are the pieces held together? Report your findings to the class.

Police Officer

uniform
radio
siren
laws
badge
station
squad car
protect

Can you think of another word to add to this list of terms that you might use when talking about what police officers do? Use your Spelling Dictionary to look up any unfamiliar words.

■ GETTING AT MEANING

Working in Pairs Since police officers often work in pairs, find the pairs of list words that belong in each category.

TWO things a police officer wears.

TWO places a police officer might be found.

Divide and Conquer Sometimes it helps to study hard words piece by piece. Study the words below syllable by syllable. Then cover them and write them.

ra • di • o
u • ni • form

Thanks!

Take a few minutes to think about how important police officers are in helping people in a community lead peaceful, orderly lives. With a partner, write down three ways police help out in your community. Share your ideas with the class.

TWO things
police officers use to let others know where they are.

TWO important concerns
for a police officer:

Seeing that ___ are obeyed.

Working to ___ citizens from danger.

clay
wheel
shape
pot
bowl
glaze
kiln
fire

Pottery

Can you add another word to this list of terms that people who make pottery use? The Spelling Dictionary will help you with any unfamiliar words.

■ GETTING AT MEANING

Not Words Use the "not" clues to match list words with definitions that tell what potters do.

1. Spinning disk that potters use as they shape the clay	**NOT what turns around on a bicycle or car**
2. To put clay figures in a kiln to bake at a very high temperature	**NOT to tell someone that they have lost their job**
3. A dish with wide open top, that is not too deep, often made of clay	**NOT playing a game rolling a big ball to knock down ten pins**
4. A container, often made of clay, and used to hold plants	**NOT another name for a pan**
5. To form clay with one's hands	**NOT a word meaning the outside form of something**

Start to Finish Use list words to finish this description of what a potter does.

Potters begin with a soft, sticky kind of earth called (6). When they have shaped the material into a form they like, they let it dry in the air and then bake at a high temperature in a special oven called a (7). Often they decorate the baked piece of pottery with a special coating called a (8). This coating is also baked on to make the finished pot durable and waterproof.

Magic Pottery

Folk tales from all over the world tell of magic pots that will give you any kind of food you want to eat. Draw what you think such a magic pot should look like. In your drawing, leave a clue about what kind of food you'd want to see come bubbling out.

■ SPELL WELL

Spelling New Words Think about how each word below is spelled. Write each word.

9. glaze
10. kiln

Writer's Handbook

INTRODUCTION

A carpenter follows plans to make a building. A cook follows recipes to make a meal. A writer uses the writing process to create something for someone else to read. This handbook will review the writing process, capitalization rules, and punctuation rules.

CONTENTS

The Writing Process

This section reviews the five steps of the writing process: prewriting, drafting, revising, proofreading, and presenting.

1. PREWRITING

What should I do before I begin writing?

Think about and plan your writing before you actually put any words on paper. Time you spend prewriting is time well spent. Follow these steps and suggestions.

- **Select a topic** by listing ideas, looking through books or magazines for ideas, or rereading a personal journal or diary.
- **Know your purpose and audience.** Your purpose is your reason for writing. It may be to tell how you feel, describe or explain something, give or get information, persuade, or tell a story. Your audience could be your teacher or a friend.
- **Narrow your topic.** You need to focus on one specific idea. To do this, you might write questions about the topic, make a word web, or list and group key words to explore.

- **Find details about your topic.** You might need to look in books and magazines for information. You could talk about your topic with other people. You might think about how things look, sound, and feel.
- **Organize your information.** Decide on the order in which you want to tell things. Will you describe something from top to bottom? Will you tell events in the order they happened, first to last? Will you tell the most important thing first?

2. DRAFTING

How do I actually begin to write the paper?

Gather your prewriting notes, pencils, and paper. Find a good place to write. It should be well lit with a good writing surface. Here are some helpful hints.

- **Ignore** the telephone. Turn off the radio and TV.
- **Set a goal.** Decide how much you are going to write during this writing time.
- **Read** your notes to find an idea for the first paragraph.
- **Begin** with a sentence that tells the main idea of the paragraph. Then get your ideas on paper.
- **Keep writing** without worrying about perfect spelling, punctuation, or capitalization.

3. REVISING

How do I start revising?

Revising means to read what you've written and find ways to make it better. To begin, you might

- **read your draft to yourself** to catch mistakes such as unclear sentences or words left out.
- **have a conference** with other students or your teacher.

What kinds of changes should I make?

You might do any or all of the following:

- **Add** words or ideas.
- **Take out** extra words, sentences, or paragraphs.
- **Move** words, sentences, or paragraphs.
- **Change** words or ideas to improve your draft.

What kinds of questions should I ask myself?

The questions you'll ask will depend on your purpose, audience, and the type of writing you're doing. These questions will help you get started:

- Did I say what I wanted to say?
- Are my details in the best possible order?
- Do I have a clear beginning, middle, and end?
- Does each paragraph have a topic sentence and stick to one idea?
- Can I take out extra words or replace inexact ones?
- Are all facts and figures correct?

Ask yourself these questions!

4. PROOFREADING

Why should I proofread? When do I do it?

Proofreading a paper means to read it carefully to find mistakes in grammar, punctuation, and spelling. Proofread after you have revised your first draft. Be sure that you have made all corrections. Then also proofread your final copy.

Use proofreading symbols like those in the box to clearly mark the corrections to be made.

☰	Make a capital.
/	Make a small letter.
∧	Add something.
ℓ	Take out something.
⊙	Add a period.
¶	New paragraph

What should I look for when I proofread?

Use the following questions as a proofreading checklist:

- Are all my sentences complete thoughts?
- Is each sentence correctly punctuated?
- Did I capitalize the first word of each sentence?
- Did I capitalize proper nouns and adjectives?
- Did I indent each paragraph?
- Did I check spelling and meaning of unfamiliar words?
- Is my handwriting clear and easy to read?

5. PRESENTING

How should I present my final work?

The way you present your work will depend on your teacher and on the assignment. Here are some suggestions for regular assignments.

- Write neatly on the front side only of white lined paper. If you're using a computer, type out your paper carefully.
- Put your name, the subject, and the date in the top right-hand corner of the first page.
- Center the title of your composition on the second line.
- Leave a one-inch margin on the sides of the paper and leave the last line blank.

Special ways to present writing include hanging it on a bulletin board, sharing it in a young author's conference, binding it in an illustrated book, publishing it in a newspaper, and reading it aloud.

Taking Writing Tests

Be a confident writer. These guidelines can help you write better on writing tests.

GENERAL GUIDELINES FOR WRITING TESTS

- **Listen carefully to test instructions.** Know how much time you have. Do you need pen or pencil?
- **Read the assignment and identify the key words.** Know what key words like these mean:

  Categorize or Classify: Group facts or ideas.
  Compare or Contrast: Point out similarities (compare) or differences (contrast).
  Define: Tell what something is or means.
  Describe: Create a word picture with details.
  Discuss: Explain what something means to you.
  Explain: Make something clear by giving reasons, examples, or steps.
  Summarize: State main points, or retell important parts of a story or article.

Look for these key words!

- **Plan how you'll use your time.** Allow time for prewriting, writing, and revising.
- **Write a strong opening** to interest your reader. It should state the topic clearly.
- **Use specific facts and details** to develop the topic.
- **Write an interesting conclusion** that will summarize what you have written.

WRITING A DESCRIPTION

Descriptive writing uses details that appeal to the senses—sight, sound, smell, taste, and touch—to create a vivid picture for the reader.

KEY WORDS IN ASSIGNMENTS

- **Tell** what you **see** or **hear** or **smell** or **feel** or **taste**.
- **Describe** what it **looks like**. . . **sounds like**. . . **and so on**.

SAMPLE ASSIGNMENTS

- Your little sister or brother got into your parents' closet and got dressed up. Describe the outfit!
- Describe a favorite outdoor place, such as a playground or park, on a busy day. What does it look like? What are people doing? What sounds do you hear?

A PLAN OF ATTACK

- Know what you must write about. In the first assignment describe the sights, sounds, and smells of a dressed-up child. In the second, tell what details would help in the identification.
- Note vivid sensory details. Think of colorful, precise words. What comparisons can you use?
- Choose an order to describe details. You might use **spatial order** to describe the outfit from head to toe or your favorite place from left to right.

FOLLOW-UP CHECKLIST

- Does the topic sentence tell about your topic in an interesting way?
- Are your details precise? Do they focus on your topic?
- Do you follow the order you've decided upon?

WRITING INSTRUCTIONS

Well-written instructions are clear and easy to follow. They tell you how to do something in step-by-step order.

KEY WORDS IN ASSIGNMENTS

- **Explain how to**. . .
- **Describe the steps** you would take to. . .

SAMPLE ASSIGNMENTS

- Rrrrring! It's the fire alarm. Explain the fire drill procedure for your school or your home.
- Eat right! Explain how to make your favorite healthy snack.

A PLAN OF ATTACK

- Know exactly what you must write about. List the materials the reader would need, if any, and the steps involved in the process.
- Instructions are usually written in **step-by-step order,** beginning with the first step. Use words like *first, next, then,* and *last* to show the correct order.
- Choose clear, precise words to describe what the reader must do in each step.

FOLLOW-UP CHECKLIST

- Does the topic sentence state what the reader will learn to make or do?
- Are the steps arranged in a logical order?
- Are any steps missing?
- Are time-order words used to help the reader understand the order of the steps?
- Is all capitalization, punctuation, and spelling correct?

WRITING A FRIENDLY LETTER

Writing a friendly letter should be like speaking to a friend in person. Some reasons for writing a friendly letter are to keep in touch, to thank someone, to send an invitation, or to reply to one.

KEY WORDS IN ASSIGNMENTS

- **Write to** . . .
- **Respond to**. . .

SAMPLE ASSIGNMENTS

- Write a friendly letter to a favorite relative telling about what you've been doing lately.
- Write an invitation to a parent, relative, or friend for a classroom performance of a play.

A PLAN OF ATTACK

- Know the purpose of the letter. The first assignment is to tell about recent events. The second is to extend an invitation.
- List the events you want to mention to your relative. For the invitation, list important dates, times, and places.
- Decide on an order to put your details in. A friendly letter is usually organized in time order, though it doesn't have to be.

FOLLOW-UP CHECKLIST

- Does the letter have the five basic parts: heading, greeting, body, closing, and signature? (See the model on page 245.)
- Is the tone informal and conversational?
- Are important dates, times, and places included in the invitation?
- Is all spelling and punctuation correct?

WRITING A PERSONAL NARRATIVE

A story about something you did or something that happened to you is called a personal narrative.

KEY WORDS IN ASSIGNMENTS

- **Tell what happened** to **you**. . .
- Write about **your** most . . .

SAMPLE ASSIGNMENTS

- Ha! Ha! Ha! What's the funniest thing that's ever happened to you? Write about it.
- Learning how to do something new is challenging. Write about a time when you learned something new.

A PLAN OF ATTACK

- For both assignments, choose a topic to write about that will be interesting and entertaining.
- Jot down the details describing the event you are writing about. Think of strong verbs and colorful adjectives and adverbs to use to relate your story.
- A narrative is usually organized in time order. List words like *first, then,* and *next* that you might use.

FOLLOW-UP CHECKLIST

- Does the topic sentence interest the reader?
- Does the narrative follow time order?
- Does the story have a beginning, middle, and end?
- Are the events told about with strong, clear verbs, adverbs, and adjectives?
- Is all capitalization, punctuation, and spelling correct?

WRITING A TALL TALE

A tall tale is a humorous story about things that couldn't possibly happen in real life. Usually, these things happen as a result of a character's superhuman abilities. Paul Bunyan and Pecos Bill are famous heroes of American tall tales.

KEY WORDS IN ASSIGNMENTS

- Write a modern **tall tale**. . .
- **Exaggerate** to create. . . **hero**. . . **deeds**. . .

SAMPLE ASSIGNMENTS

- Think of a familiar character from a tall tale. Write a new adventure for him or her.
- Most tall tales take place in the country. Create a hero or heroine who lives in the city. Then write a tall tale that takes place in a city.

A PLAN OF ATTACK

- Decide upon a character for your tall tale. List adjectives and adverbs to describe him or her. Use exaggeration to make your character superhuman in some way.
- Develop the plot of the tall tale. List what happens in the beginning, the middle, and the end. Organize the details of the plot in time order.
- Decide what things you will exaggerate to make the tall tale amazing and funny.

FOLLOW-UP CHECKLIST

- Does the topic sentence introduce the hero or heroine?
- Are the events in the plot easy to follow?
- Is exaggeration used to make the tale funny?
- Is all spelling and punctuation correct?

WRITING A PERSUASIVE PARAGRAPH

The goal of a persuasive paragraph is to make the reader agree with your opinion. To do this, you must support your opinion with good reasons.

KEY WORDS IN ASSIGNMENTS

- **Persuade** your teacher. . .
- Write a . . . **convincing**. . . **to agree**. . .

SAMPLE ASSIGNMENTS

- You would like to start a recess soccer league at your school. Write a paragraph persuading your classmates that it would be a good idea.
- You feel that your bedtime is too early. Write a paragraph convincing your parents that you should be allowed to stay up later.

A PLAN OF ATTACK

- Clearly state the opinion you intend to support.
- List at least three good reasons to support your opinion.
- Organize your reasons in **order of importance.** Usually writers save their strongest reason for last.
- List persuasive words to use in your paragraph.

FOLLOW-UP CHECKLIST

- Does the topic sentence clearly state your opinion?
- Are the supporting reasons organized from least important to most important?
- Are the reasons logical and sensible?
- Does the conclusion summarize the opinion and reasons?
- Is all capitalization, punctuation, and spelling correct?

Rules, Guidelines, and Models

CAPITALIZATION

Capitalize the following in your writing:

Names, initials, and titles used with names:

> Dr. Leo S. Ruiz, Jr.   Reverend Jill Jones

Proper adjectives:

> Eastern accent   Italian leather   Asian art

The pronoun *I*:

> Andy and I were both late.

Names of cities, states, countries, continents:

> Boston   Iowa   Japan   Africa

Names of lakes, rivers, mountains:

> Fox Lake   Ohio River   Wasatch Mountains

Names of streets and street abbreviations:

> Fir Street   Elm Ave.   Red Rd.   East Market

Days, months, holidays:

> Tuesday   Wed.   July   Jan.   Memorial Day

First, last, and all important words in movie, book, story, play, and TV show titles:

> Beauty and the Beast   Rascal
>
> "The Necklace"

First word in a sentence:

> Eight is an even number.

First word inside quotation marks:

> Luis said, "Let's go to the park."

Both letters of the United States Postal Service state abbreviations:

AL (Alabama)	**LA** (Louisiana)	**OH** (Ohio)
AK (Alaska)	**ME** (Maine)	**OK** (Oklahoma)
AZ (Arizona)	**MD** (Maryland)	**OR** (Oregon)
AR (Arkansas)	**MA** (Massachusetts)	**PA** (Pennsylvania)
CA (California)	**MI** (Michigan)	**RI** (Rhode Island)
CO (Colorado)	**MN** (Minnesota)	**SC** (South Carolina)
CT (Connecticut)	**MS** (Mississippi)	**SD** (South Dakota)
DE (Delaware)	**MO** (Missouri)	**TN** (Tennessee)
FL (Florida)	**MT** (Montana)	**TX** (Texas)
GA (Georgia)	**NE** (Nebraska)	**UT** (Utah)
HI (Hawaii)	**NV** (Nevada)	**VT** (Vermont)
ID (Idaho)	**NH** (New Hampshire)	**VA** (Virginia)
IL (Illinois)	**NJ** (New Jersey)	**WA** (Washington)
IN (Indiana)	**NM** (New Mexico)	**WV** (West Virginia)
IA (Iowa)	**NY** (New York)	**WI** (Wisconsin)
KS (Kansas)	**NC** (North Carolina)	**WY** (Wyoming)
KY (Kentucky)	**ND** (North Dakota)	

PUNCTUATION

Use **periods**

- to end declarative and imperative sentences:

  Matt plays hockey.   Do your homework now.

- after most abbreviations:

  Mrs.   Feb.   Sun.   Jr.   St.   A.M.   Dr.

Use **exclamation marks**

- after sentences that show strong feeling:

  I'm so happy!

Use **question marks**

- after interrogative sentences:

  Have you met the new principal?

Use **commas**

- between the day and the year in a date:
    March 15, 1997

- between the name of a city and state:
    Houston, Texas

- after the greeting and closing of a letter:
    Dear Adam,   Yours truly,

- between series of words in a sentence:
    You will need paper, pencils, and an eraser.

- before the word that joins a compound sentence:
    Howie struck out, and our team lost the game.

- to separate a noun after a direct address:
    Dad, is that you?   Yes, it is, Ed.

- before quotation marks or inside the end quotation marks:
    Al said, "I like radishes and cucumbers."
    "I don't believe that," said Lynn.

Use **quotation marks**

- around the exact words someone used when speaking:
    "Sailing is fun," said Auntie Deb.

- around titles of stories, poems, and songs:
    "The Gold Bug"   "Fire and Ice"   "Summertime"

Underline titles of books and movies:
    <u>Henry Huggins</u>   <u>Rudy</u>

Use **apostrophes**

- to form the possessive of a noun:
    dentist's   cousins'   women's

- in contractions in place of dropped letters:
    isn't (is not)   don't (do not)   I'll (I will)

FRIENDLY LETTER FORM

Writing a friendly letter should be like talking to your friend in person. Some purposes for writing a friendly letter are to keep in touch, to thank someone, to extend an invitation, or to reply to one.

A friendly letter has five parts: the **heading**, the **greeting**, the **body**, the **closing**, and the **signature**. Study the model letter. Notice the correct capitalization and punctuation in each part. If you are writing to someone you know well, you may leave out your address from the heading.

123 Callan Avenue
Evanston, IL 60202
October 21, 20_ _

Heading

Dear John,

Greeting

I saw the photograph of you and your scout troop on the cover of the <u>Evanston Journal</u>. Now I know a celebrity! What was your Cub Scout troop doing at the train station in Evanston?

Third grade is fun so far. My favorite subject is science. Our class is taking a field trip to the Chicago Academy of Science next week. We are going to learn about animal habitats.

Body

Our soccer team isn't as good as it was last year. We all miss having you as goalie! Maybe you can come and see one of our games.

Your friend,

Closing

Chris

Signature

Spelling Dictionary

Look at the dictionary entry below. Each part of the entry is labeled. This entry will help you when you look up a word in the Spelling Dictionary.

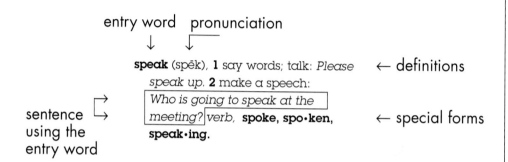

The **entry word** is the word you want to look up.

The **pronunciation** tells you how to pronounce or say the entry word.

The **definition** tells you what the entry word means. An entry word may have more than one definition.

The **sentence using the entry word** can help you understand what the entry word means.

The **special form** shows another form of the entry word.

Full Pronunciation Key

a	hat, cap	**p**	paper, cup
ā	age, face	**r**	run, try
ä	father, far	**s**	say, yes
â	care, hair	**sh**	she, rush
		t	tell, it
b	bad, rob	**th**	thin, both
ch	child, much	**ŦH**	then, smooth
d	did, red		
		u	cup, butter
e	let, best	**ú**	full, put
ē	equal, be	**ü**	rule, move
ėr	term, learn		
		v	very, save
f	fat, if	**w**	will, woman
g	go, bag	**y**	young, yet
h	he, how	**z**	zero, breeze
		zh	measure, seizure
i	it, pin		
ī	ice, five	**ə**	represents:
			a in about
j	jam, enjoy		e in taken
k	kind, seek		i in pencil
l	land, coal		o in lemon
m	me, am		u in circus
n	no, in		
ng	long, bring		
o	hot, rock		
ō	open, go		
ȯ	all, saw		
ô	order, store		
oi	oil, voice		
ou	house, out		

A

act (ɑkt), **1** something done; deed: *Sharing the candy was a generous act.* **2** doing: *I was caught in the act of hiding the presents.* **3** to do something: *The firemen acted promptly and saved the burning house.* **4** to perform on the stage, in motion pictures, on television, or over the radio; play a part: *He acts the part of a doctor in a TV series.* **5** a main division in a play or opera: *This play has three acts.* **1,2,5** *noun,* **3,4** *verb.*

ac·tiv·i·ty (ɑk tiv′ə tē), **1** a being active; use of power; movement: *Children like physical activity.* **2** an action: *The activities of groups of interested citizens have brought about many new laws.* **3** a thing to do: *Jogging is a popular outdoor activity. noun, plural* **ac·tiv·i·ties.**

ac·tor (ɑk′tər), a person who acts on the stage, in motion pictures, on television, or over the radio. *noun.*

ad·mi·ra·tion (ad′mə rā′shən), a feeling of wonder, pleasure, and approval: *I expressed my admiration for the painting. noun.*

a·fraid (ə frād′), **1** frightened; feeling fear: *afraid of the dark, afraid of heights.* **2** sorry to have to say: *I'm afraid you are wrong about that. adjective.*

Af·ri·ca (af′rə kə), the continent south of Europe and east of the Atlantic Ocean. Only one other continent, Asia, is larger than Africa. *noun.*

af·ter·noon (af′tər nün′), the part of the day between noon and evening. *noun.*

a·gain (ə gen′), another time; once more: *Come again to play. Say that again. adverb.*

a·go (ə gō′), **1** gone by; past: *I met her two years ago.* **2** in the past: *He lived in this town long ago.* **1** *adjective,* **2** *adverb.*

a·gree·ment (ə grē′mənt), **1** an understanding reached by two or more persons, groups of persons, or nations. **2** harmony in feeling or opinion: *There was perfect agreement between the two friends. noun.*

actor

The **actors** are performing in a play.

aircraft

a low-flying **aircraft**

aim (ām), **1** to point or direct something in order to hit: *She aimed carefully at the target.* **2** the act of pointing or directing at something: *She hit the target because her aim was good.* **3** a purpose: *Her aim was to become a lawyer.* **1** *verb,* **2,3** *noun.*

air·craft (âr′kraft′), a machine that flies. Airplanes, airships, helicopters, and balloons are aircraft. *noun, plural* **air·craft.**

air·plane (âr′plān′), an aircraft heavier than air, that has wings and is driven by a propeller or jet engine. *noun.*

al·ien (ā′lyən), **1** a person who is not a citizen of the country in which he or she lives: *The aliens in the book came from Mars.* **2** of another country; foreign: *They came from an alien land.* **1** *noun, plural* **al·iens; 2** *adjective.*

al·most (ȯl′mōst), nearly: *It is almost ten o'clock. I almost missed the train. adverb.*

a·lone (ə lōn′), **1** apart from other persons or things: *After my friends left, I was alone. One tree stood alone on the hill.* **2** without help from others: *I solved the problem alone.* **1** *adjective,* **1,2** *adverb.*

al·ways (ȯl′ wāz), **1** every time; in each case: *Night always follows day.* **2** all the time: *Their home is always open to their friends.* **3** forever: *There will always be stars in the sky. adverb.*

a·maze (ə māz′), to surprise greatly; strike with sudden wonder: *She was amazed at their courage. The talking bird was amazing. verb,* **a·maz·es, a·mazed, a·maz·ing.**

A·mer·i·ca (ə mer′ə kə), **1** the United States of America. **2** North America. **3** North America and South America. The two continents are sometimes called **the Americas.** *noun.* [The name *America* was made up by a German map maker in 1507 from the name *Amerigo Vespucci.* He was an Italian navigator who lived from 1451 to 1512. He claimed to have explored the Atlantic coast of South America.]

am·ox·i·cil·lin (ə mok′sə sil′in), an antibiotic medication used to treat infections. *noun.*

am·phib·i·an (am fib′ē ən), **1** one of a group of cold-blooded animals that have a backbone and can live both in water and on land. Frogs and toads are amphibians. **2** a tank, truck, or other vehicle able to travel across land or water. *noun, plural* **am·phib·i·ans.** [*Amphibian* is from a Greek word meaning "living in two ways." The word was used for this group of animals because they can live both on land and in water.]

A·na·sa·zi (ä′nə sä′zē), the name of a people who lived in the American Southwest long ago. *noun.*

and (ənd *or* and), **1** as well as; also: *Yesterday we went to the beach and to the zoo.* **2** added to; with: *4 and 2 make 6. I like ham and eggs.* **3** in addition; then; while: *I washed the dishes and my brother dried them. conjunction.*

an·gry (ang′grē), **1** feeling or showing anger: *My parents were very angry when I disobeyed them.* **2** suggesting anger; stormy or threatening; *The angry waves pounded the beach. adjective,* **an·gri·er, an·gri·est.**

an·i·mal (an′ə məl), **1** any living thing that is made up of many cells, can move about, and usually has a nervous system. A human being, a dog, a bird, a fish, a snake, a fly, and a worm are animals. **2** an animal other than a human being. *noun.*

an·nounc·er (ə noun′sər), a person who announces, especially one who introduces programs or people on radio or television. *noun.*

an·oth·er (ə nuᴛʜ′ər), **1** one more: *Have another glass of milk. She ate a piece of candy and then asked for another.* **2** a different: *Show me another kind of hat.* **1,2** *adjective,* **1** *pronoun.*

an·swer (an′sər), **1** to speak or write in return to a question: *When I asked her a question, she answered right away.* **2** the words spoken or written in return to a question: *The boy gave a quick answer.* **3** the solution to a problem: *What is the correct answer to this math problem?* **1** *verb,* **2,3** *noun.*

an·y (en′ē), **1** one out of many: *Choose any book you like from the books on the shelf.* **2** some: *Have you any fresh fruit?* **3** every: *Any child knows that.* **4** at all: *Has my singing improved any?* **1-3** *adjective,* **2** *pronoun,* **4** *adverb.*

an·y·one (en′ē wun), any person; anybody: *Can anyone go to that movie? pronoun.*

an·y·where (en′ē hwer), in, at, or to any place: *I'll meet you anywhere you say. adverb.*

a·pol·o·gy (ə pol′ə jē), words saying one is sorry for a mistake or accident: *I made an apology to my teacher for being late. noun, plural* **a·pol·o·gies.**

ap·pear (ə pir′), **1** to be seen; come in sight: *One by one the stars appear.* **2** to seem; look: *The apple appeared sound on the outside, but it was rotten inside.* **3** to show or present oneself in public: *The singer will appear on television today. verb.*

aren't (ärnt), are not: *We aren't going today.*

amphibian
(definition 1)

							ə stands for	
a	hat	**ī**	ice	**u̇**	put		**a**	in about
ā	age	**o**	not	**ü**	rule		**e**	in taken
ä	far, calm	**ō**	open	**ch**	child		**i**	in pencil
âr	care	**ȯ**	saw	**ng**	long		**o**	in lemon
e	let	**ô**	order	**sh**	she		**u**	in circus
ē	equal	**oi**	oil	**th**	thin			
ėr	term	**ou**	out	**ᴛʜ**	then			
i	it	**u**	cup	**zh**	measure			

ar·ray (ə rā′), **1** a display or collection of persons or things: *The team had an impressive array of fine players.* **2** an arrangement of objects or numbers in rows and columns. *noun.*

ar·rest (ə rest′), **1** to take to jail or court by authority of the law: *The police arrested the burglar.* **2** a stopping; seizing: *We saw the arrest of the burglar.* 1 *verb,* 2 *noun.*

art·ist (är′tist), **1** a person who paints pictures. **2** a person who is skilled in any of the fine arts, such as sculpture, music, or literature. **3** a public performer, especially an actor or singer. *noun.*

astronaut

Franklin Chang

a·shamed (ə shāmd′), **1** uncomfortable because one has done something wrong, bad, or silly: *I was ashamed of the lies I had told.* **2** unwilling because of fear of shame: *I was ashamed to tell my parents I had failed math.* *adjective.*

a·sleep (ə slēp′), **1** not awake; sleeping: *The cat is asleep.* **2** into a state of sleep: *The tired children fell asleep.* **3** numb: *My foot is asleep.* 1,3 *adjective,* 2 *adverb.*

as·tro·naut (as′trə nòt), a member of the crew of a spacecraft. *noun,* *plural* **as·tro·nauts.** [*Astronaut* comes from two Greek words meaning "star" and "sailor."]

ate (āt). See **eat.** *We ate our dinner.* *verb.*

a·way (ə wā′), **1** from a place: *Stay away from the fire.* **2** at a distance; a way off: *His home is miles away.* **3** absent; gone: *My friend is away today.* 1,2 *adverb.* 2,3 *adjective.*

badge

a space shuttle **badge**

B

back·bone (bak′bōn′), **1** the main bone along the middle of the back in human beings, horses, birds, snakes, frogs, fish, and many other animals; spine. **2** the most important part: *The Constitution is the backbone of our legal system.* *noun.*

back·fire (bak′fīr′), **1** an explosion of gas occurring at the wrong time or in the wrong place in a gasoline engine. **2** to have a result opposite to the expected result: *His plan backfired, and instead of getting rich he lost his money.* 1 *noun,* 2 *verb,* **back·fires, back·fired, back·fir·ing.**

back·yard (bak′yärd′), the piece of ground behind a house or building. *noun.*

bac·ter·i·a (bak tir′ē ə), certain living things made of one cell that can usually be seen only through a microscope. Certain bacteria cause diseases such as pneumonia; others form a sticky, colorless film on teeth. *noun plural of* **bac·ter·i·um** (bak tir′ē əm).

badge (baj), something worn to show that a person belongs to a certain occupation, school, or club: *She wore a police badge.* *noun.*

baf·fle (baf′əl), to be too hard for a person to understand or solve; bewilder: *This puzzle baffled me.* *verb,* **baf·fles, baf·fled, baf·fling.**

bal·loon (bə lün′), **1** an airtight bag filled with some gas lighter than air, so that it will rise and float in the air. Some balloons have a basket or container for carrying persons or instruments. **2** a child's toy made of thin rubber filled with air or some gas lighter than air. *noun.*

band·age (ban′dij), **1** a strip of cloth or other material used to wrap or cover a wound or injury. **2** to wrap or cover with a bandage. 1 *noun,* 2 *verb,* **band·ag·es, band·aged, band·ag·ing.**

bank (bangk), **1** a place of business for keeping, lending, exchanging, and issuing money. **2** a small container with a slot through which coins can be dropped to save money. **3** any place where reserve supplies are kept: *a blood bank.* *noun.*

bar (bär), **1** an evenly shaped piece of some solid, longer than it is wide or thick: *a bar of soap, a chocolate bar.* **2** a rod or pole put across an opening to close it off: *There's an iron bar across that old door.* *noun.*

bar·be·cue (bär′bə kyü), **1** an outdoor meal in which food is cooked over an open fire. **2** a grill or open fireplace for cooking food, usually over charcoal. **3** to cook over an open fire or hot charcoal. **4** to cook meat, fish, or fowl in a highly flavored sauce. 1,2 *noun,* 3,4 *verb,* **bar·be·cues, bar·be·cued, bar·be·cu·ing.** [*Barbecue* comes from a Spanish word meaning "framework for roasting meat." The Spanish word was taken from a Central American Indian word.]

bare·foot (bâr′fút′), wearing nothing on the feet: *The children ran barefoot around the yard. adjective, adverb.*

bar graph (bär′ graf′), a graph that shows amounts by parallel bars which differ in length in proportion to the difference in amount.

bath·tub (bath′tub′), a tub to bathe in. *noun.*

bat·ter (bat′ər), a player whose turn it is to bat in baseball, cricket, and similar games. *noun.*

bat·ter·y (bat′ər ē), **1** a single electric cell: *Most flashlights work on two batteries.* **2** a set of two or more electric cells that produce electric current. Batteries provide the current that starts automobile and truck engines. *noun, plural* **bat·ter·ies.**

be (bē). *Be* is a very common verb that has several different forms. We say: I *am,* you (we, they) *are,* he (she, it) *is,* I (he, she, it) *was,* you (we, they) *were. verb,* **am** (am), **are** (är), **is** (iz); **was, were; been** (bin); **be·ing.**

bear[1] (bâr), **1** to carry or support; hold up: *The ice is too thin to bear your weight.* **2** to put up with: *He cannot bear any more pain.* **3** to bring forth; produce: *This tree bears fine apples.* **4** to give birth to: *Our cat will soon bear kittens. verb,* **bears, bore** (bôr), **borne** (bôrn) or **born** (bôrn), **bear·ing.**

bear[2] (bâr), a large animal with thick, coarse fur and a very short tail. *noun.*

beard (bird), **1** the hair growing on a man's chin and cheeks. **2** something like this. The long hair on the chin of a goat is a beard. *noun.*

beau·ti·ful (byü′tə fəl), very pleasing to see or hear: *a beautiful park, beautiful music. adjective.*

be·cause (bi kȯz′), for the reason that; since: *Because we were late, we ran the whole way home. conjunction.*

bed·room (bed′rüm′), a room to sleep in. *noun.*

be·fore (bi fôr′), **1** earlier than: *Come before noon.* **2** earlier: *Come at five o'clock, not before.* **3** until now; in the past: *You were never late before.* 1 *preposition,* 2,3 *adverb.*

be·gan (bi gan′). See **begin.** *Snow began to fall. verb.*

be·gin (bi gin′), **1** to do the first part; start: *When shall we begin? I began reading the book yesterday.* **2** to come into being: *The club began years ago. verb,* **be·gins, be·gan, be·gun** (bi gun′), **be·gin·ning.**

be·hav·ior (bi hā′vyər), a way of acting; actions: *Her sullen behavior showed that she was angry. noun.*

be·ing (bē′ing). **1** *Being* is a form of **be.** *The dog is being fed.* **2** a person; living creature: *a human being.* **3** life; existence: *The world came into being long ago.* 1 *verb,* 2,3 *noun.*

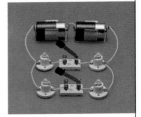

battery (definition 2)

a	hat	**ī**	ice	** u̇**	put	**ə** stands for
ā	age	**o**	not	**ü**	rule	**a** in about
ä	far, calm	**ō**	open	**ch**	child	**e** in taken
âr	care	**ȯ**	saw	**ng**	long	**i** in pencil
e	let	**ô**	order	**sh**	she	**o** in lemon
ē	equal	**oi**	oil	**th**	thin	**u** in circus
ėr	term	**ou**	out	**ᵗH**	then	
i	it	**u**	cup	**zh**	measure	

board (definition 1)
boards for constructing
a house

be·lief (bi lēf′), what is held to be true or real; thing believed: *One of my beliefs is that if you try hard you can succeed.* noun, plural **be·liefs.**

be·lieve (bi lēv′), **1** to think something is true or real: *Who doesn't believe that the earth is round?* **2** to think somebody tells the truth: *I believe you.* **3** to think; suppose: *I believe we are going to have a test soon.* verb, **be·lieves, be·lieved, be·liev·ing.**

be·long·ings (bi lòng′ingz), things that belong to a person. noun plural.

blush (blush), **1** to become red in the face because of shame, confusion, or excitement: *The little boy blushed when everyone laughed at his mistake.* **2** to be ashamed: *I blushed at my sister's bad table manners.* verb, **blush·es, blushed, blush·ing.**

board (bôrd), **1** a broad, thin piece of wood for use in building: *We used boards 10 inches wide for shelves.* **2** to cover with such pieces of wood: *We board up the windows of our summer cottage in the fall.* **3** a flat piece of wood or other material used for one special purpose: *an ironing board, a drawing board.* **4** a group of persons managing something; council: *a school board, a board of directors.* 1,3,4 noun, 2 verb.

board·er (bôr′dər), a person who pays for meals, or for room and meals, at another's house. noun.

bod·y (bod′ē), **1** the whole material or physical part of a person or animal: *I exercise to keep my body strong and healthy.* **2** the main part of an animal, not the head, limbs, or tail. **3** the main part of anything. noun, plural **bod·ies.**

boulder
boulders on a cliff

bor·der (bôr′dər), **1** the side, edge, or boundary of anything: *We pitched our tent on the border of the lake.* **2** to touch at the edge or boundary: *Canada borders on the United States.* 1 noun, 2 verb.

boul·der (bōl′dər), a large rock, rounded or worn by the action of water and weather: *Boulders fell down the cliff.* noun, plural **boul·ders.**

bowl (bōl), **1** a hollow, rounded dish, usually without handles: *a mixing bowl.* **2** the amount that a bowl can hold: *She had a bowl of soup for lunch.* noun.

bread (bred), a food made of flour or meal mixed with milk or water and baked: *She likes toasted bread.* noun.

break·fast (brek′fəst), **1** the first meal of the day. **2** to eat breakfast: *I like to breakfast alone.* 1 noun, 2 verb. [*Breakfast* comes from the phrase *break* (one's) *fast*, meaning "to end a period of not eating."]

bright (brīt), **1** giving much light; shining: *The stars are bright, but sunshine is brighter.* **2** very light or clear: *It is a bright day. Dandelions are bright yellow.* **3** clever; intelligent: *A bright student learns quickly. She can always think of a bright idea.* adjective.

bron·chi·tis (brong kī′tis), soreness and swelling of the mucous membrane that lines the bronchial tubes. Bronchitis usually causes a deep cough. noun.

broth·er (bruṭH′ər), **1** the son of the same parents. A boy is a brother to the other children of his parents. **2** male member of the same group, club, union, or religious organization. noun.

brush (brush), **1** a tool for sweeping, scrubbing, smoothing, or painting. Brushes are made of bristles, hair, or wire set in a stiff back or fastened to a handle. **2** to sweep, scrub, smooth, or paint with a brush; use a brush on: *I brushed my hair until it was shiny.* 1 noun, plural **brush·es;** 2 verb.

buck·et (buk′it), **1** a container for carrying liquids, sand, or the like; pail. **2** bucketful: *Pour in about four buckets of water.* noun.

buf·fa·lo (buf′ə lō), **1** a wild animal of North America, with a great, shaggy head and a large hump over the shoulders; bison. **2** any of several kinds of large animals related to cattle: *water buffalo. noun, plural* **buf·fa·loes, buf·fa·los,** or **buf·fa·lo.**

bur·glar (bėr′glər), a person who breaks into a house or other building to steal something. *noun.*

bus·y (biz′ē), **1** having plenty to do; working; active: *The principal of our school is a busy person.* **2** full of work or activity: *Main Street is a busy place. adjective,* **bus·i·er, bus·i·est.**

but·ter·fly (but′ər flī′), an insect with a slender body and two pairs of large, usually brightly colored, wings. Butterflies fly mostly in the daytime. *noun, plural* **but·ter·flies.**

but·ton (but′n), **1** a round, flat piece of plastic, metal, or the like, sewn onto clothes as fasteners or for decoration. **2** to fasten the buttons of: *Button your coat.* **1** *noun,* **2** *verb.*

C

cab·i·net (kab′ə nit), a piece of furniture with shelves or drawers, used to hold different articles for use or display. *noun.*

cake (kāk), **1** a baked mixture of flour, sugar, eggs, flavoring, and other things: *I baked a chocolate cake.* **2** to form into a solid mass; harden: *Mud cakes as it dries.* **1** *noun,* **2** *verb,* **cakes, caked, cak·ing.**

cal·en·dar (kal′ən dər), **1** a chart showing the months, weeks, and days of the year. A calendar shows the day of the week on which each day of the month falls. **2** a list or schedule: *The newspaper has a calendar of events. noun.*

camp (kamp), **1** to live away from home for a time outdoors or in a tent or hut: *The scout troop is camping at the foot of the mountain.* **2** a place where one lives in a tent or hut or outdoors: *Last year I spent a week at summer camp.* **1** *verb,* **camps, camped, camp·ing;** **2** *noun, plural* **camps.**

can (kan *or* kən), **1** to be able to: *You can run fast.* **2** to know how to: *She can speak Spanish.* **3** to have the right to: *Anyone can cross the street here.* **4** may: *Can I go now? verb, past tense* **could.**

car·di·nal (kärd′n əl), **1** one of the high officials of the Roman Catholic Church, appointed by the Pope and ranking next below him. Cardinals wear red robes and red hats. **2** a North American songbird. The male has bright-red feathers marked with black. **3** a bright, rich red. **1,2** *noun,* **3** *adjective.*

car·di·nal di·rec·tions (kärd′n əl də rek′shənz), the four basic directions: north, south, east, west.

care (kâr), **1** attention: *A pilot's work requires great care.* **2** to feel interest: *Musicians care about music.* **1** *noun,* **2** *verb,* **cares, cared, car·ing.**

care·ful (kâr′fəl), **1** thinking about what you say or do: *Be careful with my new bicycle!* **2** done with thought or effort; exact: *Math requires careful work. adjective.*
—**care′ful·ly,** *adverb*
—**care′ful·ness,** *noun.*

care·less (kâr′lis), **1** not thinking about what you say or do; not careful: *I was careless and broke the cup.* **2** done without enough thought or effort: *careless work.* **3** not caring or troubling: *Some people are careless about their appearance. adjective.*

butterfly

a	hat	ī	ice	u̇	put	ə *stands for*	
ā	age	o	not	ü	rule	a	in about
ä	far, calm	ō	open	ch	child	e	in taken
âr	care	ȯ	saw	ng	long	i	in pencil
e	let	ô	order	sh	she	o	in lemon
ē	equal	oi	oil	th	thin	u	in circus
ėr	term	ou	out	₮H	then		
i	it	u	cup	zh	measure		

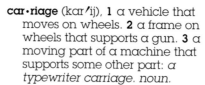

castle (definition 1)

a **castle** in Wales

caterpillar

A **caterpillar** looks like a worm.

car·riage (kar′ij), **1** a vehicle that moves on wheels. **2** a frame on wheels that supports a gun. **3** a moving part of a machine that supports some other part: *a typewriter carriage.* noun.

cas·tle (kas′əl), **1** a large building or group of buildings with thick walls, towers, and other defenses against attack. Most castles were built during the Middle Ages. **2** one of the pieces in the game of chess; rook. noun.

catch (kach), **1** to take and hold something moving: *Catch the ball with both hands.* **2** to attract: *The bright display caught my attention.* **3** to take or get: *Paper catches fire easily. Put on a warm coat or you will catch cold.* verb, **catch·es, caught, catch·ing.**

catch·er (kach′ər), **1** a person or thing that catches. **2** a baseball player who stands behind the batter to catch the ball thrown by the pitcher. noun.

cat·er·pil·lar (kat′ər pil′ər), the wormlike larva of a butterfly or a moth. Caterpillars are often colorful, and many are furry or have bristles. noun.

caught (kot). See **catch.** *I caught the ball.* verb.

cause (koz), **1** a person, thing, or event that makes something happen: *The flood was the cause of much damage.* **2** to make happen; bring about: *The fire caused much damage.* **3** something in which many people are interested and to which they give their support: *World peace is the cause she works for.* 1,3 noun, 2 verb, **caus·es, caused, caus·ing.**

cent (sent), a coin of the United States and Canada; penny. One hundred cents make one dollar. noun, *plural* **cents.**

cen·ter (sen′tər), **1** the middle point, place, or part: *the center of a room.* **2** a place to which people or things go for a particular purpose: *The family went skating at the recreation center.* noun.

chain (chān), **1** a row of links joined together: *The dog is fastened to a post by a chain.* **2** to fasten with a chain: *The dog was chained to a post.* 1 noun, 2 verb.

chalk (chok), **1** a soft, white mineral used for writing or drawing. Chalk is made up mostly of very small fossil seashells. **2** a white or colored substance like chalk, used for writing or drawing on a chalkboard. noun.

chance (chans), **1** a favorable time; opportunity: *I saw a chance to earn some money selling newspapers.* **2** a possibility: *There's a good chance that you will be well enough to return to school next week.* noun.

char·ac·ter (kar′ik tər), **1** personality. The special way in which you think, feel, and act makes up your character. *She has an honest, dependable character.* **2** moral strength: *Her courage in the face of suffering showed her character.* **3** a person or animal in a play, poem, story, book, or motion picture: *My favorite character in "Charlotte's Web" is Wilbur, the pig.* noun.

chase (chās), **1** to run after to catch or kill: *The cat chased the mouse.* **2** to drive; drive away: *The blue jay chased the squirrel from its nest.* **3** to follow; pursue: *The children chased the ball as it rolled downhill.* verb, **chas·es, chased, chas·ing.**

cheer (chir), **1** a shout of support or praise: *Give three cheers for the players who won the game.* **2** to show praise and approval by cheers: *We all cheered loudly.* **3** make glad; comfort: *It cheered me to have my friends visit me while I was sick.* 1 noun, 2,3 verb.

cheer·ful (chir′fəl), **1** full of cheer; joyful; glad: *She is a smiling, cheerful girl.* **2** pleasant; bringing cheer: *This is a cheerful, sunny room.* adjective.

cheese (chēz), a solid food made from the curds of milk. noun.

chim·ney (chim′nē), **1** a structure of brick or stone, connected with a fireplace or furnace, to make a draft and carry away smoke. **2** a glass tube placed around the flame of a lamp. *noun, plural* **chim·neys.**

chim·pan·zee (chim′pan zē′ *or* chim pan′zē), an African ape smaller than a gorilla. Chimpanzees are very intelligent. *noun.*
[The chimpanzee was first found in west Africa. Explorers got the word for this animal from the people who lived there.]

choc·o·late (chȯk′lit *or* chȯk′ə lit), **1** a substance made by roasting and grinding cacao seeds. **2** a drink made of chocolate with hot milk or water and sugar. **3** a candy made of chocolate. **4** made of or flavored with chocolate: *chocolate cake.* 1–3 *noun*, 4 *adjective.*
[The name for the drink was borrowed from a Mexican Spanish word. Spanish settlers got it from the American Indian name for the food.]

Christ·mas (kris′məs), the yearly celebration of the birth of Christ; December 25. *noun, plural* **Christ·mas·es.**

cir·cle (sėr′kəl), **1** a round line. Every point on a circle is the same distance from the center. **2** anything shaped like a circle; ring: *We sat in a circle around the teacher. noun.*

cir·cus (sėr′kəs), a traveling show of acrobats, clowns, and wild animals. *noun, plural* **cir·cus·es.**

cit·i·zen (sit′ə zən), **1** a person who by birth or choice is a member of a nation. Citizens owe loyalty to that nation and are given certain rights by it. **2** an inhabitant of a city or town. *noun, plural* **cit·i·zens.**

cit·y (sit′ē), **1** a large, important center of population and business activity. New York, Buenos Aires, and Shanghai are major world cities. **2** of the city; in the city: *He loved the city lights.* 1 *noun, plural* **cit·ies;** 2 *adjective.*

claw (klȯ), **1** a sharp, hooked nail on a bird's or animal's foot. **2** the pincers of a lobster or crab. *noun, plural* **claws.**

clay (klā), a sticky kind of earth that can be easily shaped when wet and hardens when it is dried or baked. Bricks and dishes are made from various kinds of clay. *noun.*

clear (klir), **1** not cloudy or hazy: *A clear sky is free of clouds.* **2** easy to see through: *I looked through the clear glass.* **3** to make clean and free; get clear: *After dinner, we cleared the table. She cleared her throat.* 1,2 *adjective,* 3 *verb.*

cliff dweller (klif′ dwel′ər), member of a group of prehistoric people who lived in houses built in cliffs in the southwestern United States; Anasazi.

clin·ic (klin′ik), a place where people can receive medical treatment, sometimes at a reduced cost. A clinic is often connected with a hospital or medical school: *an eye clinic, a dental clinic. noun.*
[The word *clinic* comes from a Greek word meaning "a physician who visits patients who are sick in bed."]

clock (klok), **1** an instrument for measuring and showing time. **2** to measure the time or speed of: *I clocked the runners with a stopwatch.* 1 *noun,* 2 *verb.*
[*Clock* comes from a Latin word meaning "bell." It was called this because bells were used before the invention of modern clocks to mark the hours.]

chimpanzee

circus
a **circus** under the big top

						ə stands for	
a	hat	**ī**	ice	**u̇**	put	**a**	in about
ā	age	**o**	not	**ü**	rule	**e**	in taken
ä	far, calm	**ō**	open	**ch**	child	**i**	in pencil
âr	care	**ȯ**	saw	**ng**	long	**o**	in lemon
e	let	**ô**	order	**sh**	she	**u**	in circus
ē	equal	**oi**	oil	**th**	thin		
ėr	term	**ou**	out	**ŦH**	then		
i	it	**u**	cup	**zh**	measure		

close (klōz), **1** to shut: *Close the door.* **2** to come or bring to an end: *The meeting closed with a speech by the president. verb,* **clos·es, closed, clos·ing.**

clothes (klōz), coverings for the body: *I bought a jacket, jeans, and other clothes. noun plural.*

clue (klü), something which helps to solve a mystery: *The police could find no clues to help them in solving the robbery. noun.*

clum·sy (klum′zē), awkward in moving: *The cast on my broken leg made me clumsy. adjective,* **clum·si·er, clum·si·est.**

coach (kōch), **1** a large, closed carriage with seats inside and often on top. **2** a passenger car of a railroad train. **3** a person who teaches or trains an athlete or athletic teams: *a swimming coach. noun, plural* **coach·es.**

coast·line (kōst′līn′), the outline of a coast: *From their spacecraft, the astronauts could see the coastline of Africa. noun, plural* **coast·lines.**

coat (kōt), **1** a piece of outer clothing with long sleeves: *It is cold enough for your winter coat.* **2** any outer covering: *a dog's coat of hair.* **3** a thin layer: *a coat of paint. noun.*

coat of arms (kōt əv ärms), a design or pattern, usually on a shield, that in former times was a symbol for a knight or lord. Some families, schools, and other groups now have coats of arms. *plural* **coats of arms.**

cold (kōld), **1** much less warm than the body: *Snow and ice are cold.* **2** feeling cold or chilly: *Put on a sweater, or you will be cold. adjective.*

cold-blood·ed (kōld′blud′id), creatures having blood that is about the same temperature as the air or water around them. Turtles are cold-blooded; dogs are warm-blooded. *adjective.*

col·lar (kol′ər), **1** the part of a coat, a dress, or a shirt that makes a band around or just below the neck. **2** a leather or plastic band or a metal chain for the neck of a dog or other pet animal. *noun.*

col·umn (kol′əm), **1** a line of objects or numbers from top to bottom in an array. **2** anything that seems tall and slender like a column: *You add a column of figures.* **3** a line of persons or things following one behind another: *How many columns are there? noun, plural* **col·umns.**

com·mu·ni·cate (kə myü′nə kāt), to give or exchange information or news: *Since my brother is away at school, I communicate with him by telephone. verb,* **com·mu·ni·cates, com·mu·ni·cat·ed, com·mu·ni·cat·ing.**

com·mu·ni·ty (kə myü′nə tē), **1** all the people living in the same place: *This lake provides water for six communities.* **2** a neighborhood; the area where people live: *There is a post office in our community. noun, plural* **com·mu·ni·ties.**

com·pa·ny (kum′pə nē), **1** a group of people joined together for some purpose: *a company of tourists, a company of actors.* **2** a business firm: *I have worked for two companies that make furniture.* **3** a guest or guests: *We are having company for dinner tonight. noun, plural* **com·pa·nies.**

com·pass rose (kum′pəs rōz′), a device for showing directions on a map.

com·pe·ti·tion (kom′pə tish′ən), **1** a trying hard to win or gain something wanted by others. **2** a contest. *noun.*

com·plain (kəm plān′), **1** to say that something is wrong: *We complained that the room was too cold.* **2** to make an accusation or charge: *I complained to the police about the barking of my neighbor's dog. verb.*

com·put·er (kəm pyü′tər), an electronic machine that can store, recall, or process information. Computers keep files, play games, solve mathematical problems, and control the operations of other machines. *noun.*

con·cert (kon′sərt), a musical show in which one or more musicians take part: *The school orchestra gave a free concert. noun.*

coastline

a **coastline** in southern Australia

coat of arms

a family's **coat of arms**

cone (kōn), **1** a solid object that has a flat, round base and narrows to a point at the top. **2** anything shaped like a cone: *an ice-cream cone, the cone of a volcano. noun.*

con·fuse (kən fyüz′), **1** to throw into disorder; mix up: *So many people talking at once confused me.* **2** to be unable to tell apart: *People often confuse this girl with her twin sister. verb,* **con·fus·es, con·fused, con·fus·ing.**

con·ver·sa·tion (kon′vər sā′shən), a friendly talk; exchange of thoughts by talking together. *noun.*

cook·ie or **cook·y** (ku̇k′ē), a small, flat, sweet cake. *noun, plural* **cook·ies.** [The words *cookie* and *cooky* look as if they come from the word *cook*. Actually they come from a Dutch word meaning "little cake."]

co·or·di·nates (kō ôrd′n its), integers in an ordered pair giving the location of a point in a coordinate plane; a number pair. *noun plural.*

core (kôr), **1** the hard, central part containing the seeds of fruits like apples and pears: *After eating the apple he threw the core away.* **2** the central or innermost part of the earth. *noun.*

could (ku̇d), **1** was able; was able to: *She could ski very well. See* **can.** **2** might be able to: *Perhaps I could go with you tomorrow. verb.*

could·n't (ku̇d′nt), could not.

count (kount), to name numbers in order: *The child can count from one to ten. verb.*

cous·in (kuz′n), a son or daughter of one's uncle or aunt. *noun.*

crack·er (krak′ər), a thin, crisp wafer. *noun, plural* **crack·ers.**

cray·on (krā′on *or* krā′ən), a stick of colored wax, used for drawing or writing. *noun.*

cre·a·tive (krē ā′tiv), having the power to create: *He has a very creative mind, always full of new ideas. adjective.*

croc·o·dile (krok′ə dīl), a large reptile with a long body, four short legs, a thick skin, a pointed snout, and a long tail. *noun.*

crown (kroun), **1** a head covering of precious metal and jewels, worn by a king or queen. **2** the part of a tooth above the gum, or an artificial substitute for it. *noun.*

crust (krust), **1** the hard outside part of bread. **2** the solid outside part of the earth. *noun.*

cry (krī), **1** to call loudly: *The drowning man cried, "Help!"* **2** to shed tears: *My little sister was crying after she fell. verb,* **cries, cried, cry·ing.**

cube (kyüb), **1** a solid object with 6 square sides. **2** anything shaped like a cube: *ice cubes, a cube of sugar. noun.*

cul·ture (kul′chər), the customs, arts, and tools of a nation or people at a certain time: *She spoke on the culture of the ancient Egyptians. noun.*

cup (kup), **1** a hollow, rounded dish to drink from. Most cups have handles. **2** a unit of measure equal to 8 fluid ounces. *noun.*

cup·board (kub′ərd), a cabinet with shelves for dishes and food supplies. *noun.*

cur·i·ous (kyu̇r′ē əs), eager to know: *Small children are very curious, and they ask many questions. adjective.*

crown (definition 1) the British Imperial State **Crown**

a	hat	**ī**	ice	**u̇**	put	**ə** stands for
ā	age	**o**	not	**ü**	rule	**a** in about
ä	far, calm	**ō**	open	**ch**	child	**e** in taken
âr	care	**ȯ**	saw	**ng**	long	**i** in pencil
e	let	**ô**	order	**sh**	she	**o** in lemon
ē	equal	**oi**	oil	**th**	thin	**u** in circus
ėr	term	**ou**	out	**ᴛʜ**	then	
i	it	**u**	cup	**zh**	measure	

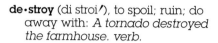

cus·tom (kus′təm), a long-established or accepted way of doing things: *The social customs of many countries differ from ours.* noun.

cyl·in·der (sil′ən dər), a hollow or solid object shaped like a round pole or tube. Tin cans and rollers are cylinders. noun.

D

dan·ger·ous (dān′jər əs), likely to cause harm; not safe; risky: *Shooting off firecrackers can be dangerous.* adjective.

da·ta (dā′tə or dat′ə), a collection of gathered information that has not been organized. noun plural.

day (dā), **1** the time of light between sunrise and sunset: *Days are longer in summer than in winter.* **2** the 24 hours of day and night. noun.

dead (ded), **1** not alive; no longer living: *The flowers in my garden are dead.* **2** dull; quiet: *This beach is crowded now, but in the winter it's dead.* adjective.

deep (dēp), **1** going a long way down from the top: *The pond is deep in the middle.* **2** far down; far on: *They dug deep before they found water.* **3** far down or back: *I had a deep cut on my finger.* 1,3 adjective, 2 adverb.

deer (dir), a swift, graceful animal. The male deer has antlers which are shed and grow again every year. noun, plural **deer**. [*Deer* comes from an earlier English word meaning "a wild animal."]

dem·o·crat·ic (dem′ə krat′ik), of a democracy; like a democracy. adjective.

de·nom·i·na·tor (di nom′ə nā′tər), the number below or to the right of the line in a fraction: *In ¾, 4 is the denominator, and 3 is the numerator.* noun.

den·tist (den′tist), a doctor whose work is the care of teeth. noun.

deer

A fawn is a young **deer**.

de·stroy (di stroi′), to spoil; ruin; do away with: *A tornado destroyed the farmhouse.* verb.

did·n't (did′nt), did not.

die (dī), **1** to stop living; become dead: *The flowers in the garden died from frost.* **2** to lose force or strength; come to an end; stop: *The motor sputtered and died.* verb, **dies, died, dy·ing.**

dif·fer·ent (dif′ər ənt), not alike; not like: *People have different names. A boat is different from an automobile.* adjective.

di·no·saur (dī′nə sôr), one of a group of extinct reptiles that lived many millions of years ago. Some dinosaurs were bigger than elephants. Some were smaller than cats. noun.

dirt (dėrt), **1** mud, dust, or the like. **2** earth; soil: *Before I planted my garden I had to take lots of stones out of the dirt.* noun.

dis·ap·point (dis′ə point′), to fail to satisfy: *The circus disappointed him, for there was no elephant.* verb.

dis·cour·age (dis kėr′ij), **1** to take away the courage of; destroy the hopes of: *Failing again and again discourages anyone.* **2** to try to prevent by disapproving: *All her friends discouraged her from such a dangerous swim.* verb, **dis·cour·ag·es, dis·cour·aged, dis·cour·ag·ing.**

dis·ease (də zēz′), a sickness; illness: *People, animals, and plants can all suffer from disease. Cleanliness helps prevent disease.* noun.

do (dü), **1** to carry through to an end any action or piece of work: *Do your work well.* **2** to take care of: *Who is doing the dishes at your house?* **3** to act; behave: *You did very well today.* **4** to be satisfactory: *That hat will do.* verb, **does, did, done** (dun), **do·ing.**

does (duz). See **do.** *She does all her work. Does he sing well?* verb.

does·n't (duz′nt), does not.

dog·house (dȯg′hous′), a small shelter for a dog. *noun, plural* **dog·houses** (dȯg′hou′ziz).

dol·lar (dol′ər), a unit of money in the United States and Canada equal to 100 cents. $1.00 means one dollar. *noun.*

door·knob (dôr′nob′), a handle on a door. *noun.*

drag (drag), **1** to pull or draw along the ground: *A team of horses dragged the big log out of the forest.* **2** to trail on the ground: *The little girl's blanket was dragging behind her. verb,* **drags, dragged, drag·ging.**

drag·on (drag′ən), a huge, winged lizard in old stories, supposed to breathe out fire and smoke. *noun.*

drawer (drôr), a box with handles, built to slide in and out of a table, desk, or dresser: *He kept his shirts in the dresser drawer. noun.*

draw·ing (drȯ′ing), **1** a picture or sketch done with pen, pencil, or crayon. **2** the making of such a sketch or picture: *She is good at drawing and painting. noun.*

dream (drēm), **1** something seen during sleep: *I had a bad dream last night.* **2** to see during sleep; have dreams: *The little boy dreamed that he was flying.* **1** *noun,* **2** *verb,* **dreams, dreamed** or **dreamt** (dremt), **dream·ing.**

dream·er (drē′mər), **1** a person who has dreams. **2** a person whose ideas do not fit real conditions. *noun.*

dress (dres), **1** a piece of clothing worn by women and girls. A dress is a top and skirt made as one piece or sewed together. **2** to put clothes on: *Please dress the baby.* **3** to care for. To dress a cut or sore is to treat it with medicine and bandages. **1** *noun, plural* **dress·es;** **2,3** *verb,* **dress·es, dressed, dress·ing.**

drink (dringk), **1** to swallow anything liquid: *A person must drink water to stay alive.* **2** a liquid swallowed or to be swallowed: *Water is a good drink to quench one's thirst.* **1** *verb,* **drinks, drank** (drangk), **drunk** (drungk), **drink·ing;** **2** *noun.*

drum (drum), **1** a musical instrument that makes a sound when it is beaten. A drum is hollow with a cover stretched tight over the ends. **2** to beat, tap, or strike again and again: *Stop drumming on the table with your fingers.* **1** *noun,* **2** *verb,* **drums, drummed, drum·ming.**

dry (drī), **1** not wet; not moist: *The paint is dry now.* **2** to make or become dry: *We washed and dried the dishes after dinner.* **1** *adjective,* **dri·er, dri·est;** **2** *verb,* **dries, dried, dry·ing.**

duck[1] (duk), **1** a wild or tame swimming bird with a flat bill, short neck, short legs, and webbed feet. **2** a female duck. The male is called a drake. **3** the flesh of a duck used for food: *roast duck. noun.*

duck[2] (duk), to lower the head or bend the body quickly to keep from being hit or seen: *She ducked to avoid a low branch. verb.*

due (dü *or* dyü), **1** owed as a debt: *The money due her for her work was paid today.* **2** looked for; expected: *The train is due at noon. Your report is due tomorrow. adjective.*

dump (dump), **1** to empty out; throw down: *The truck dumped the coal on the sidewalk.* **2** a place for throwing rubbish: *Garbage is taken to the city dump.* **3** a dirty, shabby, or untidy place. **1** *verb,* **2,3** *noun.*

drawing (definition 1)

duck[1] (definition 1)
a **duck** with her family of ducklings

							stands for
a	hat	ī	ice	u̇	put	ə	
ā	age	o	not	ü	rule	a	in about
ä	far, calm	ō	open	ch	child	e	in taken
âr	care	ȯ	saw	ng	long	i	in pencil
e	let	ô	order	sh	she	o	in lemon
ē	equal	oi	oil	th	thin	u	in circus
ėr	term	ou	out	ŦH	then		
i	it	u	cup	zh	measure		

E

ear·ly (ėr′lē), **1** in the beginning; in the first part: *The sun is not hot early in the day.* **2** before the usual time: *Please come early.* adverb, adjective, **ear·li·er, ear·li·est.**

earth (ėrth), **1** Also, **Earth.** the planet on which we live. **2** ground: *The earth in the garden is soft.* noun.

earth (definition 1)
a view of the **Earth**
from Apollo 17

earth·quake (ėrth′kwāk′), a shaking or sliding of the earth's crust, caused by the sudden movement of rock far beneath the earth's surface: *Earthquakes can cause great destruction.* noun.

earth·shak·ing (ėrth′shā′king), very important: *an earthshaking development.* adjective.

earth·worm (ėrth′wėrm′), a reddish-brown or grayish worm that lives in the soil; angleworm. Earthworms help loosen the soil. noun.

eas·y (ē′zē), **1** not hard to do or get: *Washing a few dishes was easy work.* **2** free from pain, difficulty, or worry; pleasant: *The pampered poodle led an easy life.* adjective, **eas·i·er, eas·i·est.**

eas·i·ly (ē′zə lē), **1** without trying hard: *The simple tasks were quickly and easily done.* **2** without pain or trouble; *A few hours after the operation, the patient was resting easily.* adverb.

eat (ēt), **1** to chew and swallow food: *Cows eat grass and grain.* **2** to have a meal: *Where shall we eat?* verb, **eats, ate, eat·en** (ēt′n), **eat·ing.**

edge (ej), **1** the line or place where something begins or ends: *A page of notebook paper has four edges.* **2** a segment where two faces of a polyhedron meet. **3** the thin side that cuts: *The knife had a very sharp edge.* noun.

elephant

eight (āt), one more than seven; 8. Four and four make eight. noun, adjective.

eighth (ātth), **1** next after the seventh. **2** one of eight equal parts. adjective, noun, plural **eighths.**

e·lec·tion (i lek′shən), **1** a choosing by vote: *Our city elections occur every two years.* **2** a selection by vote: *An honest campaign resulted in her election.* noun, plural **e·lec·tions.**

el·e·phant (el′ə fənt), the largest land animal now living. It has a long snout called a trunk, and ivory tusks. noun, plural **el·e·phants** or **el·e·phant.**

else (els), **1** other; different: *Will somebody else speak? What else could I say?* **2** in addition; more: *The Browns are here; do you expect anyone else?* adjective.

em·bar·rass (em bar′əs), to make uneasy and ashamed: *She embarrassed me by asking me if I really liked her.* verb.

e·nam·el (i nam′əl), **1** a paint used to make a smooth, hard, glossy surface. **2** the hard outer layer that covers and protects a tooth. noun.

en·e·my (en′ə mē), **1** a person or group that hates or tries to harm another; foe: *Two countries fighting against each other are enemies.* **2** anything that will harm: *Frost is an enemy of flowers.* noun, plural **en·e·mies.**

en·joy (en joi′), **1** be happy with; take pleasure in: *The children enjoyed their visit to the museum.* **2** to have as an advantage or benefit: *He enjoys good health.* verb.

e·rase (i rās′), to rub out; wipe out: *He erased the wrong answer and wrote in the right one.* verb, **e·ras·es, e·rased, e·ras·ing.**

e·rupt (i rupt′), to burst out: *Lava and ashes erupted from the volcano.* verb.

es·say (es′ā), a short piece of writing about one subject. noun.

e·ven (ē′vən), **1** level; flat; smooth: *The country is even, with no high hills.* **2** at the same level: *The snow was even with the window.* adjective.

eve·ry (ev′rē), each one of the entire number of: *Read every word on the page.* adjective.

eve·ry·bod·y (ev′rə bud′ē or ev′rē bod′ē), every person: *Everybody likes the new principal.* pronoun.

eve·ry·one (ev′rē wun or ev′rē wən), each one; everybody: *Everyone in the class is here.* pronoun.

eve·ry·thing (ev′rē thing), **1** every thing; all things: *She did everything she could to help her friend.* **2** something extremely important: *This news means everything to us.* 1 pronoun, 2 noun.

F

face (fās), **1** the front part of the head: *Your eyes, nose, and mouth are parts of your face.* **2** a look; expression: *His face was sad.* **3** a flat surface that is part of a polyhedron. noun.

fa·cial (fā′shəl), of or for the face: *We laughed at the facial expressions of the children as they watched the magician.* adjective.

fac·tor (fak′tər), **1** a number to be multiplied: *Multiply factors 2 and 5 to get 10.* **2** A number that divides evenly into a given second number is a factor of that number. noun, plural **fac·tors.**

fair[1] (fâr), giving the same treatment to all: *Try to be fair, even to people you dislike.* adjective.

fair[2] (fâr), a showing of farm products and goods of a certain region: *Prizes were given for the best farm animals at the state fair.* noun.

false (fóls), **1** not true; not correct; wrong: *They gave us false information about the accident.* **2** not real; artificial: *false teeth.* adjective, **fals·er, fals·est.**

fan·tas·tic (fan tas′tik), **1** very odd: *The firelight cast weird, fantastic shadows on the walls.* **2** very good: *The class prepared a fantastic science exhibition.* adjective.

fan·ta·sy (fan′tə sē), **1** a product of the imagination: *Fairy tales are fantasies.* **2** a picture existing only in the mind: *I have a fantasy in which I win a million dollars.* noun, plural **fan·ta·sies.**

far·a·way (fär′ə wā′), distant; far away: *He read of faraway places in geography books.* adjective.

farm·er (fär′mər), a person who raises crops or animals on a farm. noun.

farm·ing (fär′ming), the business of raising crops or animals on a farm; agriculture. noun.

fau·cet (fó′sit), a device for turning on or off a flow of liquid from a pipe. noun.

fault (fólt), **1** something that is not as it should be: *Her dog has two faults; it eats too much, and it howls at night.* **2** a cause for blame; responsibility: *Whose fault was it?* noun.

fa·vor·ite (fā′vər it), **1** liked better than others: *What is your favorite flower?* **2** the one liked better than others: *He is a favorite with everybody.* 1 adjective, 2 noun.

fear (fir), **1** a feeling that danger or evil is near: *I have a fear of high places.* **2** to be afraid of: *Our cat fears big dogs.* **3** to feel fear: *I fear that I am late.* 1 noun, 2,3 verb.

feath·er (feŦH′ər), one of the light, thin growths that cover a bird's skin. Because feathers are soft and light, they are used to fill pillows. noun.

face (definition 2)
a happy, young **face**

a	hat	**ī**	ice	**u̇**	put	**ə** stands for	
ā	age	**o**	not	**ü**	rule	**a**	in about
ä	far, calm	**ō**	open	**ch**	child	**e**	in taken
âr	care	**ȯ**	saw	**ng**	long	**i**	in pencil
e	let	**ô**	order	**sh**	she	**o**	in lemon
ē	equal	**oi**	oil	**th**	thin	**u**	in circus
ėr	term	**ou**	out	**ŦH**	then		
i	it	**u**	cup	**zh**	measure		

festival

a Mardi Gras **festival**

in Bolivia

fes·ti·val (fes′tə vəl), **1** a special time of rejoicing or feasting, often in memory of some great happening: *Christmas is a Christian festival; Hanukkah is a Jewish festival.* **2** a program of entertainment, often held annually: *summer music festivals. noun, plural* **fes·ti·vals.**

fifth (fifth), **1** next after the fourth. **2** one of five equal parts: *Three-fifths is more than half. adjective, noun, plural* **fifths.**

fi·nal (fī′nl), **1** at the end; coming last: *I just read the final chapter.* **2** deciding completely; settling the question: *The boss makes the final decisions. adjective.*

fi·nal·ist (fī′nl ist), person who takes part in the last of a series of contests. *noun.*

fi·nal·ly (fī′nl ē), at the end; at last: *The lost dog finally came home. adverb.*

find (fīnd), **1** to meet with; come upon: *I found a dime on the sidewalk.* **2** to locate: *Did you find your other shoe? verb,* **finds, found, find·ing.**

fin·ish (fin′ish), **1** to complete; bring to an end; reach the end of: *to finish one's dinner, to finish painting a picture.* **2** an end: *a fight to the finish.* **1** *verb,* **2** *noun, plural* **fin·ish·es.**

fire (fīr), **1** the flame, heat, and light caused by something burning. **2** to dry thoroughly with heat; bake: *Bricks are fired to make them hard.* **1** *noun,* **2** *verb,* **fires, fired, fir·ing.**

fire·fight·er (fīr′fī′tər), a person whose work is putting out fires. *noun.*

fish (fish), **1** one of a group of cold-blooded animals with a long backbone that live in water and have gills instead of lungs. **2** to catch fish; try to catch fish: *We will go fishing today.* **1** *noun, plural* **fish** or **fish·es;** **2** *verb,* **fished, fish·ing.**

fix (fiks), **1** to make ready; prepare: *He fixes our breakfast every day.* **2** to mend; repair: *to fix a watch. verb,* **fix·es, fixed, fix·ing.**

forest (definition 1)

a **forest** of birch trees

fla·min·go (flə ming′gō), a tropical wading bird with very long legs and neck, and feathers that vary from rosy-pink to bright red. *noun, plural* **fla·min·gos** or **fla·min·goes.**

floss (flòs), **1** a strong thread that has not been twisted: *Dental floss is used for cleaning between the teeth.* **2** to use dental floss, or use dental floss on: *I flossed my teeth this morning.* **1** *noun,* **2** *verb.*

fly¹ (flī), any of a large group of insects that have two wings, especially houseflies. *noun, plural* **flies.**

fly² (flī), **1** to move through the air with wings: *These birds fly long distances.* **2** to cause to float or wave in the air: *The children are flying kites. verb,* **flies, flew** (flü), **flown** (flōn), **flied, fly·ing.**

fly ball (flī′ bòl′), in baseball, a ball that flies high before falling.

fly·ing sau·cer (flī′ing sò′sər), an unidentified disklike object reported in the sky over many parts of the world; UFO.

foot (fùt), **1** the end part of a leg. **2** the part opposite the head of something: *the foot of a bed. noun.*

foot·hill (fùt′hil′), a low hill at the base of a mountain or mountain range. *noun.*

foot·print (fùt′print′), a mark made by a foot. *noun.*

fo·reign·er (fôr′ə nər), a person from another country; outsider: *The foreigners arrived by boat. noun, plural* **fo·reign·ers.**

fo·rest (fôr′ist), **1** thick woods, often covering many miles. **2** of the forest: *Help prevent forest fires.* **1** *noun,* **2** *adjective.*

for·get·ful (fər get′fəl), apt to forget; having a poor memory: *If I get too tired, I become forgetful. adjective.*

fos·sil (fos′əl), the hardened remains or traces of something which lived in a former age: *fossils of dinosaurs. noun.*
[*Fossil* comes from a Latin word meaning "to dig up." Fossils were called this because they are dug up out of the earth.]

found (found). See **find.** *We found the treasure. The lost child was found.* verb.

frac·tion (frak′shən), **1** one or more of the equal parts of a whole. $\frac{1}{2}$, $\frac{1}{3}$, and $\frac{3}{4}$ are fractions; so are $\frac{4}{3}$ and $\frac{10}{6}$. **2** a very small part: *I had time to do only a fraction of my homework.* noun.

fresh (fresh), **1** newly made, grown, or gathered: *fresh footprints, fresh coffee, fresh flowers.* **2** not spoiled; not stale: *Is this milk fresh?* adjective.

Fri·day (frī′dē), the sixth day of the week; the day after Thursday. noun. [*Friday* is from an earlier English word meaning "Frig's day." Frig is the name of the Norse goddess of love.]

friend (frend), a person who knows and likes another: *We are good friends.* noun, plural **friends.**

frus·trate (frus′trāt), to defeat; block: *Heavy rain frustrated our plans for a picnic.* verb, **frus·trates, frus·trat·ed, frus·trat·ing.**

fry (frī), to cook in hot fat: *We fried the potatoes in a deep pan: Are you frying the eggs?* verb, **fries, fried, fry·ing.**

ful·crum (ful′krəm), the point on which a lever turns and is supported. noun.

fur (fėr), the soft hair covering the skin of many animals. noun.

fur·nace (fėr′nis), an enclosed space to make a very hot fire in. Furnaces are used to heat buildings, melt metals, and make glass. noun.

fur·ni·ture (fėr′nə chər), movable articles needed in a room, house, or office. Beds, chairs, tables, and desks are furniture. noun.

G

gal·ax·y (gal′ək sē), a group of billions of stars forming one system. The earth and sun are in the Milky Way galaxy. Many galaxies outside our own can be seen with a telescope. noun, plural **gal·ax·ies.**

gal·lon (gal′ən), a unit for measuring liquids equal to 4 quarts. noun.

gar·den (gärd′n), **1** a piece of ground used for growing vegetables, flowers, or fruits. **2** to take care of a garden: *I garden as a hobby.* 1 noun, 2 verb.

get (get), **1** to come to have; obtain; receive: *I got a present.* **2** to reach; arrive: *I got home early last night.* **3** to become: *It is getting colder.* verb, **gets, got** (got), **got** or **got·ten** (got′n), **get·ting.**

gift (gift), something given; present. noun.

gill (gil), a part of the body of a fish, tadpole, crab, or other water animal by which the animal gets oxygen from water. A tadpole has gills. noun, plural **gills.**

glad (glad), **1** happy; pleased: *She is glad to see us.* **2** willing; ready: *I will be glad to go if you need me.* adjective, **glad·der, glad·dest.**

glaze (glāz), **1** a smooth, glassy surface or glossy coating: *A glaze of ice on the walk is dangerous.* **2** to cover with a shiny, smooth coating: *The pottery is glazed at the factory.* 1 noun, 2 verb, **glaz·es, glazed, glaz·ing.**

glue (glü), **1** a substance used to stick things together. **2** to stick together with glue: *We glued the two surfaces.* 1 noun, 2 verb, **glues, glued, glu·ing.**

garden (definition 2)
gardening in the backyard

gift
a **gift** for my sister

a	hat	ī	ice	u̇	put	**ə** stands for	
ā	age	o	not	ü	rule	a	in about
ä	far, calm	ō	open	ch	child	e	in taken
âr	care	ȯ	saw	ng	long	i	in pencil
e	let	ô	order	sh	she	o	in lemon
ē	equal	oi	oil	th	thin	u	in circus
ėr	term	ou	out	ŦH	then		
i	it	u	cup	zh	measure		

go (gō), **1** to move along: *Cars go on the road.* **2** to move away; leave: *Don't go yet.* **3** to be in motion; act; work; run: *Make the washing machine go.* **4** to proceed; advance: *to go to New York.* **5** to take part in the activity of: *to go skiing, to go swimming.* **6** to pass: *Summer had gone. Vacation goes quickly.* **7** to have its place; belong: *This book goes on the top shelf.* **8** to make a certain sound: *The cork went "pop!"* verb, **goes, went, gone** (gon), **go·ing.**

gold (gōld), **1** a heavy, bright-yellow, precious metal. Gold is used in making coins, watches, and rings. **2** made of this metal: *a gold watch.* **3** bright-yellow. 1 *noun*, 2,3 *adjective.*

good (gùd), **1** having high quality; well done: *The teacher said my report was good.* **2** right; as it ought to be: *good health, good weather.* **3** behaving well; that does what is right: *a good child.* adjective, **bet·ter** (bet/ər), **best** (best).

goods (gùdz), **1** belongings; personal property: *We shipped our household goods in a van.* **2** a thing or things for sale. *noun plural.*

goose (güs), **1** a tame or wild bird like a duck, but larger and with a longer neck. A goose has webbed feet. **2** a female goose. The male is called a gander. **3** the flesh of a goose used for food. **4** a silly person. *noun, plural* **geese** (gēs).

gov·ern·ment (guv/ərn mənt), **1** a group of people who make laws, see that the laws are obeyed, and settle arguments about what the laws mean: *Good government depends on informed citizens.* **2** a person or persons ruling a country, state, district, or city at any time: *The government of the United States consists of the President and the cabinet, the Congress, and the Supreme Court.* noun.

gov·er·nor (guv/ər nər), an official elected as the head of a state of the United States. The governor of a state carries out the laws made by the state legislature. *noun.*

greenhouse
Tropical plants grow in a
greenhouse.

guard (definition 1)
He is **guarding**
St. James's Palace.

grace·ful (grās/fəl), **1** beautiful in form or movement: *a graceful dancer.* **2** pleasing; agreeable: *a graceful speech of thanks.* adjective.

gram (gram), a unit of weight in the metric system. Twenty-eight grams weigh about one ounce. *noun.*

grand·fa·ther (grand/fä/ᵮᴇr), the father of one's father or mother. *noun.*

grand·moth·er (grand/muᵮ/ər), the mother of one's mother or father. *noun.*

greed·i·ness (grē/dē nəs), the state of being greedy, of wanting more than one's share. *noun.*

green·house (grēn/hous/), a building with a glass or plastic roof and sides, kept warm for growing plants; hothouse. *noun, plural* **green·hous·es** (grēn/hou/ziz).

grid (grid), a pattern of evenly spaced lines running up and down and across. Grids are used on maps, charts, and graphs. *noun.*

grue·some (grü/səm), horrible; causing fear or horror: *a gruesome crime.* adjective.

guard (gärd), **1** to watch over; take care of: *The dog guarded the child day and night.* **2** to keep from escaping; hold back: *Guard the prisoners. Guard your tongue.* **3** to take precautions: *Guard against cavities by brushing your teeth regularly.* verb.

guess (ges), **1** to form an opinion when one does not know exactly: *Do you know this or are you just guessing?* **2** to get right by guessing: *Can you guess the answer to that riddle?* **3** an opinion formed without really knowing: *My guess is that it will rain tomorrow.* 1,2 *verb*, 3 *noun, plural* **guess·es.**

guide (gīd), **1** to show the way; lead: *The scout guided us through the wilderness.* **2** a person or thing that shows the way: *Tourists sometimes hire guides.* 1 *verb*, **guides, guid·ed, guid·ing;** 2 *noun.*

gum (gum), the flesh around the teeth. *noun.*

H

had·n't (had′nt), had not.

hair (hâr), **1** a fine threadlike growth from the skin of people and animals. **2** a mass of such growths: *I combed my hair.* noun.

Hal·low·een or **Hal·low·e'en** (hal′ō ēn′), the evening of October 31. noun.

halves (havz), more than one half. Two halves make one whole. noun plural.

ham·mer (ham′ər), **1** a tool with a metal head and a handle, used to pound nails. **2** to hit with a hammer: *I hammered a nail into the wall to hold up a picture.* 1 noun, 2 verb.

hap·pen (hap′ən), **1** to take place; occur: *What happened at the party yesterday?* **2** to be or take place by chance: *Accidents will happen.* verb.

hap·pi·ly (hap′ə lē), **1** in a happy manner; with pleasure, joy, and gladness: *They lived happily forever after.* **2** by luck; with good fortune: *Happily, I saved you from falling.* adverb.

hap·pi·ness (hap′ē nis), a state of being happy; gladness. noun.

hap·py (hap′ē), **1** glad; pleased; contented: *She is happy in her work.* **2** showing that one is glad: *a happy smile, a happy look.* adjective, **hap·pi·er, hap·pi·est.**

hard (härd), **1** solid and firm to the touch; not soft: *a hard nut.* **2** firmly; solidly: *Don't hold my hand so hard.* **3** needing much ability, effort, or time: *a hard job, a hard lesson.* **4** acting with energy: *He is a hard worker and gets a lot done.* **5** with violence or vigor: *It is raining hard.* 1,3,4 adjective, 2,5 adverb.

has·n't (haz′nt), has not.

haunt·ed (hòn′tid), visited by ghosts: *They were afraid to go into the haunted house.* adjective.

have·n't (hav′ənt), have not.

Ha·wai·i (hə wī′ē), a state of the United States in the northern Pacific, consisting of the Hawaiian Islands. *Abbreviation:* HI *Capital:* Honolulu. noun.
[*Hawaii* comes from the Hawaiian name of the largest island in the group. According to legend, the original settlers of Hawaii named it for their homeland.]

head (hed), **1** the top part of the human body or the front part of most animal bodies where the eyes, ears, nose, mouth, and brain are. **2** the top part of anything: *the head of a pin.* noun, plural **heads.**

hear (hir), **1** to take in a sound or sounds through the ear: *We couldn't hear in the back row. I can hear my watch tick.* **2** to listen to: *You must hear what he has to say.* **3** to receive information: *Have you heard from your sister?* verb, **hears, heard, hear·ing.**

heard (hèrd). See **hear.** *The sound was heard a mile away.* verb.

heart (härt), **1** the part of the body that pumps the blood. **2** courage; enthusiasm: *The losing team still had plenty of heart.* **3** the middle; center: *in the heart of the forest.* **4** a figure shaped somewhat like this: ♥: *The valentine was covered with hearts.* noun.

heav·y (hev′ē), **1** hard to lift or carry; of much weight: *The washing machine was a heavy load for them to carry.* **2** greater than usual; large: *a heavy rain, a heavy vote.* **3** hard to bear or endure: *Their troubles became heavier.* adjective, **heav·i·er, heav·i·est.**

happy (definition 1-2)

a	hat	**ī**	ice	**ù**	put	**ə** stands for	
ā	age	**o**	not	**ü**	rule	**a**	in about
ä	far, calm	**ō**	open	**ch**	child	**e**	in taken
âr	care	**ȯ**	saw	**ng**	long	**i**	in pencil
e	let	**ô**	order	**sh**	she	**o**	in lemon
ē	equal	**oi**	oil	**th**	thin	**u**	in circus
ėr	term	**ou**	out	**ŦH**	then		
i	it	**u**	cup	**zh**	measure		

holiday

waving flags for a

holiday

height (hīt), how tall a person is; how high anything is: *the height of a mountain. noun.*

hel·lo (he lō′ or hə lō′), **1** a call of greeting. We usually say "hello" when we call or answer a call on the telephone. "*Hello, Mother!*" the boy said. **2** a call or shout: *The girl gave a loud hello to let us know where she was.* **1** *interjection,* **2** *noun, plural* **hel·los.**

hel·met (hel′mit), a covering to protect the head. Knights wore helmets as part of their armor. Soldiers wear steel helmets. *noun.*

help (help), **1** to give or do what is needed or useful: *My father helped me with my homework.* **2** the act of helping; aid: *I need some help with this job.* **1** *verb,* **2** *noun.*

help·ful (help′fəl), giving help; useful. *adjective.*
—**help·ful·ly,** *adverb*
—**help·ful·ness,** *noun.*

her·it·age (her′ə tij), what is handed down from one generation to the next: *The heritage of freedom is precious to Americans. noun.*

he's (hēz), **1** he is. **2** he has.

him·self (him self′), **1** *Himself* is used to make a statement stronger. *He himself did it. Did you see Roy himself?* **2** *Himself* is used instead of *he* or *him* in cases like: *He cut himself. He kept the toy for himself.* **3** his real or true self: *He feels like himself again. pronoun.*

his (hiz), **1** of him; belonging to him: *His name is Bill. This is his book.* **2** the one or ones belonging to him: *My books are new; his are old.* **1** *adjective,* **2** *pronoun.*

hole (hōl), **1** an open place: *a hole in a stocking.* **2** a hollow place in something solid: *a hole in the road. Rabbits dig holes in the ground to live in. noun.*

hol·i·day (hol′ə dā), a day when one does not work; a day for pleasure and enjoyment: *The Fourth of July is a holiday for everyone. noun.* [*Holiday* comes from earlier English words meaning "holy day" or "time of a religious festival."]

hot (definition 1)
The firefighter hoses down
the **hot** blaze.

home (hōm), **1** the place where a person or family lives: *Her home is at 25 South Street.* **2** (in sports) played in a team's hometown: *a home game.* **1** *noun,* **2** *adjective.*

home·work (hōm′wėrk′), a lesson to be studied or prepared outside the classroom. *noun.*

hop (hop), **1** to jump, or move by jumping, on one foot: *How far have you hopped on your right foot?* **2** to jump, or move by jumping, with both or all feet at once: *Both kangaroos went hopping off.* **3** a jump or leap: *He came up each step with a hop.* **1,2** *verb,* **hops, hopped, hop·ping;** **3** *noun.*

hope (hōp), **1** a feeling that what you desire will happen: *Her friendly smile gave me hope.* **2** to wish and expect: *I am hoping to do well in school this year. She hoped to arrive on time.* **1** *noun,* **2** *verb,* **hopes, hoped, hop·ing.**

hor·ri·ble (hôr′ə bəl), **1** causing horror: *a horrible disease.* **2** extremely unpleasant: *a horrible smell. adjective.*

hot (hot), **1** much warmer than the body: *That fire is hot.* **2** warmer than it usually is: *The weather is hot for April.* **3** feeling hot or warm: *That long run has made me hot.* **4** having a sharp, burning taste: *Pepper and mustard are hot.* **5** violent; fiery: *He has a hot temper. adjective,* **hot·ter, hot·test.**

hour (our), **1** one of the 12 equal periods of time between noon and midnight, or between midnight and noon. 60 minutes make an hour. **2** the time of day: *The clock strikes the hours and half hours each day. noun.*

house (hous), **1** a building in which people live. **2** the people living in a house: *The noise woke up the whole house.* **3** a building for any purpose: *a tool house, a movie house. noun, plural* **hous·es** (hou′ziz).

hun·dred (hun′drəd), ten times ten; 100. There are one hundred cents in a dollar. *noun, adjective.*

hun·gry (hung′grē), **1** feeling a desire or need for food: *I missed breakfast and was hungry all morning.* **2** showing hunger: *The stray cat had a hungry look. adjective,* **hun·gri·er, hun·gri·est.**

hunt·er (hun′tər), **1** a person who hunts. **2** a horse or dog trained for hunting. *noun.*

hur·ry (hėr′ē), **1** to move or act more quickly than usual; rush: *She hurried to get to work on time.* **2** eagerness to have quickly or do quickly: *She was in a hurry to meet her friends.* 1 *verb,* **hur·ries, hur·ried, hur·ry·ing;** 2 *noun.*

hus·tle (hus′əl), **1** to move quickly; hurry: *I had to hustle to get the lawn mowed before it rained.* **2** to push or shove roughly: *Guards hustled the demonstrators away from the mayor's office. verb,* **hus·tles, hus·tled, hus·tling.**

I

i·de·a (ī dē′ə), **1** a belief, plan, or picture in the mind: *Swimming is her idea of fun.* **2** a thought; opinion: *I had no idea that the job would be so hard.* **3** the point or purpose: *The idea of a vacation is to get a rest. noun.*

i·dle (ī′dl), doing nothing; not busy; not working: *the idle hours of a holiday. adjective,* **i·dler, i·dlest.**

I'm (īm), I am.

inch (inch), **1** a unit of length; 12 inches make a foot. **2** to move slowly or little by little: *The worm inched along.* 1 *noun, plural* **inch·es;** 2 *verb.*

inclined plane (in klīnd′ plān′), a simple machine that has a plane surface with one end higher than the other.

in·fec·tion (in fek′shən), **1** a causing of disease in people and other living things by bringing into contact with germs. **2** a disease caused in this manner that can spread from one person to another. *noun.*

in·field·er (in′fēl′dər), a baseball player who plays in the infield. *noun.*

in·stead (in sted′), in another's place; as a substitute: *She stayed home, and her sister went riding instead. adverb.*

in·tel·li·gent (in tel′ə jənt), able to learn and know; quick at learning: *Elephants are intelligent animals. adjective.*

in·ven·tor (in ven′tər), a person who invents. *noun.*

in·vis·i·ble (in viz′ə bəl), not visible; not able to be seen: *Thought is invisible. Germs are invisible to the naked eye. adjective.*

i·ron (ī′ərn), **1** the commonest and most useful metal, from which tools and machinery are made. Steel is made from iron. **2** made of iron: *an iron fence.* **3** an implement with a flat surface which is heated and used to press clothing. **4** to press with a heated iron. 1,3 *noun,* 2 *adjective,* 4 *verb.*

its (its), of it; belonging to it: *The dog wagged its tail. adjective.*

it's (its), **1** it is. **2** it has.

I've (īv), I have.

inventor

the American **inventor** T.A. Edison in his chemistry lab

J

jack·et (jak′it), **1** a short coat. **2** an outer covering: *a book jacket. noun.*

jam (jam), fruit boiled with sugar until thick: *raspberry jam. noun.*

a	hat	**ī**	ice	**u̇**	put	**ə** stands for	
ā	age	**o**	not	**ü**	rule	**a**	in about
ä	far, calm	**ō**	open	**ch**	child	**e**	in taken
âr	care	**ȯ**	saw	**ng**	long	**i**	in pencil
e	let	**ô**	order	**sh**	she	**o**	in lemon
ē	equal	**oi**	oil	**th**	thin	**u**	in circus
ėr	term	**ou**	out	**ᴛʜ**	then		
i	it	**u**	cup	**zh**	measure		

jellyfish

the helmet **jellyfish**

kiln

a **kiln** for firing pottery

jeal·ous (jel′əs), **1** fearful that somebody you love may love someone else better: *The child was jealous when anyone paid attention to the new baby.* **2** full of envy: *He is jealous of his brother's good grades. adjective.*

jeans (jēnz), pants made of a strong cotton cloth. *noun plural.* [*Jeans* comes from an earlier English word meaning "of Genoa," a city in Italy. The cloth from which jeans are made was called jean because it was first made in Genoa.]

jel·ly (jel′ē), fruit juice boiled with sugar and then cooked until firm. *noun, plural* **jel·lies.** [*Jelly* comes from a Latin word meaning "frozen" or "stiffened." Jelly was called this because it is liquid that has become stiff.]

jel·ly·bean (jel′ē bēn′), a small candy made of jellied sugar, usually shaped like a bean. *noun.*

jel·ly·fish (jel′ē fish′), a sea animal like a lump of jelly. Most jellyfish have long, trailing tentacles that can sometimes sting. *noun, plural* **jel·ly·fish** or **jel·ly·fish·es.**

jew·el·ry (jü′əl rē), **1** jewels: *Mother keeps her jewelry in a small locked box.* **2** rings, bracelets, or other ornaments to be worn. *noun.*

joke (jōk), **1** something said or done to make somebody laugh; something funny. **2** to make jokes; say or do something as a joke: *As it got colder, we joked about the possibility of snow in July.* 1 *noun,* 2 *verb,* **jokes, joked, jok·ing.**

jour·ney (jėr′nē), **1** a traveling from one place to another; trip: *a journey around the world.* **2** to travel; take a trip: *She journeyed to Europe last summer.* 1 *noun,* *plural* **jour·neys;** 2 *verb.* [*Journey* comes from a Latin word meaning "daily." Originally a journey was a trip that took a day to finish. Another English word from the same Latin word is *journal.* A journal is something that you write in every day.]

jump (jump), **1** to spring from the ground; leap: *How high can you jump? Jump across the puddle.* **2** a spring from the ground; leap: *The horse made a fine jump.* **3** to leap over: *to jump a stream. The speeding car jumped the curb and crashed.* **4** to rise suddenly: *The price of orange juice jumped when the orange crop was ruined.* 1,3,4 *verb,* 2 *noun.*

K

keep (kēp), **1** to have for a long time or forever: *You may keep this book.* **2** to have and not let go: *Can you keep a secret?* **3** to hold back; prevent: *Keep the baby from crying.* **4** to be faithful to: *keep a promise. verb,* **keeps, kept, keep·ing.**

kept (kept). See **keep.** *He kept the book I gave him. The milk was kept cool. verb.*

kiln (kil or kiln), a furnace or oven for burning, baking, or drying something. Bricks and pottery are baked in a kiln. *noun.*

kind·li·ness (kīnd′lē nis), **1** a kindly feeling or quality. **2** a kindly act. *noun.*

kind·ness (kīnd′nis), **1** a kind nature; being kind: *We admire his kindness.* **2** a kind act: *They showed me many kindnesses. noun, plural* **kind·ness·es.**

kiva (kē′və), an American Indian word for a large underground room. It was used for special ceremonies. *noun.*

knee (nē), the joint between the thigh and the lower leg. *noun.*

knife (nīf), a thin, flat metal blade fastened in a handle so that it can be used to cut or spread. *noun, plural* **knives** (nīvz).

knight (nīt), **1** (in the Middle Ages) a man raised to an honorable military rank and pledged to do good deeds. **2** one of the pieces in the game of chess. *noun.*

knock (nok), **1** a hit: *That knock on my head really hurt.* **2** to hit and cause to fall: *The speeding car knocked over a sign.* **3** to hit and make a noise: *She knocked on the door.* 1 *noun*, 2,3 *verb.*

know (nō), **1** to have the facts of; be skilled in: *She knows math. The teacher really knew his subject.* **2** to be acquainted with: *I know her very well. verb,* **knows, knew** (nü), **known** (nōn), **know·ing.**

knowl·edge (nol′ij), **1** what one knows: *a gardener's knowledge of flowers.* **2** all that is known or can be learned: *Science is a part of knowledge. noun.*

L

la·bel (lā′bəl), **1** a slip of paper or other material attached to anything and marked to show what or whose it is, or where it is to go. **2** to put or write a label on: *The bottle is labeled "Poison."* 1 *noun, plural* **la·bels;** 2 *verb.*

lad·der (lad′ər), a set of rungs or steps fastened into two long pieces of wood, metal, or rope, for use in climbing up and down. *noun.*

la·dy (lā′dē), **1** a woman having good manners. **2** a polite term for any woman. "Ladies" is often used in speaking or writing to a group of women. *noun, plural* **la·dies.** [*Lady* comes from an earlier English word originally meaning "one who kneads a loaf of bread" or "mistress of the house."]

lamp·post (lamp′pōst′), post used to support a street lamp. *noun.*

land·fill (land′fil′), a dump where city trucks unload trash and garbage. *noun.*

lan·guage (lang′gwij), **1** human speech, spoken or written: *Civilization would be impossible without language.* **2** the speech of one nation, tribe, or other large group of people: *the French language. noun.*

large (lärj), of more than the usual size, amount, or number; big: *America is a large country. Ten thousand dollars is a large sum of money. Large crowds come to see our team play. adjective,* **larg·er, larg·est.**

la·ser (lā′zər), a device that makes a very narrow and very strong beam of light. Laser beams are used to cut or melt hard materials, remove diseased body tissues, and send television signals. *noun.*

last (last), **1** coming after all others: *Z is the last letter; A is the first.* **2** after all others: *She came last in the line.* 1 *adjective,* 2 *adverb.*

laugh (laf), **1** to make the sounds and movements that show one is happy or amused: *We all laughed at the clown's funny tricks.* **2** the sound made when a person laughs: *She gave a hearty laugh at the joke.* 1 *verb,* 2 *noun.*

laun·dry (lȯn′drē), **1** a room or building where clothes and linens are washed and ironed. **2** clothes and linens that have been washed or are to be washed. *noun, plural* **laun·dries.**

la·va (lä′və), **1** the hot, melted rock flowing from a volcano. **2** the rock formed by the cooling of this melted rock. *noun.*

law (lȯ), a rule made by a country or state for all the people who live there: *Good citizens obey the laws. noun.*

lava (definition 1)
The **lava** is flowing from a Hawaiian volcano.

a	hat	**ī**	ice	**u̇**	put	**ə stands for**	
ā	age	**o**	not	**ü**	rule	**a**	in about
ä	far, calm	**ō**	open	**ch**	child	**e**	in taken
âr	care	**ȯ**	saw	**ng**	long	**i**	in pencil
e	let	**ô**	order	**sh**	she	**o**	in lemon
ē	equal	**oi**	oil	**th**	thin	**u**	in circus
ėr	term	**ou**	out	**ŦH**	then		
i	it	**u**	cup	**zh**	measure		

library (definition 1-2)

lawn (lȯn), a piece of land covered with grass kept closely cut, especially near or around a house. *noun.* [An earlier spelling of *lawn* was *laund.* This came from an old French word meaning "a wooded ground" or "a wasteland."]

law·yer (lȯ′yər), a person who knows the laws and gives advice about matters of law or acts for others in a court of law. *noun.*

leaf (lēf), **1** one of the thin, flat, green parts of a tree or other plant that grow on the stem or grow up from the roots. **2** a thin sheet or piece: *a leaf of a book. noun, plural* **leaves.**

leash (lēsh), a strap or chain for holding an animal in check: *He led the dog on a leash. noun.*

leaves (lēvz), more than one leaf. *noun plural.*

left (left), **1** belonging to the side of the less-used hand (in most people): the opposite of right: *I sprained my left ankle.* **2** on or to the left side: *Turn left.* **1** *adjective,* **2** *adverb.*

lem·on (lem′ən), **1** the sour, light-yellow, juicy fruit of a tree grown in warm climates. **2** flavored with lemon. **1** *noun,* **2** *adjective.*

length (lengkth *or* length), **1** how long a thing is; longest way a thing can be measured: *the length of a room, eight inches in length.* **2** how long something lasts or goes on: *the length of a visit, the length of a book. noun.*

les·son (les′n), something to be learned or taught; something that has been learned or taught: *Children study many different lessons in school. noun.*

let (let), to allow; permit: *Let the dog have a bone. She lets me use her clothes brush. verb,* **lets, let, let·ting.**

let's (lets), let us.

let·ter (let′ər), **1** a mark or sign that stands for any one of the sounds that make up words. There are 26 letters in our alphabet. **2** a written or printed message: *He told me about his vacation in a letter. noun.*

lighthouse
The **lighthouse** is a welcome sight.

lev·er (lev′ər *or* lē′vər), a bar or board used for lifting a weight at one end by pushing down at the other end. A lever is a simple machine. *noun.*

li·brar·y (lī′brer′ē), **1** a collection of books, magazines, films, or recordings. Libraries may be public or private. **2** a room or building where such a collection is kept for public use and borrowing. *noun, plural* **li·brar·ies.**

light·house (līt′hous′), a tower with a bright light that shines far over the water. It warns ships of danger and helps guide them. *noun, plural* **light·hous·es** (līt′hou′ziz).

light·ning (līt′ning), a flash of electricity in the sky. The sound that it makes is thunder. *noun.*

line drive (līn′ drīv′), baseball hit so that it goes in almost a straight line, usually close to the ground; liner.

lis·ten (lis′n), to try to hear; pay attention to in order to hear: *I like to listen to music. verb.*

li·ter (lē′tər), the basic unit for measuring liquid in the metric system. It is equal to about a quart. *noun.*

lit·ter (lit′ər), **1** things scattered about: *We picked up the litter.* **2** to scatter things about; make untidy: *You have littered the room with your papers.* **3** the young animals produced at one time: *a litter of puppies.* **1,3** *noun,* **2** *verb.*

lit·tle (lit′l), **1** not big or large; small. **2** not much: *A very sick child can eat only a little food.* **3** short; not long in time or in distance: *Wait a little while and I'll go a little way with you. adjective,* **less** (les) *or* **less·er** (les′ər), **least** (lēst), *or* **lit·tler, lit·tlest.**

live·ly (līv′lē), **1** full of life and spirit; active: *A good night's sleep made us all lively again.* **2** cheerful: *a lively conversation. adjective,* **live·li·er, live·li·est.**

load (lōd), **1** what one is carrying: *The cart has a load of hay.* **2** to put in or put on whatever is to be carried: *to load a ship.* **1** *noun,* **2** *verb.*

lo·cate (lō′kāt), **1** to find out the exact position of: *We followed the stream until we located its source.* **2** to state or show the position of: *Can you locate Africa on the globe? verb,* **lo·cates, lo·cat·ed, lo·cat·ing.**

lock·er (lok′ər), a chest, small closet, or cupboard that can be locked. *noun.*

log·ging (lȯ′ging), the work of cutting down trees, sawing them into logs, and moving the logs out of the forest. *noun.*

lone·ly (lōn′lē), feeling oneself alone and longing for company or friends: *He was lonely while his brother was away. adjective.* **lone·li·er, lone·li·est.**

long (lȯng), **1** measuring much from end to end: *An inch is short; a mile is long. I read a long story.* **2** in length: *My table is three feet long. adjective,* **long·er** (lȯng′gər), **long·est** (lȯng′gist).

lose (lüz), **1** to not have any longer. **2** to be unable to find: *to lose a book.* **3** to fail to win; be defeated: *Our team lost. verb,* **los·es, lost, los·ing.**

lot (lot), **a lot,** a great deal: *I feel a lot better. adverb.*

loz·enge (loz′inj), a small tablet of any shape used as medicine or candy. Cough drops are sometimes called lozenges. *noun.*

luck·y (luk′ē), having or bringing good luck: *This is a lucky day. adjective,* **luck·i·er, luck·i·est.**

lung (lung), either one of a pair of organs found in the chest of human beings and certain other animals that breathe air. Lungs give the blood the oxygen it needs, and take away carbon dioxide. *noun.*

M

mad (mad), **1** very angry: *The insult made me mad.* **2** foolish; unwise: *Trying to row across the ocean is a mad undertaking.* **3** blindly and unreasonably fond: *My friend is mad about swimming. adjective,* **mad·der, mad·dest.**

mag·ma (mag′mə), hot melted rock deep under the surface of the earth. *noun.*

mail·box (māl′boks′), **1** a public box from which mail is collected. **2** a private box at one's home or business to which mail is delivered. *noun, plural* **mail·box·es.**

Maine (mān), one of the northeastern states of the United States. *Abbreviation:* Me. or ME *Capital:* Augusta. *noun.*
[*Maine* probably comes from the English phrase *the maine,* that is, the mainland. Explorers who found many islands off the coast may have used the term to refer to the mainland.]

mam·mal (mam′əl), one of a group of warm-blooded animals with a backbone and usually having hair. Human beings, cattle, dogs, and whales are all mammals. *noun.*

man·ag·er (man′ə jər), a person who manages: *She is the manager of the department store. noun.*

man·tle (man′tl), **1** anything that covers or conceals: *The ground had a mantle of snow.* **2** the layer of the earth lying between its crust and its core. *noun.*

man·y (men′ē), **1** consisting of a great number: *There are many children in the city.* **2** a large number of people or things: *There were many at the dance.* **1** *adjective,* **more** (môr), **most; 2** *noun, pronoun.*

mantle (definition 1)
a **mantle** of snow

a	hat	ī	ice	u̇	put	**ə stands for**	
ā	age	o	not	ü	rule	a	in about
ä	far, calm	ō	open	ch	child	e	in taken
âr	care	ȯ	saw	ng	long	i	in pencil
e	let	ô	order	sh	she	o	in lemon
ē	equal	oi	oil	th	thin	u	in circus
ėr	term	ou	out	ᴛH	then		
i	it	u	cup	zh	measure		

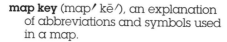

map key (map′ kē′), an explanation of abbreviations and symbols used in a map.

march (märch), **1** to walk as soldiers do, in time and with steps of the same length: *Our band marches in every parade.* **2** to walk or go steadily: *He marched to the front of the room.* verb, **march·es, marched, march·ing.**

Mars (märz), the planet next beyond the earth. It is the fourth in distance from the sun. noun.

marsh·mal·low (märsh′mal′ō or märsh′mel′ō), a soft, white, spongy candy, covered with powdered sugar. noun.

math (math), mathematics. noun.

may (mā), **1** to be permitted or allowed to: *May I have an apple? May I go now?* **2** to be possible that it will: *It may rain tomorrow.* verb, past tense **might.**

meat (mēt), **1** animal flesh used for food. Fish and poultry are not usually called meat. **2** food of any kind: *meat and drink.* noun.

me·chan·ic (mə kan′ik), a person skilled at working with tools, especially someone who repairs machines: *an automobile mechanic.* noun.

meet (mēt), **1** to come face to face with something or someone: *Our car met another car on a narrow road.* **2** to come together: *Two roads met near the bridge.* **3** to keep an appointment with: *Meet me at one o'clock.* verb, **meets, met** (met), **meet·ing.**

Mer·cur·y (mėr′kyər ē), the planet closest to the sun. noun.

me·sa (mā′sə), a high, steep hill that has a flat top and stands alone. noun.

me·ter (mē′tər), the basic unit of length in the metric system. It is equal to about 39⅓ inches. noun.

mid·dle (mid′l), **1** the point or part that is the same distance from each end or side; center: *the middle of the road.* **2** halfway between; in the center: *the middle house in the row.* **1** noun, **2** adjective.

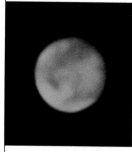

Mars

the planet **Mars**

Mercury

the planet **Mercury**

might (mīt). See **may.** *Mother said that we might play in the barn. He might have done it when you were not looking.* verb.

mile (mīl), a unit for measuring length or distance equal to 5280 feet: *She walked two miles.* noun, plural **miles.**

mil·lion (mil′yən), one thousand thousands; 1,000,000. noun, adjective.

min·ute (min′it), **1** one of the 60 equal periods of time that make up an hour; 60 seconds. **2** a short time; an instant: *I'll be there in five minutes.* noun, plural **min·utes.**

mis·be·have (mis′bi hāv′), to behave badly: *Some of the children were misbehaving at the picnic.* verb, **mis·be·haves, mis·be·haved, mis·be·hav·ing.**

mis·chie·vous (mis′chə vəs), **1** full of mischief; naughty: *The mischievous child poured honey all over the kitchen.* **2** full of playful tricks and teasing fun: *My friends were feeling mischievous and hid my glasses.* adjective.

mix (miks), **1** to put together; combine and stir well: *The cook mixes butter, sugar, and milk together.* **2** a preparation that is already mixed: *I used a cake mix.* **1** verb, **mix·es, mixed, mix·ing;** **2** noun, plural **mix·es.**

Mon·day (mun′dē), the second day of the week; the day after Sunday. noun.
[*Monday* comes from an earlier English word meaning "the moon's day." It was called this because it follows Sunday, that is, the sun's day.]

mon·key (mung′kē), **1** an animal of the group most like human beings. Monkeys are very intelligent animals. **2** one of the smaller animals in this group, not a chimpanzee, gorilla, or other large ape. It usually has a long tail. noun, plural **mon·keys.**

mon·ster (mon′stər), **1** an imaginary creature of strange or horrible appearance, such as a dragon. **2** a huge creature or thing. noun.

month (munth), one of the twelve periods of time into which a year is divided. *noun.*

morn·ing (môr′ning), the early part of the day, ending at noon. *noun.*

most (mōst), **1** greatest in amount, degree, or number: *The winner gets the most money.* **2** the greatest amount, degree, or number: *We did most of the work around the house.* **1** *adjective, superlative of* **much** (much) *and* **many;** **2** *noun.*

moth·er (muᴛʜ′ər), **1** a female parent. **2** to take care of: *She mothers her baby sister.* **1** *noun,* **2** *verb.*

mov·a·ble (mü′və bəl), able to be moved, or to be carried from place to place: *movable furniture. adjective.*

move (müv), **1** to change the place or position of: *Do not move your hand. Move your chair to the table.* **2** to change place or position: *The child moved in his sleep. verb,* **moves, moved, mov·ing.**

mov·er (mü′vər), a person or company whose business is moving furniture from one house or place to another. *noun.*

mov·ie (mü′vē), **1** a motion picture: *I enjoyed that movie.* **2** the movies, a showing of motion pictures: *We went to the movies last night. noun.*

mov·ing van (mü′ving van′), a large truck used to move furniture from one place to another.

mul·ti·pli·ca·tion (mul′tə plə kā′shən), the operation of multiplying one number by another: *12 times 3 = 36 is a simple multiplication. noun.*

mul·ti·ply (mul′tə plī), to add a number a given number of times: *To multiply 6 by 3 means to add 6 three times, making 18. verb,* **mul·ti·plies, mul·ti·plied, mul·ti·ply·ing.**

my (mī), of me; belonging to me: *I learned my lesson. adjective.*

N

nail (nāl), **1** a slender piece of metal having a point at one end and usually a flat or rounded head at the other end. **2** to fasten with a nail or nails: *I nailed the poster to the wall.* **1** *noun,* **2** *verb.*

near (nir), **1** close; not far; to or at a short distance: *The holiday season is drawing near.* **2** close to: *Our house is near the river.* **1** *adverb,* **2** *preposition.*

near·ness (nir′nes), a closeness to: *Her nearness made us feel safe. noun.*

neck (nek), **1** the part of the body that connects the head with the shoulders. **2** the part of a garment that fits the neck: *the neck of a shirt.* **3** any narrow part like a neck: *She held the bottle by the neck. noun.*

neck·lace (nek′lis), a string of jewels, gold, silver, or beads worn around the neck as an ornament. *noun.*

need·n't (nēd′nt), need not.

neigh·bor (nā′bər), **1** someone who lives in the next house or nearby **2** a person or thing that is near or next to another: *The big tree brought down several of its smaller neighbors as it fell. noun.*

nerv·ous (nėr′vəs), **1** of the nerves: *nervous energy.* **2** easily excited or upset: *A person who has been overworking is likely to become nervous.* **3** restless or uneasy; timid: *Are you nervous about staying alone at night? adjective.*

nick·el (nik′əl), a coin of the United States and Canada equal to 5 cents. Twenty nickels make one dollar. *noun.*

a	hat	**ī**	ice	**u̇**	put	**ə** <u>stands for</u>	
ā	age	**o**	not	**ü**	rule	**a**	in about
ä	far, calm	**ō**	open	**ch**	child	**e**	in taken
âr	care	**ȯ**	saw	**ng**	long	**i**	in pencil
e	let	**ô**	order	**sh**	she	**o**	in lemon
ē	equal	**oi**	oil	**th**	thin	**u**	in circus
ėr	term	**ou**	out	**ᴛʜ**	then		
i	it	**u**	cup	**zh**	measure		

nick·name (nik′nām′), **1** a name added to a person's real name, or used instead of it: *"Ed" is a nickname for "Edward."* **2** to give a nickname to: *They nicknamed the redheaded girl Rusty.* 1 *noun,* 2 *verb,* **nick·names, nick·named, nick·nam·ing.**

night (nīt), **1** the time between evening and morning; time from sunset to sunrise, especially when it is dark. **2** evening: *What night is the play? noun.*

night·mare (nīt′mâr′), **1** a terrible dream: *I had a nightmare about falling off a high building.* **2** a terrible experience: *The hurricane was a nightmare. noun.*

no (nō), **1** a word used to say that you can't or won't, or that something is wrong: *Will you come? No. Can a cow fly? No.* **2** not any: *Dogs have no wings.* **3** not at all: *He is no better.* 1,3 *adverb,* 2 *adjective.*

noise (noiz), **1** a sound that is not musical or pleasant: *The noise kept me awake.* **2** any sound: *the noise of rain on the roof. noun.*

no·where (nō′hwâr), **1** in no place; at no place; to no place. **2** a place that is not well-known or is far from everything else: *Our car broke down in the middle of nowhere.* 1 *adverb,* 2 *noun.*

number pair (num′bər pâr′), a pair of numbers arranged so there is a first number and a second number, used to locate a point on a grid.

nu·me·ra·tor (nü′mə rā′tər or nyü′mə rā′tər), the number above or to the left of the line in a fraction, which shows how many equal parts of the whole make up the fraction: *In ⅜, 3 is the numerator and 8 is the denominator. noun.*

nurse (nėrs), **1** a person who is trained to take care of the sick, the injured, or the old. **2** to be or act as a nurse for sick people: *They nursed their children through the flu.* 1 *noun,* 2 *verb,* **nurs·es, nursed, nurs·ing.**

nurse (definition 1)
a surgical **nurse** in the operating room

oat·meal (ōt′mēl′), **1** oats partially ground up and flattened into small flakes. **2** a cooked cereal made from this: *We often have oatmeal for breakfast. noun.*

o·cean (ō′shən), **1** the great body of salt water that covers almost three-fourths of the earth's surface; the sea. **2** any of its four main divisions—the Atlantic, Pacific, Indian, and Arctic Oceans. *noun.*

off (ȯf), **1** from the usual position or condition: *I took off my hat.* **2** from; away from; far from: *He pushed me off my seat. We are miles off the main road.* 1 *adverb,* 2 *preposition.*

O·hi·o (ō hī′ō), one of the north central states of the United States. *Abbreviation:* O. or OH; *Capital:* Columbus. *noun.* [*Ohio* got its name from the Ohio River. It may have come from an Iroquois Indian word meaning "fine" or "beautiful."]

oil (oil), **1** any of several kinds of thick, fatty or greasy liquids. Animal and vegetable oils, such as olive oil, are used in cooking. **2** to put oil on or in: *to oil the squeaky hinges of a door.* 1 *noun,* 2 *verb.*

once (wuns), **1** one time: *Read it once more.* **2** when; if ever: *Most people like to swim, once they have learned how.* 1 *adverb,* 2 *conjunction.*

one (wun), **1** the number 1. **2** a single: *one person, one apple.* **3** a single person or thing: *I like the ones in that box.* 1,3 *noun,* 2 *adjective.*

o·pen (ō′pən), **1** not shut; not closed: *She climbed in through the open window.* **2** to make or become open: *Open the window. The door opened.* 1 *adjective,* 2 *verb.*

op·po·nent (ə pō′nənt), a person who is on the other side in a fight, game, or discussion: *She defeated her opponent in the election. noun.* [*Opponent* comes from two Latin words meaning "place against."]

o·range (ôr'inj), **1** the round, reddish-yellow, juicy fruit of a tree grown in warm climates. Oranges are good to eat. **2** reddish-yellow. **1** *noun,* **2** *adjective.*
[Oranges were first grown in northern India. The name of the fruit comes from a Persian word.]

O·re·gon (ôr'ə gon *or* ôr'ə gən), one of the Pacific states of the United States. *Abbreviation:* Oreg. *or* OR; *Capital:* Salem. *noun.*
[*Oregon* probably got its name from the Oregon River, a name once given to the Columbia River.]

ounce (ouns), **1** a unit of weight equal to ¹⁄₁₆ of a pound. **2** a unit for measuring liquids; fluid ounce. 16 ounces = 1 pint. *noun.*

our (our), of us; belonging to us: *We need our coats now. adjective.*

out·field·er (out'fēl'dər), a baseball player who plays in the outfield. *noun.*

out·side (out'sīd'), **1** the side or surface that is out; outer part: *to polish the outside of a car; the outside of a house.* **2** on or to the outside; outdoors: *Run outside and play.* **1** *noun,* **2** *adverb.*

P

page (pāj), one side of a sheet or piece of paper: *a page in this book. noun.*

paint·er (pān'tər), **1** a person who paints pictures; artist. **2** a person who paints houses or woodwork. *noun.*

pair (pâr), **1** a set of two; two that go together: *a pair of shoes, a pair of horses.* **2** a single thing consisting of two parts that cannot be used separately: *a pair of scissors, a pair of trousers. noun, plural* **pairs** *or* **pair.**

pan·da (pan'də), **1** a bearlike animal of Tibet and parts of China, mostly white with black legs, often called the **giant panda.** **2** a reddish-brown animal somewhat like a raccoon, that lives in the mountains of India. *noun.*

pan·sy (pan'zē), a flower somewhat like a violet but much larger. *noun, plural* **pan·sies.**
[*Pansy* comes from an old French word meaning "thought." The flower was called this because it was considered the symbol of thought or remembrance.]

pa·per (pā'pər), **1** a material used for writing, printing, drawing, wrapping packages, and covering walls. **2** a piece or sheet of paper. **3** an article; essay: *The teacher read a paper on the teaching of science. noun.*

par·a·med·ic (par'ə med'ik), a person who is trained to assist a physician, especially one who gives medical treatment at the scene of an emergency. *noun.*

par·ty (pär'tē), **1** a group of people having a good time together: *She invited her friends to both parties.* **2** a group of people doing something together: *a dinner party. noun, plural* **par·ties.**

pas·ture (pas'chər), **1** grassy land on which cattle, sheep, or horses can feed: *These pastures are getting green now.* **2** grass and other growing plants: *These lands supply good pasture. noun, plural* **pas·tures.**

pen·cil (pen'səl), **1** a pointed tool to write or draw with. **2** to mark or write with a pencil. **1** *noun,* **2** *verb.*

pen·i·cil·lin (pen'ə sil'ən), a very powerful drug used to kill the bacteria that cause certain diseases. It is made from a fungus mold. *noun.*

pansy
colorful **pansies** from the garden

pasture (definition 1)
cattle grazing in the **pasture**

a	hat	ī	ice	u̇	put	ə *stands for*	
ā	age	o	not	ü	rule	a	in about
ä	far, calm	ō	open	ch	child	e	in taken
âr	care	ȯ	saw	ng	long	i	in pencil
e	let	ô	order	sh	she	o	in lemon
ē	equal	oi	oil	th	thin	u	in circus
ėr	term	ou	out	ᵀʜ	then		
i	it	u	cup	zh	measure		

pitcher

The **pitcher** tries to throw a strike.

pen·ny (pen/ē), a cent; coin of the United States and Canada. One hundred pennies make one dollar. *noun, plural* **pen·nies.**

peo·ple (pē/pəl), **1** men, women, and children; persons: *There were ten people present.* **2** a race; nation: *Asian peoples, the American people. noun, plural for definition* 2 **peo·ples.**

pep·pe·ro·ni (pep/ə rō/nē), a very highly spiced Italian sausage. *noun, plural* **pep·pe·ro·nis** *or* **pep·pe·ro·ni.**

phar·ma·cist (fär/mə sist), a druggist. *noun.*

pic·nic (pik/nik), **1** a pleasure trip or party, with a meal in the open air: *We had a picnic at the beach.* **2** to go on such a trip: *Our family often picnics at the beach.* **1** *noun,* **2** *verb,* **pic·nics, pic·nicked, pic·nick·ing.**

pic·to·graph (pik/tə graf), **1** a picture used as a sign or symbol: *The symbols used in written Chinese developed from pictographs.* **2** a chart or diagram showing facts or information by using such pictures. *noun.*

pic·ture (pik/chər), **1** a drawing, painting, portrait, or photograph; printed copy of any of these: *The book contains a good picture of a tiger.* **2** to form a picture of in the mind; imagine: *It is hard to picture life a hundred years ago.* **3** an image on a television set. **1,3** *noun,* **2** *verb,* **pic·tures, pic·tured, pic·tur·ing.**

pierce (pirs), **1** to go into; go through: *A tunnel pierces the mountain.* **2** to make a hole in; bore into or through: *She had her ears pierced.* **3** to force a way through or into: *The cold wind pierced our clothes. A sharp cry pierced the air. verb,* **pierc·es, pierced, pierc·ing.**

pint (pīnt), a unit for measuring liquids equal to half a quart or 16 fluid ounces or 2 cups. *noun.*

pitch·er (pich/ər), a player on a baseball team who throws a ball to the batter to hit. *noun.*

planet

the **planet** Saturn

plan (plan), **1** a way of making or doing something that has been worked out beforehand: *Our summer plans were upset by mother's illness.* **2** to think out beforehand how something is to be made or done: *Have you planned your trip?* **3** to have in mind as a purpose: *I am planning to go to New York next week.* **1** *noun,* **2,3** *verb,* **plans, planned, plan·ning.**

plane¹ (plān), **1** flat; level. **2** an airplane. **1** *adjective,* **2** *noun.*

plane² (plān), a tool with a blade for smoothing wood. *noun.*

plan·et (plan/it), one of the heavenly bodies that moves around the sun. Mercury, Venus, Earth, Mars, Jupiter, Saturn, Uranus, Neptune, and Pluto are planets. *noun, plural* **plan·ets.**
[*Planet* comes from a Greek word meaning "wandering." People of ancient times thought of the planets as stars that moved about while the other stars stayed in one place.]

plaque (plak), a thin film containing germs, which forms on the teeth. Plaque can cause tooth decay. *noun.*

play·er (plā/ər), a person who plays: *a baseball player, a card player, a flute player. noun.*

play·ful (plā/fəl), **1** full of fun; fond of playing: *a playful puppy.* **2** joking; not serious: *a playful remark. adjective.*

plur·al (plùr/əl), more than one in number. *Cat is singular; cats is plural. adjective.*

po·et·ry (pō/i trē), **1** poems: *Have you read much poetry?* **2** the art of writing poems: *Shakespeare was a master of English poetry. noun.*

point (point), **1** a sharp end: *the point of a needle.* **2** to show direction with the finger: *He pointed the way to the village.* **1** *noun,* **2** *verb.*

po·lice (pə lēs/), **1** persons whose duty is keeping order and arresting people who break the law. **2** to keep in order: *to police the streets.* **1** *noun,* **2** *verb,* **po·lic·es, po·liced, po·lic·ing.**

pol·lute (pə lüt′), to make dirty or impure: *The water at the bathing beach was polluted by refuse from the factory.* verb, **pol·lutes, pol·lut·ed, pol·lut·ing.**

pop·corn (pop′kôrn′), **1** a kind of corn, the kernels of which burst open and puff out when heated. **2** the white, puffed-out kernels. *noun.*

pop-up (pop′up′), in baseball, a ball hit straight up, but not very high; a pop fly. *noun.*

pot (pot), a round container used to hold many things: *a pot of soup, a pot of flowers.* noun.

po·ta·to (pə tā′tō), **1** a round or oval, starchy vegetable with a thin skin. *Potatoes grow underground.* **2** a sweet potato. *noun, plural* **po·ta·toes.**

pot·ter·y (pot′ər ē), pots, dishes, or vases made from clay and hardened by heat. *noun.*

pound (pound), a unit of weight equal to 16 ounces. *noun.*

prair·ie (prâr′ē), a large area of level or rolling land with grass but few or no trees. *noun.*

prank (prangk), a playful trick; piece of mischief: *On April Fools' Day people play pranks on each other.* noun.

pre·scribe (pri skrīb′), to order as medicine or treatment: *The doctor prescribed penicillin.* verb, **pre·scribes, pre·scribed, pre·scrib·ing.**

pre·scrip·tion (pri skrip′shən), a written direction or order for preparing and using a medicine: *The doctor wrote a prescription for my cough.* noun.

pres·ent[1] (prez′nt), at hand; not absent: *Every member of the class was present. Oxygen is present in the air.* adjective.

pres·ent[2] (pri zent′), to give: *They presented flowers to their teacher.* verb.

pre·tend (pri tend′), **1** to make believe: *Let's pretend that we are grown-ups.* **2** to claim falsely: *I pretended to like the meal so that my host would be pleased.* verb, **pre·tends, pre·tend·ed, pre·tend·ing.**

pret·ty (prit′ē), pleasing; attractive: *a pretty face, a pretty tune.* adjective, **pret·ti·er, pret·ti·est.**

prod·uct (prod′əkt), a number found by multiplying two or more numbers together: *40 is the product of 5 and 8.* noun.

pro·tect (prə tekt′), to shield from harm or danger: *Proper food protects a person's health.* verb.

pud·dle (pud′l), **1** a small pool of water, especially dirty water: *a puddle of rain water.* **2** a small pool of any liquid: *a puddle of ink.* noun.

pull (pul), **1** to move something toward oneself: *Pull the door open. I pulled the sled uphill.* **2** to take hold of and tug: *to pull a person's hair, to pull at someone's sleeve.* verb.

pul·ley (pul′ē), a wheel with a grooved rim in which a rope can run, and so lift weights; a simple machine. *Our flag is raised to the top of a pole by a rope and two pulleys.* noun, plural **pul·leys.**

pulp (pulp), the soft inner part of a tooth, containing blood vessels and nerves. *noun.*

pottery
a **pottery** jar

pulley
A **pulley** helps ease the work.

a	hat	**ī**	ice	**u̇**	put	**ə** *stands for*	
ā	age	**o**	not	**ü**	rule	**a**	in about
ä	far, calm	**ō**	open	**ch**	child	**e**	in taken
âr	care	**ȯ**	saw	**ng**	long	**i**	in pencil
e	let	**ô**	order	**sh**	she	**o**	in lemon
ē	equal	**oi**	oil	**th**	thin	**u**	in circus
ėr	term	**ou**	out	**ŦH**	then		
i	it	**u**	cup	**zh**	measure		

pump·kin (pump/kin or pung/kin), the large, roundish, orange fruit of a trailing vine, used for making pies and for jack-o'-lanterns. *noun.*

pur·pose (pėr/pəs), something one has in mind to get or do: *Her purpose in coming to see us was to ask for a donation. noun.*

put (put), to place; lay; set; cause to be in some place or position: *Put away your toys. Put on your coat. verb,* **puts, put, put·ting.**

Q

quart (kwôrt), a unit for measuring liquids, equal to one-fourth of a gallon or 2 pints: *a quart of milk. noun.*

ques·tion (kwes/chən), **1** a thing asked in order to find out: *The teacher answered the children's questions about the story.* **2** to ask in order to find out: *Then the teacher questioned the children about what happened in the story.* **3** to doubt; dispute: *I question the truth of their story.* **1** *noun,* **2,3** *verb.*

R

rab·bit (rab/it), an animal about as big as a cat, with soft fur and long ears. A rabbit can make long jumps. *noun.*

rac·coon (ra kün/), a small, grayish animal with a bushy ringed tail, that lives in wooded areas near water, and is active at night. *noun.*

race (rās), **1** any contest of speed: *a horse race, a boat race.* **2** to run a race with; try to beat in a contest of speed: *I'll race you home.* **3** to make go faster than necessary: *Don't race the motor.* **1** *noun,* **2,3** *verb,* **rac·es, raced, rac·ing.**

ra·di·o (rā/dē ō), **1** a way of sending and receiving sounds without using wires to connect the sender and the receiver: *Music is broadcast by radio.* **2** the device on which these sounds may be heard or from which they may be sent. *noun, plural* **ra·di·os.**

ranch (ranch), **1** a very large farm and its buildings. **2** to work on a ranch; manage a ranch: *Feeding cattle is part of ranching.* **1** *noun,* **2** *verb.*

rap (rap), **1** a light, sharp knock; a quick, light blow: *We heard a rap on the window.* **2** to knock sharply; tap: *The chairman rapped on the table for order.* **1** *noun,* **2** *verb,* **raps, rapped, rap·ping.**

read·er (rē/dər), **1** a person who reads. **2** a book for learning and practicing reading. *noun.*

read·y (red/ē), **1** prepared for action or use at once; prepared: *Dinner is ready. We were ready to start at nine.* **2** willing: *I am ready to forget our argument. adjective,* **read·i·er, read·i·est.**

re·al (rē/əl), **1** not made up; true: *The explorer told us about a real adventure he had while on an expedition.* **2** not imitation; genuine: *This bracelet is made of real gold. adjective.*

re·al·ly (rē/ə lē), actually; truly: *We all should learn to accept things as they really are. adverb.*

re·bound (ri bound/), to spring back: *She rebounded from her injuries. verb.*

re·cep·tion (ri sep/shən), **1** an act or manner of receiving: *She got a warm reception from her friend.* **2** the quality of the sound in a radio or telephone: *Reception was poor because we were so far from the transmitter. noun.*

rec·tan·gu·lar prism (rek tang/gyə lər priz/əm), a solid shape that has six flat surfaces or faces.

re·cy·cle (rē sī/kəl), to treat or process something in order that it may be used again. Paper, aluminum, and glass products are commonly recycled. *verb,* **re·cy·cles, re·cy·cled, re·cy·cling.**

ref·e·ree (ref/ə rē/), **1** a person who rules on the plays in some games: *The referee tossed the ball up between the two centers to start the basketball game.* **2** to act as a referee. **1** *noun,* **2** *verb,* **ref·e·rees, ref·e·reed, ref·e·ree·ing.**

raccoon

raccoons in a tree

re·fill (rē fil′ *for 1;* rē′fil′ *for 2 and 3*), **1** to fill again: *I refilled my glass with milk.* **2** something to refill with: *Refills can be bought for some kinds of pens and pencils.* **3** a filling again: *I ran out of medicine and got a refill of my prescription.* 1 *verb*, 2,3 *noun.*

re·hears·al (ri hėr′səl), a rehearsing; a practicing to prepare for a public performance. *noun.*

rein·deer (rān′dir′), a large deer with branching antlers that lives in northern regions. It is used to pull sleighs and also for meat, milk, and hides. *noun, plural* **rein·deer.**

re·li·gion (ri lij′ən), **1** belief in and worship of God or gods. **2** a particular system of faith and worship: *the Christian religion, the Moslem religion. noun.*

re·mod·el (rē mod′l), to make over; change or alter: *The old barn was remodeled into a house. verb.*

re·paint (rē′pānt′), to cover or decorate again with paint. *verb.*

re·pay (ri pā′), to pay back; give back: *When can you repay me? She repaid the money she had borrowed. verb,* **re·pays, re·paid, re·pay·ing.**

re·play (rē plā′ *for 1;* rē′plā′ *for 2*), **1** to play something again. **2** a showing again of a videotape recording of a part of a game broadcast on television: *We saw the touchdown again on the replay.* 1 *verb,* 2 *noun.*

rep·tile (rep′tīl *or* rep′təl), one of a group of cold-blooded animals that have backbones and are usually covered with scales. Snakes, turtles, and crocodiles are reptiles. *noun.* [*Reptile* comes from a Latin word meaning "to crawl" or "to creep."]

re·read (rē rēd′), to read again: *to reread a good book. verb,* **re·reads, re·read** (rē red′), **re·read·ing.**

re·run (rē run′ *for 1;* rē′run′ *for 2*), **1** to run again: *The race was a tie and had to be rerun.* **2** a television program that is shown again. 1 *verb,* **re·runs, re·ran, re·run, re·run·ning;** 2 *noun.*

re·spon·si·bil·i·ty (ri spon′sə bil′ə tē), **1** a being responsible; sense of duty: *We agreed to share all responsibilities for planning the party.* **2** a thing for which one is responsible: *Keeping my room clean is one of my responsibilities. noun, plural* **re·spon·si·bil·i·ties.**

re·start (rē′stärt′), start a motor or some other device over again: *See if you can restart the car. verb.*

re·write (rē rīt′), to write again; write in a different form. *verb,* **re·writes, re·wrote** (rē rōt′), **re·writ·ten** (rē rit′n), **re·writ·ing.**

rhyme (rīm), **1** to sound alike in the last part: *"Long" and "song" rhyme. "Go to bed" rhymes with "sleepy head."* **2** a word or line having the same last sound as another: *"Cat" is a rhyme for "mat."* 1 *verb,* **rhymes, rhymed, rhym·ing;** 2 *noun.*

rhythm (riŦH′əm), any movement with a regular repetition of a beat; *the rhythm of dancing, the rhythm of music. noun.*

rich (rich), having much money, land, goods, or other property: *That movie star is a rich man. adjective.*

right (rīt), **1** good; just; lawful: *She did the right thing when she told the truth.* **2** a just claim; something that is due to a person: *Each member of the club has a right to vote. I demanded my rights.* 1 *adjective,* 2 *noun.*

remodel
Wallboard is used to **remodel** the ceiling.

reptile
This **reptile** has a hard shell.

a	hat	**ī**	ice	**u̇**	put	**ə** stands for	
ā	age	**o**	not	**ü**	rule	**a**	in about
ä	far, calm	**ō**	open	**ch**	child	**e**	in taken
âr	care	**ȯ**	saw	**ng**	long	**i**	in pencil
e	let	**ô**	order	**sh**	she	**o**	in lemon
ē	equal	**oi**	oil	**th**	thin	**u**	in circus
ėr	term	**ou**	out	**ŦH**	then		
i	it	**u**	cup	**zh**	measure		

rocket (definition 1)

ring (ring), **1** a circle: *The children danced in a ring.* **2** a thin circle of metal or other material: *a wedding ring, a key ring, a napkin ring.* **3** an enclosed space for races or games: *a circus ring, a boxing ring.* noun.

road (rōd), **1** a way between places; way made for automobiles, trucks, or other vehicles to travel on: *the road from New York to Boston.* **2** a way: *a road to peace.* noun.

roam (rōm), to go about with no special plan or aim; wander: *to roam through the fields.* verb.

rock·et (rok/it), **1** a device consisting of a tube open at one end in which an explosive or fuel is rapidly burned. The burning explosive or fuel creates gases that escape from the open end and force the tube and whatever is attached to it upward or forward. **2** to go like a rocket; move very, very fast: *The singing group rocketed to fame with its first hit record.* **1** noun, **2** verb.

root[1] (rüt), **1** a part of a plant that grows down into the soil. **2** something like a root in shape, position, or use: *the root of a tooth, the roots of the hair.* **3** to become fixed in the ground; send out roots and begin to grow: *Some plants root more quickly than others.* **1,2** noun, **3** verb.

root[2] (rüt), to cheer or support enthusiastically a team or a member of a team. *verb.*

route (rüt *or* rout), **1** a way to go; road: *Will you go to the coast by the northern route?* **2** to send by a certain way or road: *The signs routed us around the construction work and over a side road.* **1** noun, **2** verb, **routes, rout·ed, rout·ing.**

row (rō), **1** a line of people or things: *Corn is planted in rows.* **2** a line of objects or numbers from left to right in an array. noun.

roy·al (roi/əl), **1** of kings and queens: *the royal family.* **2** belonging to a king or queen: *royal power, a royal palace.* **3** rich and bright: *a royal blue.* adjective.

root[1] (definition 1)
roots of a dandelion
plant

rush (rush), **1** to move with speed or force: *The river rushes past.* **2** to send, push, or force with speed or haste: *Rush this order, please.* verb.

S

sad·ly (sad/lē), in a sad way: *He walked sadly down the street.* adverb.

sad·ness (sad/nis), a state of being sad: *A feeling of sadness came over us when our friends moved away.* noun.

said (sed), See **say.** *He said he would come.* verb.

sail·or (sā/lər), **1** a person whose work is handling a boat or other vessel. **2** a member of a ship's crew. noun.

sand·wich (sand/wich), two or more slices of bread with meat, jelly, cheese, or some other filling between them. noun, plural **sand·wich·es.**
[*Sandwich* was named for the fourth Earl of Sandwich, a British official who lived from 1718 to 1792. He is said to have invented this kind of food so that he would not have to stop in the middle of a card game to eat a regular meal.]

san·i·ta·tion work·ers (san/ə tā/shən wėr/kərz), people hired by a community to remove garbage, clean streets and alleys, and do many other jobs.

sat·is·fac·tion (sat/i sfak/shən), the condition of being satisfied, or pleased and contented: *She felt satisfaction at having done well.* noun.

Sat·ur·day (sat/ər dē), the seventh day of the week; the day after Friday. noun.
[*Saturday* comes from an earlier English word meaning "Saturn's day." It referred to the planet Saturn.]

Sat·urn (sat/ərn), the second largest planet. Saturn has a system of many rings around it. noun.

sauce (sòs), a liquid served with or on food to make it taste better. We eat mint sauce with lamb and many different sauces with ice cream. *noun.*

saw (sò), **1** a tool for cutting, made of a thin blade with sharp teeth on the edge. **2** to cut or be cut with a saw: *to saw wood. Pine saws more easily than oak.* **1** *noun,* **2** *verb,* **saws, sawed, sawed** or **sawn** (sòn), **saw·ing.**

say (sā), **1** to speak: *What did you say? "Thank you," she said.* **2** to put into words; declare: *Say what you think. verb,* **says, said, say·ing.**

scale (skāl), **1** a series of marks made along a line at regular distances to use in measuring. A thermometer has a scale. **2** the size of a plan, map, drawing, or model compared with what it represents: *This map is drawn to the scale of one inch for each 100 miles. noun.*

scan·ner (skan/ər), a person or device that examines something. *noun.*

scare (skâr), **1** to frighten: *We were scared and ran away.* **2** to frighten away; drive off: *By barking, the watchdog scared away the robber. verb,* **scares, scared, scar·ing.**

scarf (skärf), a long piece of cloth worn about the neck, shoulders, or head. *noun, plural* **scarfs, scarves** (skärvz).

scene (sēn), **1** the time and place of a play or story: *The scene of the book is laid in Boston in the year 1775.* **2** a place where something happens or takes place: *the scene of an accident. noun.*

scen·er·y (sē/nər ē), **1** the general appearance of a place: *She enjoys mountain scenery very much.* **2** the painted hangings or screens used to represent places: *The scenery pictures a moonlight garden. noun.*

sci·en·tist (sī/ən tist), a person who has expert knowledge of some branch of science. Persons specially trained in biology, chemistry, and astronomy are scientists. *noun.*

scis·sors (siz/ərz), a tool or instrument for cutting that has two sharp blades so fastened that they will work toward each other. *noun plural or singular.*

score (skôr), **1** the record of points made in a game: *The score was 9 to 2 in our favor.* **2** to make as points in a game, contest, or test: *score two runs in the second inning.* **1** *noun,* **2** *verb,* **scores, scored, scor·ing.**

screw (skrü), **1** a slender piece of metal with a ridge twisted evenly around its length. It has a slot in its head for a screwdriver to fit into, and a sharp point at the other end; a simple machine. **2** to turn as one turns a screw; twist: *to screw a lid on a jar.* **1** *noun,* **2** *verb.*

search (sėrch), **1** to try to find by looking: *We searched all day for the lost kitten.* **2** to look through; examine, especially for something concealed: *The police searched the prisoners for weapons. verb.*

se·cret (sē/krit), **1** kept from the knowledge of others: *a secret errand, a secret weapon.* **2** something secret or hidden: *Can you keep a secret?* **1** *adjective,* **2** *noun.*

see (sē), **1** to look at: *See that black cloud.* **2** to have the power of sight: *The blind do not see.* **3** to understand: *I see what you mean. verb,* **sees, saw** (sò), **seen, see·ing.**

seem (sēm), to look like; appear to be: *This apple seemed good but was rotten inside. Does this room seem hot to you? verb.*

scale (definition 1)
This **scale** measures temperature.

scientist
a **scientist** using a beaker

a	hot	ī	ice	u̇	put	ə stands for	
ā	age	o	not	ü	rule	a	in about
ä	far, calm	ō	open	ch	child	e	in taken
âr	care	ȯ	saw	ng	long	i	in pencil
e	let	ô	order	sh	she	o	in lemon
ē	equal	oi	oil	th	thin	u	in circus
ėr	term	ou	out	ᴛʜ	then		
i	it	u	cup	zh	measure		

seen (sēn). See **see.** *Have you seen Father?* *verb.*

sense·less (sens′lis), **1** unconscious: *A hard blow on the head knocked him senseless.* **2** foolish; stupid: *a senseless idea.* *adjective.*

serv·ice (sėr′vis), **1** a helpful act or acts; aid; being useful to others: *They performed many services for their community.* **2** a business or system that supplies something useful or necessary: *Bus service was good.* **3** the army, navy, or air force: *We were in the service together.* *noun, plural* **serv·ic·es.**

sew·age (sü′ij), the waste matter which passes through sewers. *noun.*

shad·ow (shad′ō), the shade made by some person, animal, or thing. Sometimes your shadow is much longer than you are, and sometimes it is much shorter. *noun.*

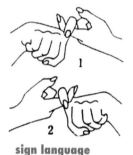

sign language

forming the word *friend*

in **sign language**

shake (shāk), **1** to move quickly backwards and forwards, up and down, or from side to side: *to shake a rug. The baby shook the rattle.* **2** to bring, throw or scatter: *She shook the snow off her clothes.* **3** to clasp hands in greeting another: *to shake hands.* **4** to tremble or make tremble: *The kitten was shaking with cold.* *verb,* **shakes, shook, shak·en** (shā′kən), **shak·ing.**

shape (shāp), **1** a form; figure; appearance: *An apple is different in shape from a banana.* **2** to form: *The child shapes clay into balls.* **1** *noun,* **2** *verb,* **shapes, shaped, shap·ing.**

shelf (shelf), a thin, flat piece of wood, stone, metal, or other material, fastened to a wall to hold things, such as books or dishes. *noun, plural* **shelves** (shelvz).

she's (shēz), **1** she is. **2** she has.

ship (ship), **1** any large boat which can travel on oceans and deep waterways. **2** an airship, airplane, or spacecraft. **3** to send or carry from one place to another by a ship, train, truck, or airplane: *Was it shipped by express or by freight?* **1,2** *noun,* **3** *verb,* **ships, shipped, ship·ping.**

shook (shùk), See **shake.** *They shook hands.* *verb.*

short (shôrt), **1** not long: *a short time, a short street.* **2** not tall: *a short man.* **3** not having enough: *We are short of food.* **4** failing to reach the point aimed at: *The arrows landed just short of the target.* **1–3,** *adjective,* **4** *adverb.*

should've (shùd′əv), should have. *verb.*

shov·el (shuv′əl), **1** a tool with a broad scoop, used to lift and throw loose matter: *a snow shovel.* **2** to lift and throw with a shovel: *She shoveled the snow from the walk.* **1** *noun,* **2** *verb.*

show (shō), **1** to let be seen; put in sight: *She showed me her rock collection.* **2** to point out: *She showed us the way to town.* **3** any kind of public exhibition or display: *We are going to the flower show and to the automobile show.* **4** a play, motion picture, or television program: *We saw a good show on television last night.* **1,2** *verb,* **shows, showed, shown** (shōn) or **showed, show·ing;** **3,4** *noun.*

sick·ness (sik′nis), illness; poor health; disease: *There has been more sickness than usual this winter.* *noun, plural* **sick·ness·es.**

side·walk (sīd′wòk′), a place to walk at the side of a street, usually paved. *noun.*

sight (sīt), **1** the power of seeing: *Birds have better sight than dogs.* **2** something worth seeing: *Niagara Falls is one of the sights of the world.* *noun.*

sign lan·guage (sīn′ lang′gwij), a language in which motions, especially of the hands, stand for words and ideas.

sil·ly (sil′ē), without sense or reason; foolish: *It's silly to be afraid of harmless insects like moths.* *adjective,* **sil·li·er, sil·li·est.**

since (sins), **1** from a past time till now: *The sun has been up since five.* **2** after: *She has worked hard since she left school.* **1** *preposition,* **2** *conjunction.*

si·ren (sī′rən), a device that makes a loud, shrill sound: *A police car went past, siren wailing and lights flashing.* *noun.*

sixth (siksth), **1** next after the fifth. **2** one of six equal parts. *adjective, noun.*

sky (skī), **1** the space overhead that seems to cover the earth like a bowl: *a blue sky, a cloudy sky.* **2** heaven. *noun, plural* **skies.** [*Sky* comes from an old Norse word meaning "cloud."]

smash (smash), to break or be broken into pieces with violence and noise: *to smash a window with a stone. The dish smashed. verb.*

smell (smel), **1** to detect or recognize by breathing in through the nose: *Can you smell the smoke?* **2** an odor: *The smell of burning rubber is not pleasant. verb,* **smells, smelled, smell·ing.**

smile (smīl), **1** to show pleasure or amusement by an upward curve of the mouth: *He is still smiling.* **2** the act of smiling: *She gave a friendly smile as she came in.* **1** *verb,* **smiles, smiled, smil·ing;** **2** *noun.*

soar (sôr), **1** to fly at a great height; fly upward: *The eagle soared without flapping its wings.* **2** to rise beyond what is common and ordinary: *Prices are soaring. verb.*

sock (sok), a close-fitting knitted covering for the foot and leg, especially one that reaches about halfway to the knee. *noun.*

soft (sôft), **1** not hard; not stiff: *Feathers, cotton, and wool are soft.* **2** smooth; pleasant to the touch; not rough or coarse: *The kitten's fur is soft. adjective.*

soil (soil), **1** the ground; earth; dirt: *Roses grow best in rich soil.* **2** a land; country: *This is my native soil. noun.*

so·lar sys·tem (sō′lər sis′təm), the sun and all the planets, satellites, and comets that revolve around it.

sol·id (sol′id), **1** something that is not a liquid or a gas. Iron, wood, and ice are solids. **2** not hollow: *A bar of iron is solid; a pipe is hollow.* **1** *noun,* **2** *adjective.*

som·er·sault (sum′ər sôlt), a run or jump, turning the heels over the head. *noun.*

some·thing (sum′thing), some thing; a particular thing not named or known: *I'm sure I've forgotten something. noun.*

some·times (sum′tīmz), now and then; at times: *They come to visit sometimes. adverb.*

sore (sôr), **1** painful; aching: *a sore finger.* **2** a painful place on the body where the skin or flesh is broken or bruised. **1** *adjective,* **sor·er, sor·est;** **2** *noun.*

space·ship (spās′ship′), spacecraft. *noun.*

spe·cial (spesh′əl), **1** of a particular kind; distinct from others; not general: *A safe has a special lock.* **2** more than ordinary; unusual; exceptional: *Lions and tigers are a topic of special interest. adjective.*

spell·ing (spel′ing), the writing or saying of the letters of a word in order: *She is poor at spelling. noun.*

sphere (sfir), **1** a solid figure with all points the same distance from the center. **2** a ball; globe. The sun, moon, Earth, and stars are spheres. A baseball is a sphere. *noun.*

spray¹ (sprā), **1** a liquid going through the air in small drops: *We were wet with the sea spray.* **2** an instrument that sends a liquid out as spray. *noun.*

spray² (sprā), a small branch or piece of some plant: *a spray of lilacs. noun.*

soar (definition 1)

soil (definition 1)
The onion bulbs are growing under the **soil.**

a	hat	**ī**	ice	**u̇**	put	**ə** stands for	
ā	age	**o**	not	**ü**	rule	**a**	in about
ä	far, calm	**ō**	open	**ch**	child	**e**	in taken
âr	care	**ȯ**	saw	**ng**	long	**i**	in pencil
e	let	**ô**	order	**sh**	she	**o**	in lemon
ē	equal	**oi**	oil	**th**	thin	**u**	in circus
ėr	term	**ou**	out	**ᴛʜ**	then		
i	it	**u**	cup	**zh**	measure		

squad car (skwäd′ kär′), police patrol car which is equipped with a special radio to keep in touch with headquarters.

squir·rel (skwėr′əl), a small, bushy-tailed animal that usually lives in trees and eats nuts. *noun.*

stair (stâr), **1** one of a series of steps for going from one level or floor to another. **2 stairs,** a set of such steps: *the top of the stairs. noun, plural* **stairs.**

stale (stāl), not fresh: *stale bread. adjective,* **stal·er, stal·est.**

stalk (stȯk), the main stem of a plant. *noun.*

start (stärt), **1** to begin to move, go, or act: *The train started on time.* **2** to begin: *I am starting to read my book. verb.*

sta·tion (stā′shən), **1** a building or place used for a definite purpose: *The suspects were taken to the police station for questioning.* **2** a building where buses or trains regularly pick up and unload passengers and baggage. *noun.*

steer (stir), **1** to guide the direction of: *to steer a car.* **2** to direct one's way or course: *Steer for the harbor. Steer away from trouble. verb.*

ster·e·o (ster′ē ō *or* stir′ē ō), a record player giving the effect of lifelike sound by using two or more sets of equipment. *noun, plural* **ster·e·os.**

still (stil), **1** without motion: *Sit still.* **2** without noise; quiet: *a still night. adjective.*

stitch (stich), **1** one complete movement of a threaded needle in sewing: *Take short stitches so the seam will be strong.* **2** a loop of thread or yarn made by a stitch: *Rip out these long stitches. noun, plural* **stitch·es.**

strat·e·gy (strat′ə jē), **1** planning and directing of military movements and operations. **2** the skillful planning and management of anything: *Strategy helped our team win the game. noun, plural* **strat·e·gies.**

study (definition 2)
taking some time to
study

straw (strȯ), **1** the stalks or stems of grain after drying and threshing. Straw is used for bedding for horses and cows, for making hats, and for many other purposes. **2** a hollow stem or stalk; something like it. Straws made of plastic or waxed paper are used for sucking up drinks. **3** made of straw: *a straw hat.* 1,2 *noun,* 3 *adjective.*

strep throat (strep′ thrōt′), an infection that causes a very sore throat.

strong (strȯng), **1** having a great deal of force or power: *A strong person can lift heavy things.* **2** having good bodily strength or health: *She was sick, but now she is well and strong. adjective,* **strong·er** (strȯng′gər), **strong·est** (strȯng′gəst).

stud·y (stud′ē), **1** the effort to learn by reading or thinking: *After an hour's hard study, I knew my lesson.* **2** to try to learn: *She studied her spelling lesson for half an hour. He is studying to be a doctor.* **3** a room for study, reading, or writing: *The author was at work in her study.* 1,3 *noun, plural* **stud·ies;** 2 *verb,* **stud·ies, stud·ied, stud·y·ing.**

such (such), **1** of that kind; of the same kind or degree: *We had never seen such a sight.* **2** of a particular kind; of the kind that: *The child had such a fever that she nearly died. adjective.*

sug·ar (shu̇g′ər), a sweet substance obtained chiefly from sugar cane or sugar beets and widely used in food products. *noun.*
[*Sugar* can be traced back to a word from an ancient language of India meaning originally "grit." Juice from sugar cane dries in the form of a sandy grit on its stalks.]

sug·gest (səg jest′ *or* sə jest′), **1** to bring to mind; call up the thought of: *The thought of summer suggests swimming.* **2** to put forward; propose: *She suggested a swim, and we all agreed. verb.*

sum·mer (sum′ər), **1** the warmest season of the year; season of the year between spring and autumn. **2** of or for summer; coming in summer: *summer heat, summer clothes.* 1 *noun,* 2 *adjective.*

sun·burn (sun′bėrn′), **1** a burning of the skin by the sun's rays. **2** to burn the skin by the sun's rays: *He is sunburned from a day on the beach.* 1 *noun,* 2 *verb,* **sun·burns, sun·burned** or **sun·burnt** (sun′bėrnt), **sun·burn·ing.**

Sun·day (sun′dē), the first day of the week. *noun.* [*Sunday* comes from an earlier English word meaning "day of the sun."]

sun·shine (sun′shīn′), the light of the sun. *noun.*

sup·pose (sə pōz′), to believe; think; imagine: *I suppose she will come as usual. verb,* **sup·pos·es, sup·posed, sup·pos·ing.**

sure (shuṙ), **1** free from doubt; certain: *Are you sure you locked the door?* **2** certain to come, to be, or to happen: *It is sure to snow this winter.* **3** surely. 1,2 *adjective,* **sur·er, sur·est;** 3 *adverb.*

sur·prise (sər prīz′), **1** something unexpected: *Our grandparents always have a surprise for us when we visit them.* **2** surprising; not expected: *a surprise party, a surprise visit.* 1 *noun,* 2 *adjective.*

swim (swim), **1** to move along on or in the water by using arms, legs, or fins: *Fish swim. We went swimming in the pool.* **2** to swim across: *He swam the river. verb,* **swims, swam, swum, swim·ming.**

sym·bol (sim′bəl), something that stands for or represents something else: *The symbols in the map key helped us find the park. noun.*

T

tack·le (tak′əl), **1** equipment; gear. The rod, line, hooks and other equipment are used as fishing tackle for catching fish. **2** to try to deal with: *We have a difficult problem to tackle.* **3** to lay hold of; seize: *I tackled the boy with the football.* 1 *noun,* 2,3 *verb,* **tack·les, tack·led, tack·ling.**

tail (tāl), **1** the part that sticks out from the back of an animal's body. Rabbits have short tails. Mice have long tails. **2** to follow closely and secretly: *The police tailed the suspected killer.* 1 *noun,* 2 *verb.*

take (tāk), **1** to hold onto: *I took her hand when we crossed the street.* **2** to accept: *Take my advice.* **3** to receive: *I took the gift with a smile of thanks.* **4** to get; have: *to take a seat.* **5** to use; make use of: *We took a train to Boston. verb.* **takes, took, tak·en, tak·ing.**

tale (tāl), **1** a story: *Grandfather told the children tales of his boyhood.* **2** a falsehood; lie. *noun.*

talk (tȯk), **1** to use words; speak: *Baby is learning to talk.* **2** an informal speech: *The coach gave the team a talk about the need for more team spirit.* 1 *verb,* 2 *noun.*

tal·ly (tal′ē), **1** a mark made for a certain number of objects in keeping account. **2** to mark on a tally; count up: *Will you tally the score?* 1 *noun, plural* **tal·lies;** 2 *verb,* **tal·lies, tal·lied, tal·ly·ing.**

tal·ly chart (tal′ē chärt′), a table to help with counting when collecting data.

tape meas·ure (tāp′ mezh′ər), a long strip of cloth or steel marked in inches and feet, or in metric units, for measuring.

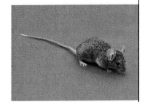

tail (definition 1)
a mouse's long, thin **tail**

tape measure
a **tape measure**
rolled up

a	hat	**ī**	ice	**u̇**	put	**ə** stands for
ā	age	**o**	not	**ü**	rule	**a** in about
ä	far, calm	**ō**	open	**ch**	child	**e** in taken
âr	care	**ȯ**	saw	**ng**	long	**i** in pencil
e	let	**ô**	order	**sh**	she	**o** in lemon
ē	equal	**oi**	oil	**th**	thin	**u** in circus
ėr	term	**ou**	out	**ᴛ͟ʜ**	then	
i	it	**u**	cup	**zh**	measure	

teacher

a music **teacher**

teach (tēch), **1** to help to learn: *He is teaching his dog to shake hands.* **2** to give lessons in: *He teaches music. verb,* **teach·es, taught** (tȯt), **teach·ing.**

teach·er (tē′chər), a person who teaches, especially one who teaches in a school. *noun.*

te·pee (tē′pē), a tent used by North American Indians, made of hides sewn together and stretched over poles arranged in the shape of a cone: *The exhibit had three tepees. noun.*

thank (thangk), to say that one is pleased and grateful for something given or done: *She thanked her teacher for helping her. verb.*

thank·ful (thangk′fəl), feeling or giving thanks: *We are thankful for good health. adjective.*
—**thank·ful·ness,** *noun.*

that'll (ŦHat′l), that will.

that's (ŦHats), that is.

thaw (thȯ), **1** to melt ice, snow, or anything frozen; free from frost: *The sun will thaw the ice on the streets.* **2** weather above the freezing point (32 degrees Fahrenheit, or 0 degrees Celsius); time of melting: *In January we usually have a thaw.* 1 *verb,* 2 *noun.*

their (ŦHâr), of them; belonging to them: *I like their house. adjective.*

then (ŦHen), **1** at that time: *Father recalled that prices were lower then.* **2** soon afterward: *The noise stopped and then began again. adverb.*

there (ŦHâr), **1** in that place; at that place; at that point: *Sit there.* **2** to or into that place: *We are going there tomorrow. adverb.*

they (ŦHā), **1** the persons, animals, things, or ideas spoken about: *They left early. Do you know where they went?* **2** some people; any people; persons: *They say we should have a new school. pronoun plural.*

they're (ŦHâr), they are.

they've (ŦHāv), they have.

tepee

a historical picture of Indian **tepees**

thick (thik), **1** with much space from one side to the opposite side; not thin: *The castle has thick stone walls.* **2** closely packed together; dense: *a thick forest.* **3** like glue or syrup; not like water: *Thick liquids pour slowly. adjective.*

thin (thin), **1** with little space from one side to the opposite side: *thin paper.* **2** slender; lean: *a thin person. adjective,* **thin·ner, thin·nest.**

think (thingk), **1** to form an idea in the mind: *I want to think about that question before I answer it.* **2** to have in the mind: *He thought that he would go.* **3** to have an opinion; believe: *Do you think it will rain? We thought it might snow. verb,* **thinks, thought, think·ing.**

third (thėrd), **1** next after the second: *C is the third letter of the alphabet.* **2** one of three equal parts: *We divided the cake into thirds.* 1 *adjective,* 2 *noun.*

thought (thȯt), **1** what a person thinks; idea; notion: *Her thought was to have a picnic.* **2** See **think.** *We thought it would snow yesterday.* 1 *noun,* 2 *verb.*
—**thought·ful·ness,** *noun.*

threat·en (thret′n), **1** to make a threat against; say what will be done to hurt or punish: *The teacher threatened to fail two students.* **2** to give warning of coming trouble: *Black clouds are threatening rain. verb,* **threat·ens, threat·ened, threat·en·ing.**

through (thrü), **1** from end to end of; from side to side of; between the parts of: *They drove through a snowstorm.* **2** from beginning to end; from one side to the other: *She read the book all the way through.* 1 *preposition,* 2 *adverb.* Also spelled **thru.**

Thurs·day (thėrz′dē), the fifth day of the week; the day after Wednesday. *noun.*
[*Thursday* comes from an earlier English word meaning "Thur's day." Thur or Thunor is the name of a Norse god of thunder.]

tick·et (tik′it), **1** a card or piece of paper that gives its holder a right or privilege: *a ticket to the theater.* **2** a written order to appear in court, given to a person accused of breaking a traffic law or a parking regulation: *a ticket for speeding, a parking ticket.* noun.

ti·ger (tī′gər), a large cat of Asia with dull-yellow fur striped with black. noun.

tight (tīt), **1** firm; held firmly; packed or put together firmly: *a tight knot.* **2** firmly: *The rope was tied too tight.* **3** fitting closely; close: *tight clothing.* 1,3 adjective, 2 adverb. —**tight·ness,** noun.

time (tīm), **1** all the days there have been or ever will be; the past, present, and future. **2 times,** multiplied by. The sign for this in math is ×. *Four times three is twelve.* 1 noun, 2 preposition.

tired (tīrd), weary; wearied; exhausted: *I'm tired, but I must get back to work.* adjective.

to (tü, tù, or tə), **1** in the direction of: *Go to the right.* **2** for the purpose of; for: *She soon came to the rescue.* **3** *To* is used to show action toward: *Give the book to me. Speak to her.* preposition.

toast (tōst), **1** slices of bread browned by heat. **2** to brown by heat: *We toasted the bread.* 1 noun, 2 verb.

to·day (tə dā′), **1** this day; the present time: *Today is Wednesday.* **2** on or during this day: *What are you doing today?* 1 noun, 2 adverb.

to·geth·er (tə geTH′ər), **1** with each other; in company: *They were standing together.* **2** with united action; in cooperation: *Let's work together and get the job done quickly.* adverb.

too (tü), **1** also: *We, too, are going away.* **2** more than what is proper or enough: *I ate too much.* **3** very; exceedingly: *I am only too glad to help.* adverb.

took (tùk). See **take.** *She took the car an hour ago.* verb.

tooth (tüth), one of the hard, bonelike parts in the mouth, used for biting and chewing. noun, *plural* **teeth** (tēth).

tooth·ache (tüth′āk′), a pain in a tooth. noun.

tooth·paste (tüth′pāst′), a paste used in cleaning the teeth. noun.

tor·pe·do (tôr pē′dō), **1** a large cigar-shaped metal tube that contains explosives and travels through water by its own power. **2** to attack or destroy with a torpedo or torpedoes: *After the warship was torpedoed, it sank.* 1 noun, *plural* **tor·pe·does;** 2 verb, **tor·pe·does, tor·pe·doed, tor·pe·do·ing.**

touch (tuch), **1** to put the hand or some other part of the body on or against and feel: *I touched the soft, furry kitten.* **2** to put one thing against another: *He touched the post with his umbrella.* **3** to be against; come against: *Your sleeve is touching the butter.* verb.

tour·ist (tùr′ist), a person traveling for pleasure: *Each year many tourists go to Canada.* noun.

toy (toi), something for a child to play with; plaything. *Dolls are toys; so are electric trains.* noun.

tra·di·tion (trə dish′ən), the handing down of beliefs, opinions, customs, and stories from parents to children, especially by word of mouth or by practice. noun, *plural* **tra·di·tions.**

tiger
A **tiger** is a large, fierce mammal.

a	hat	**ī**	ice	**ù**	put	**ə** stands for	
ā	age	**o**	not	**ü**	rule	**a**	in about
ä	far, calm	**ō**	open	**ch**	child	**e**	in taken
âr	care	**ȯ**	saw	**ng**	long	**i**	in pencil
e	let	**ô**	order	**sh**	she	**o**	in lemon
ē	equal	**oi**	oil	**th**	thin	**u**	in circus
ėr	term	**ou**	out	**ŦH**	then		
i	it	**u**	cup	**zh**	measure		

trail (definition 1)
a marked **trail**

trail (trāl), **1** a path across a wild or unsettled region: *The scouts followed mountain trails for days.* **2** a track or smell: *The dogs found the trail of the rabbit.* **3** to follow, fall, or lag behind, as in a race, game, or the like: *Our team trailed by three runs with one turn at bat left.* 1,2 *noun,* 3 *verb.*

train (trān), **1** a connected line of railroad cars moving along together: *A very long freight train of 100 cars rolled by.* **2** a line of people, animals, wagons, trucks, or the like, moving along together: *The early settlers crossed the continent by wagon train.* **3** to bring up; rear; teach: *They trained their child to be thoughtful of others.* **4** to make or become fit by exercise and diet: *The runners trained for races.* 1,2 *noun,* 3,4 *verb.*

trav·el (trav′əl), **1** to go from one place to another; journey: *She is traveling in Europe this summer.* **2** a going in trains, airplanes, ships, cars, and the like, from one place to another: *She loves travel.* 1 *verb,* 2 *noun.*

treas·ure (trezh′ər), **1** wealth or riches stored up; valuable things: *The pirates buried treasure along the coast.* **2** to value highly: *She treasures her train more than all her other toys.* 1 *noun,* 2 *verb,* **treas·ures, treas·ured, treas·ur·ing.**

trick (trik), **1** something done to deceive or cheat: *The false message was a trick to get her to leave the house.* **2** to deceive; cheat: *We were tricked into buying a stolen car.* **3** a clever act; feat of skill: *We enjoyed the tricks of the trained animals.* **4** a piece of mischief; prank; joke: *Hiding my lunch was a mean trick.* 1,3,4 *noun,* 2 *verb.*

tried (trīd), See **try**. *I tried to call you. She tried on the blouse. verb.*

tro·phy (trō′fē), an award, often in the form of a statue or cup. A trophy is often awarded as a prize in a race or contest. *noun, plural* **tro·phies.**

truck
The **truck** dumps its load of dirt.

truck (truk), a strongly built motor vehicle for carrying heavy loads. *noun.*
[*Truck* is believed to come from a Greek word meaning "wheel."]

true (trü), correct; right; accurate; not false: *It is true that 4 and 6 are 10. The story I told is true; I did not make it up. adjective,* **tru·er, tru·est.**

try (trī), **1** to attempt; make an effort: *He tries to do the work. Try harder if you wish to succeed.* **2** to find out about by using; experiment on or with; test: *Try this candy and see if you like it.* **3** to judge in a court of law: *They were tried and found guilty of robbery. verb,* **tries, tried, try·ing.**

Tues·day (tüz′dē or tyüz′dē), the third day of the week; the day after Monday. *noun.*
[*Tuesday* comes from an earlier English word meaning "Tiw's day." Tiw is the name of the ancient German god of war.]

tur·key (tėr′kē), **1** a large North American bird with brown or white feathers and a bare head and neck. **2** its flesh, used for food. *noun, plural* **tur·keys.**

twirl (twėrl), to revolve rapidly; spin; whirl: *The skater twirled like a top. verb.*

two (tü), one more than one; 2. *We count one, two, three, four. noun, plural* **twos;** *adjective.*

U

un·but·ton (un but′n), to unfasten the button or buttons of. *verb.*

un·cle (ung′kəl), a brother of one's father or mother. *noun.*

un·clear (un klir′), not clear; confusing: *Your directions were unclear and we got lost. adjective.*

un·con·scious (un kon′shəs), not able to feel or think; not conscious: *He was knocked unconscious by the blow. adjective.*

un·de·feat·ed (un′di fē′tid), always winning; not losing: *undefeated army, undefeated football team.* *adjective.*

un·der·ground (un′dər ground′ *for 1;* un′dər ground′ *for 2*), **1** beneath the surface of the ground: *Miners work underground.* **2** being, working, or used beneath the surface of the ground: *an underground passage.* 1 *adverb,* 2 *adjective.*

un·der·stand (un′dər stand′), **1** to get the meaning of: *Now I understand the teacher's question.* **2** to know well: *My parents understand Russian.* **3** to be informed; learn: *I understand that she is moving to another town.* *verb,* **un·der·stands, un·der·stood, un·der·stand·ing.**

un·der·stood (un′dər stüd′). See **understand.** *Have you understood the lesson? I understood what she said.* *verb.*

un·e·ven (un ē′vən), not level: *uneven ground.* *adjective.*

un·fold (un fōld′), to open the folds of; spread out: *to unfold a napkin, to unfold your arms.* *verb.*

un·hap·py (un hap′ē), without gladness; sad; sorrowful: *an unhappy face.* *adjective,* **un·hap·pi·er, un·hap·pi·est.**

un·i·den·ti·fied (un′ī den′tə fīd), not identified; not recognized. *adjective.*

u·ni·form (yü′nə fôrm), the clothes worn by the members of a group when on duty. Soldiers, police officers, and nurses wear uniforms so that they may be easily recognized. *noun.*

U·nit·ed States (yü nī′tid stāts′), a country in North America, extending from the Atlantic to the Pacific and from the Gulf of Mexico to Canada. Alaska, the 49th state, lies northwest of Canada. Hawaii, the 50th state, is an island group in the Pacific.

un·load (un lōd′), **1** to take a load from: *They unloaded the car.* **2** to remove bullets or shells from a gun. *verb.*

un·luck·y (un luk′ē), not lucky; unfortunate; bringing bad luck. *adjective,* **un·luck·i·er, un·luck·i·est.**

un·pack (un pak′), **1** to take out things packed in a box, trunk, or other container: *I unpacked my clothes.* **2** to take things out of: *to unpack a trunk.* *verb.*

un·planned (un pland′), not planned. *adjective.*

un·pleas·ant (un plez′nt), not pleasant; disagreeable: *an unpleasant odor.* *adjective.*

un·safe (un sāf′), dangerous: *Swimming all alone is unsafe.* *adjective.*

un·tie (un tī′), to loosen; unfasten; undo: *to untie a knot. She was untying bundles.* *verb,* **un·ties, un·tied, un·ty·ing.**

un·til (un til′), **1** up to the time of: *It was cold from November until April.* **2** up to the time when: *We waited until the sun had set.* 1 *preposition,* 2 *conjunction.*

un·true (un trü′), false: *The story was untrue.* *adjective.*

un·wrap (un rap′), to remove a wrapping from; open. *verb,* **un·wraps, un·wrapped, un·wrap·ping.**

up·on (ə pon′), on: *I sat upon the rug.* *preposition.*

ur·ban (ėr′bən), of or having something to do with cities or towns: *urban planning.* *adjective.*

uniform
Uniforms are worn by football players.

						ə stands for	
a	hat	ī	ice	u̇	put	a	in about
ā	age	o	not	ü	rule	e	in taken
ä	far, calm	ō	open	ch	child	i	in pencil
âr	care	ȯ	saw	ng	long	o	in lemon
e	let	ô	order	sh	she	u	in circus
ē	equal	oi	oil	th	thin		
ėr	term	ou	out	ŦH	then		
i	it	u	cup	zh	measure		

Venus

Venus is the sixth largest planet in the solar system.

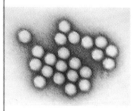

virus

a cold **virus** viewed on a slide

V

vac·cine (vak′sēn′ or vak sēn′), a medicine that can prevent a disease. Vaccines are used against polio, mumps, measles, and other diseases. *noun.* [*Vaccine* comes from a Latin word meaning "of a cow." It was called this because the vaccine used against smallpox was obtained from cows.]

val·u·a·ble (val′yü ə bəl), **1** having value; being worth something: *valuable information, a valuable friend.* **2** worth much money: *a valuable ring. adjective.*

va·por·ize (vā′pə rīz′), turn into a mist that disappears: *The space vehicle was vaporized. verb.* **va·por·ized, va·por·iz·ing.**

vege·ta·ble (vej′tə bəl or vej′ə tə bəl), a plant whose fruit, seeds, leaves, roots, or other parts are used for food: *We grow vegetables in our garden. noun.*

Ve·nus (vē′nəs), the second planet in distance from the sun and the one that comes closest to Earth. From Earth, Venus is the most brilliant of the planets. *noun.*

ver·y (ver′ē), **1** much; greatly; extremely: *The sunshine is very hot in July.* **2** absolute; exactly: *He stood in the very same place for an hour. adverb.*

vid·e·o (vid′ē ō), **1** having to do with the picture in television: *The video part of the program was off for several minutes.* **2** having or using a television screen or a screen like that of a television: *The computer has prepared this information for video display.* **3** a shortened term for a video cassette: *He watched three videos.* 1,2 *adjective,* 3 *noun, plural* **vid·e·os.** [*Video* comes from a Latin word meaning "I see."]

vi·o·lence (vī′ə ləns), **1** strong force; great force: *She slammed the door with violence.* **2** rough or harmful action or treatment: *the violence of war. noun.*

vi·o·lin·ist (vī′ə lin′ist), a person who plays the violin. *noun.*

vi·rus (vī′rəs), a germ that causes a disease. Viruses are so small that they cannot be seen through most microscopes. *noun, plural* **vi·rus·es.**

vis·it (viz′it), **1** to go to see; come to see: *Would you like to visit New Orleans?* **2** to make a call: *I visited my friend last week.* **3** an act of visiting; short stay: *My aunt paid us a visit last week.* 1,2 *verb,* 3 *noun.*

vis·i·tor (viz′ə tər), a person who visits; person who is visiting; guest: *Visitors from the East arrived last night. noun.*

voice (vois), **1** a sound made through the mouth, especially by people in speaking, singing, or shouting: *The voices of the children could be heard coming from the playground.* **2** ability as a singer: *That child has a very good voice.* **3** to express; utter: *They voiced their approval.* 1,2 *noun,* 3 *verb,* **voic·es, voiced, voic·ing.**

vol·ca·no (vol kā′nō), a mountain with an opening through which steam, ashes, rocks, and lava are sometimes forced out. *noun, plural* **vol·ca·noes** or **vol·ca·nos.** [*Volcano* comes from the Latin name of Vulcan, the Roman god of fire.]

vol·ley·ball (vol′ē bȯl′), **1** a game played by two teams of players with a large ball and a high net. The ball is hit with the hands or forearms back and forth without letting it touch the ground. **2** the ball used in this game. *noun.*

vol·ume (vol′yəm), **1** a book: *We own a library of five hundred volumes.* **2** the amount of space anything contains or fills: *The storeroom has a volume of 400 cubic feet.* **3** an amount of sound; loudness: *Please turn the volume down on the stereo. noun.*

vol·un·teer (vol′ən tir′), **1** a person who enters any branch of the armed forces by choice; one who is not drafted. **2** to offer one's services: *She volunteered for the committee.* **3** to offer freely: *He volunteered to help.* 1 *noun,* 2,3 *verb.*

vote (vōt), **1** make a choice about a proposal, a motion, or a candidate for office. In an election the person receiving the most votes is elected. **2** to cast a ballot in an election: *I voted for that senator.* **1** *noun,* **2** *verb,* **votes, vot·ed, vot·ing.**

W

wag·on (wag′ən), **1** a four-wheeled vehicle for carrying loads, usually pulled by a horse: *a milk wagon.* **2** a child's toy cart. *noun.*

wait·er (wā′tər), a person who serves or brings food to people in a restaurant. *noun.*

walk (wȯk), **1** to go on foot: *Walk down to the post office with me.* **2** to go over, on, or through: *We were walking a steep trail.* *verb,* **walks, walked, walk·ing.**

walk·ie-talk·ie (wȯk′ē tȯk′ē), a small, portable radio set used to receive and send messages. *noun.*

want (wänt), **1** to wish for; wish: *We want a new car. I want to become an engineer.* **2** a thing desired or needed: *They live simply and have few wants.* **3** to desire to do: *We want to help them.* **1,3** *verb,* **2** *noun.*

warm (wôrm), **1** more hot than cold; giving forth gentle heat: *a warm fire. She sat in the warm sunshine.* **2** having a feeling of heat: *be warm from running.* *adjective.*

warm-blood·ed (wôrm′blud′id), creatures having blood that stays at about the same temperature no matter what the temperature is of the air or water around them. Cats are warm-blooded; snakes are cold-blooded. *adjective.*

war·ri·or (wôr′ē ər), a person experienced in fighting battles. *noun.*

was (wäz or wuz), *Was* is a form of **be.** *Once there was a queen. I was late to school yesterday. She was going to study. The candy was eaten.* *verb.*

was·n't (wäz′nt or wuz′nt), was not.

watch (wäch), **1** to look carefully: *The medical students watched the surgeon perform the operation.* **2** to look at: *Are you watching that show on television?* **3** a device for telling time. **1,2** *verb,* **3** *noun,* *plural* **watch·es.**

weak (wēk), **1** lacking bodily strength: *He was too weak to lift the chair.* **2** easily broken or torn: *My foot went through a weak board in the floor.* **3** not having much of a particular quality: *Weak tea has less flavor than strong tea.* *adjective.*

wear (wâr), **1** to have on the body: *to wear a coat, to wear black, to wear a ring.* **2** to have; show: *The gloomy old house wore an air of sadness.* *verb,* **wears, wore** (wôr), **worn** (wôrn), **wear·ing.**

weath·er (weŧH′ər), the condition of the air at a certain place and time. Weather includes facts about temperature, wind, and moisture. *noun.*

wedge (wej), **1** a piece of wood or metal thick at one end and tapering to a thin edge at the other; a simple machine. A wedge is driven in between objects to be separated or into anything to be split. **2** something shaped like a wedge or used like a wedge: *a wedge of pie.* *noun.*

Wednes·day (wenz′dē), the fourth day of the week; the day after Tuesday. *noun.* [*Wednesday* comes from an earlier English word meaning "Woden's day." Woden was one of the most important of the old English gods.]

warm-blooded
Mammals are
warm-blooded.

a	hat	**ī**	ice	**u̇**	put	**ə** *stands for*	
ā	age	**o**	not	**ü**	rule	**a**	in about
ä	far, calm	**ō**	open	**ch**	child	**e**	in taken
âr	care	**ȯ**	saw	**ng**	long	**i**	in pencil
e	let	**ô**	order	**sh**	she	**o**	in lemon
ē	equal	**oi**	oil	**th**	thin	**u**	in circus
ėr	term	**ou**	out	**ŦH**	then		
i	it	**u**	cup	**zh**	measure		

week (wēk), **1** seven days, one after another: *On Tuesday my mother left on a business trip and will be gone for a week.* **2** the time from Sunday through Saturday: *He is away most of the week and comes home on Fridays. noun.*

week·day (wēk′dā′), any day of the week except Sunday or (now often) Saturday. *noun.*

week·end (wēk′end′), Saturday and Sunday as a time for recreation: *We spent the weekend camping. noun.*

week·ly (wēk′lē), **1** of a week; for a week: *Her weekly pay is $100.* **2** done or published once a week: *She writes a weekly letter to her friend. adjective.*

weight (wāt), **1** how heavy a thing is; amount a thing weighs: *The dog's weight is 50 pounds.* **2** a unit for measuring how much a thing weighs, such as a pound or kilogram. **3** load; burden: *The pillars support the weight of the roof. noun.*

went (went), See **go.** *I went home promptly after school. verb.*

were (wėr), *Were is a form of* **be.** *Once upon a time there were dragons. They were going to finish early. verb.*

we're (wir), we are.

weren't (wėrnt), were not.

whale (hwāl), a very large animal that lives in the sea. Whales look like fish but are really mammals and breathe air. *noun, plural* **whales** or **whale.**

whistle (definition 2)

what (hwot), **1** *What is used in asking questions about persons or things. What is your name? What time is it?* **2** that which: *I know what you mean. pronoun.*

wheel (hwēl), **1** a round frame that turns on its center. **2** anything round like a wheel or moving like one. A car's wheel is used in steering. Clay is shaped into dishes on a potter's wheel. **3** to turn: *She wheeled around when I called her name.* 1,2 *noun,* 3 *verb.*

wheel and ax·le (hwēl′ ənd ak′səl), a simple machine with a center rod attached to a wheel.

when (hwen), **1** at what time: *When does school close?* **2** at the time that: *Stand up when your name is called.* **3** at any time that: *The dog comes when it is called.* **4** at which time; and then: *We had just started on our walk when it began to rain.* 1 *adverb,* 2-4 *conjunction.*

where (hwâr), **1** in what place; at what place: *Where do you live? Where is she?* **2** to what place: *Where are you going?* **3** from what place: *Where did you get that story?* **4** in which; at which: *That is the house where I was born.* 1-3 *adverb,* 4 *conjunction.*

wheth·er (hweᴛʜ′ər), **1** *Whether is used in expressing choices. He does not know whether to work or rest.* **2** if: *He asked whether he might be excused. conjunction.*

while (hwīl), **1** time; space of time: *They kept us waiting a long while.* **2** during the time that: *While I was speaking, he said nothing.* 1 *noun,* 2 *conjunction.*

whip (hwip), **1** a thing to strike or beat with, usually a stick or handle with a lash at the end. **2** to move, put, or pull quickly and suddenly: *She whipped off her coat.* **3** to defeat in a fight or contest: *She whipped her opponent in the election.* **4** to beat cream, eggs, or the like to a froth. 1 *noun,* 2-4 *verb,* **whips, whipped, whip·ping.**

whis·per (hwis′pər), **1** to speak very softly and low. **2** a very soft, low spoken sound. **3** to speak to in a whisper: *I whispered to my friend in class.* 1,3 *verb,* 2 *noun.*

whis·tle (hwis′əl), **1** to make a clear, shrill sound: *The girl whistled and her dog ran to her.* **2** an instrument for making whistling sounds. 1 *verb,* **whis·tles, whis·tled, whis·tling;** 2 *noun.*

who (hü), *Who is used in asking questions about persons. Who is your friend? Who told you? pronoun.*

who·ev·er (hü ev′ər), who; any person that: *Whoever wants the book may have it.* pronoun.

whole (hōl), **1** having all its parts; complete: *They gave us a whole set of dishes.* **2** full; entire: *He worked the whole day. We ate the whole melon.* adjective.

whole num·ber (hōl num′bər), a number such as 1, 2, 3, 4, 5, and so on, which is not a fraction or a mixed number. 15 and 106 are whole numbers; 1/2 and 7/8 are fractions; 1⅜ and 23 2/3 are mixed numbers.

why (hwī), **1** for what reason: *Why did the baby cry?* **2** because of which: *That is the reason why we left.* **1** adverb, **2** conjunction.

width (width), how wide a thing is; distance across: *The room is 12 feet in width.* noun.

will (wil), **1** am going to; is going to; are going to: *He will come tomorrow.* **2** am willing to; is willing to; are willing to: *I will go if you do.* **3** to be able to; can: *The pail will hold four gallons.* verb, past tense **would.**

win·ter (win′tər), **1** the coldest season of the year; season of the year between fall and spring. **2** of or for the winter; coming in winter: *winter clothes, winter weather.* **1** noun, **2** adjective.

with (wiŦH or with), *With* shows that persons or things are taken together in some way. **1** in the company of: *Come with me.* **2** added to: *Do you want sugar with your tea?* preposition.

won·der·ful (wun′dər fəl), **1** causing wonder; marvelous; remarkable: *a wonderful adventure, the wonderful creations of nature.* **2** excellent; splendid; fine: *We had a wonderful time at the party.* adjective.

won't (wōnt), will not.

woods (wùdz), a large number of growing trees; small forest: *We walked through the woods.* noun.

word (wėrd), **1** a sound or a group of sounds that has meaning and is a unit of speech. We speak words when we talk. **2** the letters that stand for a word: *This page is filled with words.* noun.

work (wėrk), **1** effort in doing or making something: *Gardening can be hard work.* **2** something to do; occupation; employment: *My friend is out of work.* **3** that on which effort is put: *We carried our work out onto the porch.* noun.

world (wėrld), **1** the earth: *Ships can sail around the world.* **2** all of certain parts, people, or things of the earth: *the insect world, the world of books, the world of fashion.* **3** all people; the public: *The whole world knows it.* noun.

worst (wėrst), **1** least well; most ill: *This is the worst I've been since I got sick.* **2** least good; most evil: *That was the worst movie I've ever seen.* adjective, superlative of **bad** (bad).

would (wùd), See **will.** *She said that she would come.* verb.

would·n't (wùd′nt), would not.

wrap (rap), **1** to cover by winding or folding something around: *She wrapped herself in a shawl.* **2** to wind or fold as a covering: *Wrap a shawl around yourself.* **3** to cover with paper and tie up or fasten: *Have you wrapped her birthday presents yet?* verb, **wraps, wrapped, wrap·ping.**

wres·tle (res′əl), **1** to try to throw or force an opponent to the ground. **2** a wrestling match. **1** verb, **wres·tles, wres·tled, wres·tling;** **2** noun.

winter

enjoying the **winter** season

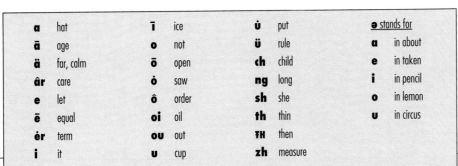

							stands for
a	hat	**ī**	ice	**ù**	put	**ə**	
ā	age	**o**	not	**ü**	rule	**a**	in about
ä	far, calm	**ō**	open	**ch**	child	**e**	in taken
âr	care	**ò**	saw	**ng**	long	**i**	in pencil
e	let	**ô**	order	**sh**	she	**o**	in lemon
ē	equal	**oi**	oil	**th**	thin	**u**	in circus
ėr	term	**ou**	out	**ŦH**	then		
i	it	**u**	cup	**zh**	measure		

zebra

The lines of the **zebra** help hide it from its enemies.

wrist·watch (rist′wäch′), a small watch worn on the wrist. *noun, plural* **wrist·watch·es.**

write (rīt), **1** to make letters or words with pen, pencil, or chalk: *You can read and write.* **2** to put down the letters or words of: *Write your name and address.* **3** to make up stories, books, poems, articles, or the like: *He writes for magazines. verb,* **writes, wrote, writ·ten** (rit′n), **writ·ing.**

wrong (rông), **1** not right; bad: *Stealing is wrong.* **2** not true; not correct; not what it should be: *She gave the wrong answer. adjective.*

wrote (rōt). See **write.** *He wrote his mother a long letter last week. verb.*

Y

yard (yärd), **1** a piece of ground near or around a house, barn, school, or other building: *You can play outside, but you must not leave the yard.* **2** a piece of enclosed ground for some special purpose or business: *a chicken yard.* **3** a space

with many tracks where railroad cars are stored, shifted around, serviced, or made up into new trains: *My dad works in the railroad yards. noun.*

year (yir), **1** 12 months or 365 days; January 1 to December 31. **2** 12 months counted from any point: *I will see you again a year from today. noun.*

year·ly (yir′lē), **1** once a year: *a yearly vacation.* **2** for a year: *a yearly salary. adjective.*

you'll (yül or yəl), **1** you will. **2** you shall.

you've (yüv or yəv), you have.

Z

Zan·zi·bar (zan′zə bär), island near the east coast of Africa. *noun.*

ze·bra (zē′brə), a wild animal of Africa that is somewhat like a horse or a donkey but has black and white stripes. *noun, plural* **ze·bras** or **ze·bra.**

Writer's Thesaurus

Introduction

Many of your spelling words have synonyms, words with similar meanings. This thesaurus lists those spelling words alphabetically, defines them, and provides synonyms. For many words, you can also look up antonyms, words with opposite meanings. This thesaurus can even introduce you to new words.

Understand a Thesaurus Entry

Entry Word   Definition

Friend means someone you like and who likes you. *When it is hot, my friends and I stand in the water from the hose.*

Synonyms →

Playmate means a person you play with often. *Tara and Jewel have been playmates since kindergarten.*

Pal means a close friend. *Esteban wants to invite a pal for dinner on Friday.*

Buddy is an informal word that means a close friend. *Norman's buddy waited for him at the corner.*

Antonym → ANTONYM: enemy

A a

Afraid means feeling fear. *Katie and I are afraid of snakes.*

Frightened means afraid. *The frightened deer leaped over the fence and ran away.*

Scared means the same as afraid but is less formal. *Levar is never scared of the dark.*

Alarmed means fearful and aware of danger. *We were all alarmed when we heard the explosion.*

ANTONYM: fearless

Alone means being away from others. *Tiffany is twelve now, old enough to stay home alone.*

Solitary means alone, often because you choose to be. *Darryl went for a long, solitary walk.*

Isolated means alone and separated from others. *My mother grew up on an isolated farm, miles from the nearest town.*

By yourself means alone. *"Are you going to the playground by yourself, Tom?" asked his mother.*

Answer means something that you say or write when someone asks a question. *When the teacher asks a question about science, Allie nearly always gives the answer first.*

Reply means an answer. It is a somewhat more formal word. It may suggest that the answer is a careful and complete one. *When Mrs. Ramirez asked the prices of new cars, the salesman gave her a reply with exact figures.*

Response means an answer. It is used about actions and about words. *The firefighters' response to the alarm was so quick that their truck arrived in five minutes.*

ANTONYM: question

B b

Beautiful means delightful to see, hear, or think about. *In the fall the colors of some trees are beautiful.*

Pretty means pleasing to see or hear. It is often used to describe girls and women. *Cassie looks like her pretty mother.*

Handsome means pleasing to see. It is often used instead of *beautiful* or *pretty* to describe a man or boy. *That handsome cowboy rides a good-looking horse.*

Good-looking means handsome or pretty. *Rick's brother has dark hair and is very good-looking.*

ANTONYM: ugly

Bright means giving a lot of light. *The bright sun caused Kara to blink.*

Shiny means reflecting a lot of light. *The shiny pan showed that Meimei had scrubbed it clean.*

Brilliant means very bright. *The brilliant outdoor lights let us play ball after dark.*

Radiant means seeming full of light. *Lupe's radiant smile showed how happy she was.*

Sunny means bright with sunshine. *Such a sunny place is perfect for a garden.*

ANTONYMS: dark, dim

WORD POOL
There are many words for what bright light can do. These words are not synonyms, but they are related words.
flicker **gleam** **glitter** **shimmer** **sparkle** **twinkle**

Lupe's **radiant** smile showed how happy she was.

WRITER'S THESAURUS

C c

WORDS FROM WORDS

care
carefree
careful
caregiver
careless
carelessly
carelessness
caring
uncaring

Careless means not careful. *Sonia was careless about shutting all the windows, and the curtains got soaked when it rained.*

Thoughtless means not thinking before doing something. *It was thoughtless of Julian to mention Lateisha's party, since Miriam wasn't invited.*

Inconsiderate means thoughtless of other people's feelings. *Our inconsiderate neighbors make a lot of noise.*

Reckless means not thinking about possible danger. *The squirrels seem reckless, but they never fall from the trees.*

ANTONYMS: careful, cautious, watchful

Complain means to say that you are unhappy about something that is wrong. *"This store never has any good candy," Teresa complained.*

Grumble means to complain in a growling, angry way. *Errol is grumbling about not getting to pitch.*

Whine can mean to complain in a sad voice about unimportant things. *When my baby sister is tired, she whines about everything.*

Gripe means to complain in a continuous, annoying way. *"If you don't stop griping, you won't get any dessert at all," said Al's mother.*

D d

Destroy means to put an end to something, often by breaking or pulling it to pieces. *We destroyed our sand castle before the ocean waves could wash it away.*

Wreck means to damage badly or completely. *Two cars were wrecked in the accident.*

Ruin means to make something worthless or useless. *Bugs that eat leaves can ruin a garden.*

Spoil means to ruin. *The paint spilled on Tyler's drawing and spoiled it.*

ANTONYMS: create, make

Do means to take a piece of work and finish it. *Eric did a nice job pulling weeds out of the garden.*

Perform means to do something that needs practice, usually in public. *The acrobats perform thrilling stunts on the high wire.*

Achieve means to succeed in doing something important and difficult. *Gina studied hard and achieved a very high mark.*

Carry out means to do. *The teachers' aides and the school janitors have different jobs to carry out.*

Eric **did** a nice job pulling weeds out of the garden.

E e

Easy means not hard to do or to use. *Counting to ten is easy.*

Simple means not hard to understand or to do. *It doesn't take long to solve a simple problem. It's simple to ride a bike.*

Effortless means needing little strength or energy. *Darryl makes diving seem effortless.*

Plain can mean easy to understand. *We will understand if you speak in plain words.*

ANTONYMS: difficult, hard

Edge means the line or place where something ends. *A square piece of paper has four edges. We live on the edge of the city.*

Margin means an area next to an edge. *Leave wide margins when you write on a sheet of paper.*

Rim means the edge of something round. *Yoko's shot hit the rim of the basket but didn't fall in.*

Border means an edge of a place or the area along the edge. *Texas forms part of the United States border with Mexico.*

F f

Fair means right and not favoring one person over another. *It is fair for every player to have a turn.*

Just means fair, based upon rules or laws. *The judge's decision was popular because it was just.*

Unbiased means trying to be completely fair. *Please find an unbiased person to settle your argument.*

Impartial means not favoring one person or one side over another. *The umpire must be impartial and say exactly what happened.*

ANTONYM: unfair

WORD STORY

Alarm comes from Italian words meaning "to arms." This was a warning to soldiers to grab their weapons.

Fear means the feeling of being scared. *The animals rushed out of the collapsing barn in fear.*

Fright means sudden fear. *Waking up to the sound of a siren gave me a terrible fright.*

Alarm means fright caused by danger. *The rabbit hopped away in alarm when we got too close to it.*

Terror means very great fear. *People in the burning building shouted in terror.*

Horror means terror and a creepy feeling. *The ghost story filled us with horror.*

Dread means great fear of something that may happen. *Nic watched in dread as the planes flew toward each other.*

ANTONYMS: bravery, courage

Fly means to move through the air by using wings. *Many birds flew up together.*

Wing can mean to fly. It is used mostly about living things. *Some butterflies may wing thousands of miles in a year.*

Flap can mean to fly with large movements of the wings. *The pigeons flap loudly from the sidewalk to the roof.*

Flutter can mean to move the wings quickly but not strongly. *Our parakeet Amigo got out of his cage and fluttered around the room.*

Friend means someone you like and who likes you. *When it is hot, my friends and I stand in the water from the hose.*

Playmate means a person you play with often. *Tara and Jewel have been playmates since kindergarten.*

Pal means a close friend. *Esteban wants to invite a pal for dinner on Friday.*

Buddy is an informal word that means a close friend. *Norman's buddy waited for him at the corner.*

ANTONYM: enemy

When it is hot, my **friends** and I stand in the water from the hose.

G g

Good means well done or of high quality. *Vicki is a very good softball player, so I hope she'll be on my team.*

Fine means very good. *Juan was happy when his teacher told him he had done a fine job.*

Excellent means extremely good. *Shamira thinks the movie was excellent and hopes her friends will like it.*

Admirable means very good. *Scout Troop 97 did an admirable job of clearing trash from the park.*

ANTONYM: bad

H h

Hurry means to move faster. *"Hurry or you'll be late for school, Cathy," said her mother.*

Rush means to move with speed or force. *Chelsea rushed out of school and wheeled herself quickly home to play with the new puppy.*

Speed means to go very fast. *The fire engines went speeding toward the blaze.*

Shake a leg and **get a move on** are idioms that mean to hurry. They are informal phrases. *"Shake a leg, Mike; your friends are all waiting for you to get a move on," called his mother.*

ANTONYMS: dawdle, slow down

I i

Idea means a picture or plan in your mind. *I have an idea about what to do after school.*

Notion means an idea. It is often used for an idea that is not fully formed. *Jim had a notion that a class picnic might be fun.*

Thought means an idea about something. *Winona offered some thoughts on where to hold the picnic.*

Brainstorm means a sudden, very good idea. *Lisa just had a brainstorm—a picnic at the amusement park!*

K k

WORDS FROM WORDS

acknowledge
acknowledgment
know
knowable
know-how
knowing
knowingly
know-it-all
knowledge
know-nothing
unknowable
unknowingly

Know means to have facts about something or someone. *My sister knows how to speak two languages. I know that our new neighbor just moved here from the Philippines.*

Understand can mean to know something well. *Richard understands sign language and likes to see it used in plays.*

Realize means to know that something is true. *Leaping Water realized that she had wandered far from the village.*

Recognize can mean to realize. *I recognize that I hurt Karen's feelings, and I'm sorry.*

L l

Last means after all others, or coming at the end. *Mandy ate the last apple, leaving the bowl empty. The last month of the year is December.*

Final means last. It emphasizes that there are no more to come. *Del scored the winning points in the final second of the game.*

Latest can mean most recent or last up to this time. *"Have you seen the latest music video by that awesome singer?" asked Marika.*

Closing can mean last. *The closing scene of the movie scared Mookie, who was glad when it ended.*

ANTONYM: first

Laugh means to show joy or amusement by making certain sounds and movements. *Flora laughs at all of Conrad's jokes. Casey laughed at the silly hat.*

Chuckle means to laugh very quietly or softly. *Lukas and Julie chuckled as they finished reading the comic strip.*

Giggle means to laugh in a silly way, with short, high-pitched sounds. *All the kindergarten children giggled when they saw the funny puppet show.*

Snicker means to laugh but try to cover it up, or laugh in a sly way. *The villain in the TV show snickered when the hero was trapped.*

Crack up is an idiom that can mean to laugh long and hard. *This new TV show is so funny, it will make you crack up.*

Little means not big, or less than normal in size. *In the dollhouse Ruth saw a little chair like the big chairs in her own house.*

Small means little. *Connie's small glass holds only five ounces of water. Some people consider Cornelius small for his age.*

Short can mean not tall. *Kenny is not too short to reach that high shelf.*

Skimpy means too little to be enough. *The skimpy snack left Amanda hungry.*

ANTONYMS: big, large

M m

Many means made up of a large number. *There were many apples on the tree before the harvest.*

Numerous means many. It emphasizes the large number. *At the library I saw numerous books about space travel.*

Countless means so many that they can hardly be counted. *In the summer night, countless fireflies flew about, flickering their tiny lights.*

Quite a few means many. *Quite a few people were at the movie, but we still found seats.*

Oodles of means many. It is also an informal phrase. *DeWayne eats oodles of noodles.*

ANTONYM: few

DeWayne eats **oodles of** noodles.

Mix means to put two or more things together. *There is always a bowl of mixed candies in Grandma's living room.*

Mingle means to mix, especially many things together. *The flavors of the meat, vegetables, and spices mingle in the stew.*

Blend means mix thoroughly. *Louisa blended the flour and eggs and other ingredients to make a cake.*

Move means to change the position of something. *Nicole moved her chair closer to the table.*

Shift means to move something to a different place or position, especially one nearby. *Annie shifted on the cushion, trying to get comfortable.*

Transfer means to change the position of something. *Chuck transferred his loose change from one pocket to the other.*

Remove means to move something from one place to another. *Luisa removed the cake carefully from the oven.*

N n

Noise means an unpleasant sound. *The noise of traffic woke Jason up.*

Racket means a clattering noise. *The carpenter hammering nails couldn't help making a racket.*

Uproar can mean the loud yelling of a crowd. *There was an uproar when the umpire called the runner out.*

Rumpus means noisy disturbance. *"Mia, tell your brothers to stop that rumpus!" called Mr. Salafsky.*

ANTONYM: silence

P p

Plan means a carefully thought-out way of doing or making something. *I like Molly's plan for surprising our teacher on her birthday.*

Program can mean a plan going from one step or event to the next. *Our city's program for cleaning up dump sites went smoothly.*

Undertaking means a plan of great imagination, danger, or difficulty. *Feeding our neighbor's six dogs was quite an undertaking for Missy.*

Plot means a secret plan, especially to do something evil. *Police uncovered a plot to rob the bank.*

Scheme means a plan of carefully chosen details. *Uncle Joe has a scheme to save on groceries by growing his own vegetables.*

WORD POOL

Here are some words for different kinds of quiet sounds. Use a dictionary to find out exactly what they mean.

hum
mumble
murmur
patter
purr
rustle
sigh
swish
whisper

WORD POOL

Here are some words for different kinds of loud sounds. Use a dictionary to find out exactly what they mean.

bang
blare
boom
clamor
clang
clank
clatter
crash
rattle

Pull means to make something move toward you, or follow along behind you. *The tractor pulls a plow.*

Jerk means to pull quickly and suddenly. *Al jerked his arm away from the cage when the tiger came close.*

Drag means to pull something along the ground or floor. *Ruth dragged a heavy chair across the room.*

Haul means to pull something big or heavy for a long distance. *A locomotive must be powerful to haul a long line of boxcars.*

ANTONYM: push

R r

Rich means having a lot of money or a lot of expensive things. *Samantha's grandfather owned a factory and became quite rich.*

Well-to-do means having enough money that you don't have to worry. *Everyone at the party was well-to-do and wore expensive clothes.*

Wealthy means very rich. *Alicia's uncles are wealthy bankers.*

Made of money is an idiom that means very rich. It is mostly used in saying that someone is not rich. *She isn't made of money, you know, and can't afford a new car right now.*

ANTONYM: poor

Everyone at the party was **well-to-do** and wore expensive clothes.

S s

Safe means out of any danger. *LaTonya tries to stay safe on her bicycle by always wearing a helmet and following traffic rules.*

Secure means safe and without fear. *The lion cubs felt secure close to their mother.*

Protected means kept safe from danger. *Many of the ants are outside the ant hill, but the queen is protected inside.*

Out of harm's way is an idiom that means away from danger. *By the time the volcano erupted, the people were out of harm's way.*

ANTONYM: dangerous

Say means to put an idea or feeling into words. *"I'm ready," Mark said. What did Aunt Marilyn say in her postcard?*

Tell can mean to give information by speech or writing. *"Don't tell anyone where we're going, Leonard," whispered Judith. Does the poster tell what the movie is about?*

Declare can mean to say something firmly and openly. *"This is the best cake I ever ate," declared Ellis.*

State means to say something in a formal way. *The manager stated that the contest was over.*

Scare means to make someone afraid. *It scares Jason when cars drive by too fast.*

Frighten means to fill someone with sudden fear. *Al's dog frightened the cat.*

Terrify means to fill someone with very great fear. *The landslide terrified the climbers on the mountain.*

Make your flesh creep and **make your hair stand on end** are idioms that mean to scare you so much that you feel it all over your body. *The scary story that Mike told as we sat around the campfire made my flesh creep. Suddenly, a sharp noise behind us in the dark made my hair stand on end.*

WORD POOL

Once in a while, a special word for *say* is exactly what you want. Here are some that you might use from time to time. These words are related, but they are not synonyms.

affirm
announce
assert
assure
blurt
comment
cry
insist
mention
mumble
murmur
mutter
proclaim
remark
report
relate
scream
whisper

See means to know with your eyes. *"From this hill you can see for miles, Gabrielle," said her father.*

Behold means to see. It is an older word, often found in stories. *The weary and thirsty desert travelers beheld a lifesaving pool of water.*

Observe means to see and give attention to. *LeVon made notes on everything he observed in the bird's nest all month, then wrote them up as his science project.*

Notice means to observe. *"Notice how close to the ground that plane is flying, Agnes," said Mr. Dragovic.*

Shape means the outward appearance of something, including its length, width, and thickness, but not its color or material. *Baseballs and softballs have the same round shape. The shape of a stop sign has eight sides. A shadow is only a shape.*

Form means a shape. *There's a snack shop in the form of a huge hot dog.*

Figure can mean a shape. *A figure with four equal sides is a square.*

Outline means a line that shows the shape of something. *When Sandar traced around his fingers with a pencil, he made an outline of his hand on the paper.*

There's a snack shop in the **form** of a huge hot dog.

Soft means tender, not hard or stiff. *Josh closed the bread bag so that the bread would stay fresh and soft.*

Many words that mean **soft** compare things to some other soft material.

Fluffy means as soft as fluff. *The young swan has short fluffy feathers.*

Mushy means as soft and wet as mush. *After the storm the soccer field will be mushy.*

Silky means as soft and smooth as silk. *Inez showed Aunt Rosa her silky new party dress.*

ANTONYM: hard

Start means to set something going. *The space shuttle flight starts with the roar of powerful engines.*

Begin means to start something, or to start doing something. *Julie began her letter, "Dear Grandma." The snow began to fall around midnight.*

Get going means to begin. *"It's time to get going on your homework, Lucille," said her dad.*

Lead off means to start something. *Jan led off story time by telling about her favorite animal.*

ANTONYMS: finish, stop

Sure means having no doubt. *Clara is sure that she saw a strange animal in the forest.*

Confident means sure, with a hopeful feeling. *Ariel is confident that with practice her reading will improve.*

Positive means sure, without any second thoughts. *Melanie is positive that she is the fastest runner in her class because she wins every race.*

Certain means sure, based on the facts. *Running Deer was certain that George Washington was the first President of the United States.*

ANTONYMS: doubtful, uncertain

WORDS FROM WORDS

assure
assuredly
insurance
insure
reassurance
reassure
sure
surefire
surefooted
surely
unsure

Surprise means to fill someone with wonder because of something unexpected. *We plan to surprise Linda with a birthday party.*

Astonish and **amaze** mean to surprise someone greatly. *The magician astonished the children by making the parrot vanish. Next, he amazed them with a card trick.*

Astound means to surprise someone completely, so that the person has trouble understanding what has happened. *It's astounding that a ten-year-old won the chess tournament.*

Startle means to make someone jump in surprise and fright. *The door slammed and startled Ms. Mackay.*

T t

Talk means to make words with your voice. *The fire chief talked about fire safety.*

Speak means to say words. *Rita speaks often of how much she liked the class trip to the museum.*

Chat means to talk with others in a light, friendly way. *Louise often chats with her friend Trish on the phone.*

Discuss means to talk about something, hearing several opinions. *We discussed a plan for collecting glass, tin cans, and newspapers.*

Louise often **chats** with her friend Trish on the phone.

Think means to use the mind in order to form ideas or understand something. *Gramps is thinking about living with us so he won't have to climb stairs.*

Reason means to think carefully in order to make a judgment or solve a problem. *Tanya reasoned her way through the difficult test.*

Concentrate can mean to pay special attention and think really hard. *The acrobat must concentrate to do this trick.*

Meditate means to think about something in a quiet and serious way. *Tor sat quietly, meditating about the death of his grandmother.*

Tired means having little energy or strength left. *After working in their garden, the kids were tired.*

Exhausted can mean having no strength or energy left at all. *At the end of 20 miles, the hikers were too exhausted to go on.*

Worn-out can mean exhausted. *The worn-out runners barely made it to the end of the long race.*

Sleepy means tired and ready to sleep. *Juanita gets sleepy about 9 o'clock.*

V v

Very means much more than usual. *After the storm, it became very hot. With binoculars, you can see very far.*

Awfully, dreadfully, and **terribly** can mean truly and deeply. *We walked an awfully long way and were dreadfully tired—but we were all terribly glad to be home!*

Extremely and **exceedingly** mean greatly. *Mr. Stratas was extremely happy to have his lost wallet returned. He was exceedingly unhappy about losing it.*

Mighty can mean very. Used this way, it is an informal word. *We were mighty glad to see land again after four days in a drifting boat.*

W w

Walk means to move on foot. *Carol and Sheila spent an hour walking around the mall.*

Step means to walk, especially a short distance. *Julio stepped over to the fountain for a drink of water.*

Stride means to take long steps. *Scott strode along the sidewalk, trying to keep up with his older brother.*

Shuffle means to walk without taking your feet from the ground. *Tonya carefully shuffled her way across the icy bridge.*

Plod means to walk slowly and heavily. *The tired puppy plodded along behind us.*

Want means to have or feel a need for something. *Everyone wants to have friends.*

Wish means to hope for something. *Lloyd wished he could find his lost watch.*

Desire means to want very much. It is a formal word. *People all over the world desire peace.*

Have your heart set on is an idiom that means to wish for something very much. *Ruben has his heart set on going to visit his cousins this summer.*

Work means effort in doing or making something. *Washing the car is an hour's work for Jon.*

Toil means long and tiring work. *After days of toil, the bird completed its nest.*

Industry can mean steady, hard work. *The children showed such industry in cleaning the basement that Mrs. Oliva took them all to a movie.*

Elbow grease is an idiom that means hard work, especially physical work. *It will take plenty of elbow grease to get all those shelves clean.*

The Word List in English and Spanish

A

actor (34) — actor
admiration (CC) — admiración
afraid (9) — tener miedo
afternoon (31) — tarde
again (23) — de nuevo
ago (10) — hace
agreement (CC) — acuerdo
aim (9) — puntería; apuntar; propósito
almost (13) — casi
alone (13) — solo, sola
a lot (13) — mucho
always (13) — siempre
America (29) — América
amphibian (CC) — anfibio
Anasazi (CC) — Anasazi
and (9) — y
angry (13) — enojado, enojada
animal (33) — animal
another (33) — otro, otra
any (8) — cualquier, cualquiera; algunos, algunas
anyone (31) — cualquiera; alguien
aren't (32) — no son, no están
array (CC) — orden
artist (34) — artista
ashamed (CC) — avergonzado, avergonzada
asleep (8) — dormido, dormida
astronauts (CC) — astronautas

B

backbone (CC) — columna vertebral
backfired (CC) — ser contraproducente (pasado)
backyard (31) — patio trasero
bacteria (CC) — bacteria
badge (CC) — placa
baffled (CC) — desconcertado, desconcertada
balloon (19) — globo
bank (1) — banco
bar graph (CC) — gráfica de barras
batter (CC) — bateador, bateadora
beautiful (27) — bello, bella

because (22) — porque
bedroom (31) — dormitorio
before (35) — antes
began (9) — comenzar (pasado)
behavior (CC) — conducta
being (35) — ser, estar
beliefs (CC) — creencias
believe (23) — creer
blushed (CC) — sonrojarse (pasado)
board (CC) — tabla
body (10) — cuerpo
boulders (CC) — canto rodados
bowl (CC) — tazón
bread (7) — pan
breakfast (7) — desayuno
bright (11) — brillante
brother (33) — hermano
brushes (4) — cepillos; cepilla
bucket (15) — cubeta
buffalo (CC) — búfalo
busy (8) — atareado, atareada; ocupado, ocupada
butterfly (31) — mariposa

C

cabinet (CC) — armario
calendar (CC) — calendario
camping (9) — camping
cardinal directions (CC) — puntos cardinales
careful (27) — cuidadoso, cuidadosa
careless (CC) — descuidado, descuidada
castle (16) — castillo
catcher (CC) — receptor
caterpillar (35) — oruga
caught (25) — atrapar (pasado)
cause (22) — causa; causar
center (3) — centro
cents (3) — centavos
chain (2) — cadena
chalk (22) — tiza
chance (15) — oportunidad
chase (15) — perseguir
cheer (29) — aplauso; aplaudir; animar
chimney (CC) — chimenea
chocolate (35) — chocolate

Christmas | erupt

Christmas (16)	Navidad
circle (3)	círculo
circus (3)	circo
cities (CC)	ciudades
citizens (CC)	ciudadanos, ciudadanas
city (8)	ciudad
claws (22)	garras
clay (CC)	arcilla
clear (29)	despejado, despejada; claro; recoger
cliff dwellers (CC)	moradores de acantilado
clinic (CC)	clínica
clock (CC)	reloj de pared
clothes (35)	ropa
clue (21)	pista
coach (10)	entrenador, entrenadora; coche
coastlines (CC)	costas
coat (10)	abrigo
cold-blooded (CC)	de sangre fría
collar (10)	collar
column (CC)	columna
communicate (CC)	comunicar
community (CC)	comunidad
compass rose (CC)	rosa náutica
cone (CC)	cono
confused (CC)	confundido, confundida
conversation (CC)	conversación
cookie (20)	galleta
core (CC)	núcleo
could (35)	podría, podía, pudo
couldn't (13)	no podría, no podía, no pudo
count (CC)	contar
cousin (35)	primo, prima
crackers (4)	galletas
crayon (9)	crayón
creative (CC)	creativo, creativa
cried (5)	gritar; llorar (pasado)
crown (CC)	corona
crust (CC)	corteza
crying (5)	gritando; llorando
cube (CC)	cubo
culture (CC)	cultura
cup (CC)	taza
curious (CC)	curioso, curiosa
customs (CC)	costumbres
cylinder (CC)	cilindro

D

data (CC)	datos
day (CC)	día
dead (7)	muerto, muerta
deep (8)	profundo, profunda
deer (29)	venado
democratic (CC)	democrático, democrática
denominator (CC)	denominador
dentist (CC)	dentista
didn't (32)	no (pasado)
died (23)	morir (pasado)
different (25)	diferente
dinosaur (35)	dinosaurio
dirt (28)	polvo
discouraged (CC)	desanimado, desanimada
disease (CC)	enfermedad
does (23)	hace
doesn't (32)	no
doing (13)	haciendo
dollar (33)	dólar
dragon (1)	dragón
drawing (22)	dibujo; dibujando
dream (1)	sueño; soñar
drink (1)	beber; bebida
drum (1)	tambor
dry (1)	seco, seca; secar
due (21)	vencido, vencida

E

early (28)	primero, primera; temprano
Earth (CC)	Tierra
earth (28)	tierra
earthquake (CC)	terremoto
easy (25)	fácil
edge (CC)	arista
eight (23)	ocho
eighths (CC)	octavos
election (CC)	elección
else (7)	otro, otra; más
embarrassed (CC)	avergonzado, avergonzada
enamel (CC)	esmalte
enemy (CC)	enemigo, enemiga
enjoy (20)	disfrutar
erase (15)	borrar
erupt (CC)	entrar en erupción

even (8)	liso, lisa; nivel
every (35)	cada
everybody (31)	todos
everyone (31)	todos
everything (31)	todo

F

face (15)	cara
faces (CC)	caras
factors (CC)	factores
fair (29)	justo, justa; feria
fantasy (CC)	fantasía
faraway (CC)	distante
farmer (34)	granjero, granjera
farming (CC)	agricultura
fault (22)	culpa
favorite (25)	preferido, preferida
fear (29)	miedo
feather (7)	pluma
festivals (CC)	festivales
fifth (25)	quinto
fifths (CC)	quintos
final (33)	final
finalist (34)	finalista
finally (27)	finalmente; por fin
finish (2)	terminar; meta
fire (CC)	cocer; fuego
firefighter (CC)	bombero, bombera
fishing (CC)	pesca
fixes (4)	prepara; repara
flies (4)	moscas; vuela
floss (CC)	hilo dental
fly (11)	volar; mosca
fly ball (CC)	batazo elevado
flying saucer (CC)	platillo volador
foot (20)	pie
foreigners (CC)	forasteros, forasteras
forest (CC)	bosque
found (13)	encontrar *(pasado)*
fraction (CC)	fracción
fresh (7)	fresco, fresca
Friday (23)	viernes
fried (5)	freír *(pasado)*; frito, frita
friend (23)	amigo, amiga
friends (4)	amigos, amigas
frustrated (CC)	frustrado, frustrada
frying (5)	friendo
fulcrum (CC)	fulcro
fur (28)	piel

G

gallon (CC)	galón
garden (33)	jardín; huerta
getting (7)	consiguiendo; hacerse
gift (1)	regalo
gills (CC)	branquias
glaze (CC)	barniz
glue (21)	pegamento; pegar
gold (10)	oro
good (20)	bueno, buena
goods (CC)	bienes
government (CC)	gobierno
graceful (27)	gracioso, graciosa
gram (CC)	gramo
grams (CC)	gramos
grandfather (31)	abuelo
grandmother (31)	abuela
grid (CC)	cuadrícula
guess (25)	conjetura; acertar; suponer
gum (CC)	encía

H

hadn't (13)	no había, no hubo
hair (29)	cabello; pelo
Halloween (8)	Halloween
halves (CC)	mitades
hammer (19, CC)	martillo
happen (19)	suceder
happily (27)	alegremente; afortunadamente
happiness (27)	felicidad
hasn't (13)	no ha
haunted (22)	embrujado, embrujada
haven't (32)	no ha
head (7)	cabeza
heard (28)	oír *(pasado)*
height (CC)	altura
hello (10)	hola; saludo
helmet (CC)	casco
helpful (27)	útil
heritage (CC)	herencia
he's (32)	él es, él está
himself (31)	él mismo
his (11)	su, sus
hole (17)	agujero
holiday (9)	día de fiesta
homework (31)	tarea

hoped (5)	esperar *(pasado)*	**lava** (CC)	lava
hoping (5)	esperando	**lawn** (22)	césped
hopped (5)	saltar *(pasado)*	**laws** (CC)	leyes
hopping (5)	saltando	**left** (1)	izquierdo, izquierda; dejar *(pasado)*
hour (17, CC)	hora		
house (15)	casa	**lemon** (33)	limón
hungry (13)	hambriento, hambrienta; tener hambre	**length** (CC)	longitud
		lesson (19)	lección
		let's (32)	vamos a
hunter (34)	cazador, cazadora	**letter** (19)	carta
hurry (19)	apurar; prisa	**lever** (CC)	palanca
		line drive (CC)	batazo de línea

I

idea (8)	idea	**listen** (16)	escuchar
I'm (32)	yo soy, yo estoy	**liter** (CC)	litro
inches (4)	pulgadas	**litter** (CC)	basura
inclined plane (CC)	plano inclinado	**little** (19)	pequeño, pequeña
infielders (CC)	jugadores de cuadro	**lively** (27)	vivaz
instead (7)	en vez de	**load** (10, CC)	carga
inventor (34)	inventor, inventora	**locate** (CC)	localizar
invisible (CC)	invisible	**locker** (15)	cajón con llave
it's (32)	es, está	**logging** (CC)	explotación forestal
I've (32)	yo he	**long** (2)	largo, larga
		lose (21)	perder

J

jacket (15)	chaqueta	**lucky** (8)	afortunado, afortunada
jam (3)	mermelada	**lungs** (CC)	pulmones
jeans (3)	pantalones vaqueros		

M

jelly (3)	jalea	**magma** (CC)	magma
joke (3)	chiste	**Maine** (9)	Maine
		mammal (CC)	mamífero

K

kept (25)	mantener; guardar *(pasado)*	**mantle** (CC)	manto
		many (8)	muchos, muchas
kiln (CC)	horno	**map key** (CC)	leyenda de mapa
kindness (27)	bondad	**marches** (4)	marcha
kiva (CC)	kiva	**Mars** (CC)	Marte
knee (16)	rodilla	**math** (9)	matemáticas
knife (16)	cuchillo	**Mercury** (CC)	Mercurio
knight (16)	caballero	**mesa** (CC)	meseta
knock (16)	toque; tocar a la puerta	**meter** (CC)	metro
know (16)	saber; conocer	**middle** (19)	central
		might (11)	posiblemente

L

labels (CC)	rótulos	**miles** (CC)	millas
ladder (19, CC)	escalera	**million** (19)	millón
ladies (4)	damas	**minutes** (CC)	minutos
landfill (CC)	basurero	**misbehaving** (CC)	comportarse mal
language (CC)	lenguaje; idioma	**mischievous** (CC)	travieso, traviesa
large (3)	grande	**mixes** (4)	mezcla
last (9)	último, última	**Monday** (25)	lunes
laugh (35)	reír	**monster** (10)	monstruo

month (CC)	mes	**picnic** (11)	comida de campo; hacer comida de campo
morning (2)	mañana		
most (10)	la mayor parte	**pictograph** (CC)	pictografía
mother (2)	madre	**picture** (25)	pintura; dibujo; retrato; foto
move (21)	trasladar; mover		
movie (21)	película	**pint** (CC)	pinta
multiplication (CC)	multiplicación	**pitcher** (CC)	lanzador, lanzadora
multiply (CC)	multiplicar	**planets** (CC)	planetas
my (11)	mi, mis	**planned** (5)	planear (pasado)

N

nail (CC)	clavo
near (29)	cerca
neck (15)	cuello
neighbor (CC)	vecino, vecina
nervous (CC)	nervioso, nerviosa
nickel (33)	moneda de 5 centavos
night (23)	noche
noise (20)	ruido
numerator (CC)	numerador
nurse (28)	enfermero, enfermera

O

off (19)	de
Ohio (10)	Ohio
oil (20)	aceite; aceitar
once (15)	una vez
one (13)	uno, una
open (33)	abierto, abierta; abrir
orange (3)	naranja; color de naranja
ounce (CC)	onza
our (17)	nuestro, nuestra
outfielders (CC)	jugadores fuera de cuadro
outside (31)	afuera

P

page (3)	página
painter (34)	pintor, pintora
pair (29)	par
paper (33)	papel
parties (4)	fiestas
pasture (CC)	pasto
pencil (3)	lápiz
penicillin (CC)	penicilina
pennies (4)	monedas de 1 centavo
people (23)	gente; personas
pharmacist (CC)	farmacéutico, farmacéutica

planning (5)	planeando
plans (CC)	planos
plaque (CC)	placa
player (34)	jugador, jugadora
poetry (CC)	poesía
point (20)	punta
police (15, CC)	policía
pollute (CC)	contaminar
popcorn (31)	palomitas de maíz
pop-up (CC)	batazo de globo
pot (CC)	maceta
pottery (CC)	alfarería
pound (CC)	libra
prescription (CC)	receta
presents (25)	regalos
pretended (CC)	fingir (pasado)
pretty (19)	bonito, bonita
product (CC)	producto
protect (CC)	proteger
puddle (19)	charco
pull (20)	tirar de
pulley (CC)	polea
pulp (CC)	pulpa dentaria
put (20)	poner; ponerse

Q

quart (CC)	cuarto de galón
question (CC)	cuestionar

R

rabbit (19)	conejo, coneja
radio (CC)	radio
ranching (CC)	ganadería
reader (34)	lector, lectora
ready (7)	preparado, preparada
real (35)	real
really (27)	realmente
rectangular prism (CC)	prisma rectangular
recycle (CC)	reciclar
refill (26)	rellenar

religion | such

religion (CC)	religión
repaint (26)	volver a pintar
repay (26)	reembolsar
replay (26)	volver a presentar; repetición
reptile (CC)	reptil
reread (26)	releer
responsibilities (CC)	responsabilidades
restart (26)	volver a arrancar
rewrite (26)	reescribir
rhyme (CC)	rima
rhythm (CC)	ritmo
rich (2)	rico, rica
rights (CC)	derechos
ring (2)	anillo
road (10)	carretera
roamed (CC)	deambular (pasado)
root (CC)	raíz
row (CC)	fila
royal (20)	real; magnífico, magnífica; azul marino
rushes (4)	apurar (pasado)

S

sadly (27)	tristemente; lamentablemente
sadness (27)	tristeza
said (23)	decir (pasado)
sailor (34)	marinero, marinera
sanitation workers (CC)	trabajadores de saneamiento ambiental
satisfaction (CC)	satisfacción
Saturday (23)	sábado
Saturn (CC)	Saturno
sauce (22)	salsa
saw (CC)	sierra
scale (CC)	escala
scared (1)	tener miedo; asustar (pasado)
scarf (1)	bufanda
scenery (CC)	paisaje
score (1)	puntaje
screw (CC)	tornillo
search (28)	búsqueda; buscar
secret (8)	secreto
seem (8)	parecer
senseless (CC)	absurdo, absurda
services (CC)	servicios
sewage (CC)	aguas cloacales
shadow (2)	sombra

shape (CC)	moldear
shelf (CC)	estante, repisa
shipped (CC)	enviar (pasado)
shook (20)	sacudir; estrechar la mano; temblar (pasado)
shovel (CC)	pala
sickness (27)	enfermedad
sight (11)	vista
silly (3)	tonto, tonta
since (15)	desde; porque
siren (CC)	sirena
sixths (CC)	sextos
sky (11)	cielo
smash (2)	destrozar
smell (7)	oler; olor
smiled (5)	sonreír (pasado)
smiling (5)	sonriendo
socks (10)	calcetines
soft (1)	blando, blanda; suave
soil (CC)	suelo
solar system (CC)	sistema solar
solid (CC)	sólido
something (2)	algo
sometimes (3)	a veces
spaceship (CC)	nave espacial
special (35)	especial
spelling (7)	ortografía
sphere (CC)	esfera
spray (9)	rociada; atomizador; ramita
squad car (CC)	carro de policía
squirrel (33)	ardilla
stairs (29)	escaleras
stalk (22)	tallo
started (5)	iniciar; comenzar (pasado)
starting (5)	iniciando; comenzando
station (CC)	estación
steer (29)	conducir, guiar
stereo (29)	tocadiscos
still (11)	inmovil; tranquilo, tranquila; aún
stitches (4)	puntadas
straw (22)	paja; popote
strep throat (CC)	inflamación de la garganta
study (21)	estudiar
such (21)	tal; tan

sugar (33)	azúcar
suggested (CC)	sugerir *(pasado)*
summer (21)	verano
Sunday (21)	domingo
sure (13)	seguro, segura
surprise (25)	sorpresa
swimming (25)	nadando
symbol (CC)	símbolo

T

tail (9, 17)	cola
tale (17)	cuento
talk (22)	hablar; discurso
tallies (CC)	marcas
tally chart (CC)	hoja de cuentas
tape measure (CC)	cinta métrica
tepees (CC)	carpas de los indios norteamericanos
thank (1)	agradecer; gracias
that's (32)	eso es, eso está
thaw (22)	descongelar
their (17)	su (de ellos, de ellas), sus (de ellos, de ellas)
then (7)	luego; entonces
there (17)	ahí; allí; allá
they (2)	ellos, ellas
they're (17)	ellos son, ellas son; ellos están, ellas están
they've (32)	ellos han, ellas han
thick (2)	grueso, gruesa; espeso, espesa
think (1)	pensar
third (28)	tercero, tercera; tercio
thought (23)	idea; pensar *(pasado)*
threatening (CC)	amenazante
through (25)	por
Thursday (28)	jueves
ticket (15)	boleto
tight (11)	apretado, apretada
times (CC)	por
tired (23)	cansado, cansada
to (17)	a
toast (10)	tostada
today (9)	hoy
together (7)	juntos, juntas
too (17)	también; demasiado, demasiada
took (20)	llevar; tomar *(pasado)*
tooth (2)	diente
touch (2)	tocar

tourist (34, CC)	turista
toys (20)	juguetes
traditions (CC)	tradiciones
trail (9)	vereda; atrasarse
travel (33)	viajar
treasure (CC)	tesoro
trick (15)	travesura; truco
tried (23)	intentar
tries (4)	intenta; intentos
truck (21)	camión
true (21)	verdadero, verdadera
Tuesday (25)	martes
turkey (28)	pavo
two (17)	dos

U

uncle (21)	tío
underground (CC)	bajo tierra
unfold (26)	desdoblar
unhappy (26)	infeliz
unidentified (CC)	no identificado, no identificada
uniform (CC)	uniforme
United States (CC)	Estados Unidos
unlucky (26)	desafortunado, desafortunada
unpack (26)	desempacar
unpleasant (CC)	desagradable
unsafe (26)	peligroso, peligrosa
untie (26)	desatar
until (13)	hasta
unwrap (26)	desenvolver
upon (35)	en
urban (CC)	urbano, urbana

V

vaccine (CC)	vacuna
vaporize (CC)	vaporizar
Venus (CC)	Venus
very (29)	muy
video (8)	vídeo
violinist (34)	violinista
virus (CC)	virus
visit (11)	visita; visitar
visitor (34)	visitante
voice (20)	voz
volcano (CC)	volcán
volume (CC)	volumen
volunteer (29)	voluntario, voluntaria
vote (CC)	votar

W

wagon (33)	vagón
waiter (34)	mesero
walking (22)	caminando
want (14)	querer
warm (14)	abrigado, abrigada; caliente
warm-blooded (CC)	de sangre caliente
was (14)	ser; estar *(pasado)*
watched (14)	mirar *(pasado)*
weak (17)	débil
wear (14)	usar
wedge (CC)	cuña
Wednesday (35)	miércoles
week (8, 17, CC)	semana
weight (CC)	peso
went (14)	ir *(pasado)*
were (28)	ser; estar *(pasado)*
we're (32)	somos; estamos
whale (14)	ballena
what (14)	qué; que
wheel (14, CC)	rueda; volante; torno de alfarero
wheels and axles (CC)	cabrias
when (14)	cuándo; cuando
where (14)	adónde; dónde; donde
while (14)	rato; mientras

whip (14)	batir
whistle (16)	silbato; silbar
who (21)	quién
whole (17, CC)	entero, entera
why (11)	por qué
width (CC)	anchura
winter (11)	invierno
with (11)	con
wonderful (27)	maravilloso, maravillosa
won't (32)	no + *(futuro)*
woods (CC)	bosque
word (28)	palabra
work (28)	trabajo; trabajar
world (28)	mundo
would (14)	ejemplo: iría *(condicional)*
wrap (16)	envolver
wrestle (16)	luchar
write (16)	escribir
wrong (16)	incorrecto, incorrecta
wrote (16)	escribir *(pasado)*

Y

year (29, CC)	año
you'll (32)	tú + *(futuro)*; usted + *(futuro)*; ustedes + *(futuro)*

Handwriting Models

a b c d e f g h i

j k l m n o p q r

s t u v w x y z

A B C D E F G H I

J K L M N O P Q R

S T U V W X Y Z